THE CONDITIONS OF DISCRETION

THE CONDITIONS OF DISCRETION
Autonomy, Community, Bureaucracy

Joel F. Handler

RUSSELL SAGE FOUNDATION
New York

The Russell Sage Foundation

The Russell Sage Foundation, one of the oldest of America's general purpose foundations, was established in 1907 by Mrs. Margaret Olivia Sage for "the improvement of social and living conditions in the United States." The Foundation seeks to fulfill this mandate by fostering the development and dissemination of knowledge about the political, social, and economic problems of America. It conducts research in the social sciences and public policy, and publishes books and pamphlets that derive from this research.

The Board of Trustees is responsible for oversight and the general policies of the Foundation, while administrative direction of the program and staff is vested in the President, assisted by the officers and staff. The President bears final responsibility for the decision to publish a manuscript as a Russell Sage Foundation book. In reaching a judgment on the competence, accuracy, and objectivity of each study, the President is advised by the staff and selected expert readers. The conclusions and interpretations in Russell Sage Foundation publications are those of the authors and not of the Foundation, its Trustees, or its staff. Publication by the Foundation, therefore, does not imply endorsement of the contents of the study.

Library of Congress Cataloging-in-Publication Data

Handler, Joel F.
  The conditions of discretion.

  Bibliography: p.
  Includes index.
  1. Handicapped children—Education—Law and legislation—Wisconsin—Madison.   2. Administrative discretion—Wisconsin—Madison.   3. Administrative discretion—United States.   4. Due process of law—United States.   I. Title.
  KFX1815.6.H36   1986   344.775′0791   85-62808
  ISBN 0-87154-349-4   347.750′4791

Cover and text design: Huguette Franco

10 9 8 7 6 5 4 3 2 1

to Betsy

· ACKNOWLEDGMENTS ·

Many people helped me with this book, and I would like to express my appreciation. Throughout the long period of research and writing, I had particularly capable research assistants, who not only helped with immediate tasks common to all scholars, but also contributed important insights and ideas. Thanks to Jeffrey Boldt, Jill Goodman, Susan McCabe, and Linda Lehnertz.

The principal empirical example in the book is the special education program of the Madison, Wisconsin, School District. Many parents, teachers, support teachers, school psychologists, parent advocates, and citizen advocates generously gave their time in the form of interviews. In addition, several officials were helpful in supporting the study and also reviewing my interpretations and ideas. I thank Lou Brown, Lee Gruenwald, and Ruth Loomis. Cindy Rose, a social worker in special education, and my neighbor during the study, gave me important leads and insights, as well as encouragement.

My thanks to several of my colleagues who read parts or all of the manuscript: Charles Anderson, Murray Edelman, William Forbath, Betsy Ginsberg, Andrew Levine, William Simon, Michael Sosin, and Mark Tushnet.

Priscilla Lewis and Ellie Dickason had the task of putting a large, unruly manuscript into readable shape. They did an excellent job and are nice to work with.

The Russell Sage Foundation provided partial support. I appreciate their confidence.

· CONTENTS ·

PART II
Construction

THE CONDITIONS OF DISCRETION

· 1 ·

The Argument

"To construct we must criticize, but criticism cannot be clear and effective unless it anticipates what is to be built."
Roberto Unger

We have witnessed profound changes in our legal culture during the past several decades. There has been an outpouring of statutory entitlements and procedural due process remedies covering diverse relationships—civil rights, welfare, education, mental health, environmental protection, occupational health and safety, consumer protection—between ordinary people and their government. There was the recognition that these relationships were valuable to people, that they were dependent on the relationships, and that they would suffer considerable harm if government acted arbitrarily. Reich (1964) captured the historical moment with the phrase, "The New Property." He argued that government was constrained by the rule of law when it interfered with the property interests of the citizen. In the modern social welfare state, relations with government in regard to welfare, education, health, and so forth, involve new forms of property, and government ought to be held to the same standards of law as with conventional or traditional property (Reich). Our historic, liberal traditions of the state were to be applied to the changing nature of the modern state.

The legal rights explosion, in turn, produced a reaction: it is argued that we now have too many laws and entitlements, too much procedure, too many lawyers and hearings, and too much litigation. Comparisons are made to Japan and other industrialized countries, which seem to get on with life without nearly all questions being decided in court. The call is for less law and procedure, for deregulation and decentralization. Whether we have too much or too little law is by no means a closed question, at least for our society as a whole (Galanter 1983; Trubek et al. 1983), but it is the thesis of this book that the system of rights and procedural remedies developed over the last several decades has not worked for the people I am most concerned with. It has failed not for the reasons usually given—the system is overused, abused, if you will—but rather that despite the impressive changes in our legal culture, justice remains largely unavailable to large sections of the population. I am including the poor, of course, but also those with incomes above poverty definitions.

In part, the reason for the failure of justice is familiar—lack of resources on the part of the citizen and maldistributions in services and structures. But my arguments go deeper. They question the basic assumptions of the approach of the legal system and argue that the system is conceptually inadequate for citizen/state relations in the modern context and fails to take account of the basic maldistribution of wealth and power in contemporary America. For these reasons, our present approach to justice in the modern state is doomed to failure.

This does not mean that justice must always be denied to large numbers of people. I believe that by reexamining basic assumptions and taking a more realistic view of the modern state we can develop structures and institutions that meet our basic ideals and values. I believe that we can preserve and enhance our core ideals of autonomy, responsibility, humaneness, and progress in the modern, bureaucratic state. In Part II—the major part of this book—I develop a theory, with a concrete, real-life example, that moves toward these goals.

This book is concerned with justice in the welfare or administrative state. The situation that I will be dealing with is the interaction between a large-scale public agency and an individual where the decision is discretionary. By discretionary, I mean that the substantive relationship is not or ought not to be governed by the rules. The primary example is the education of handicapped children, or, as it is popularly known, special education. This is a discretionary decision because for a great many of these children (for example, the mildly retarded), we really do not know why they are not performing well in school or what to do about it. There are a lot of good ideas as to both questions, but the state of the art is still experimental. This means that the evaluation and educational programs for the child should be judgmental, professional, flexible, experimental. Decisions should be based on choice (Heller 1982). In practice a great many special education decisions are based on rules—children are more or less automatically slotted on the basis of mechanical test scores—but that is not the way it should be. The decisions should be discretionary.

A contrasting example would be a highly routinized administrative program such as the Social Security old-age and survivors program. For the vast majority of claimants, eligibility and benefits are determined by specific rules. There is little room for interpretation or choice. It is a rule-bound system rather than a discretionary system.

In the real world, there are no pure types. There are discretionary issues in the old-age and survivors program, and even in well-run special education programs there are rules. Most administrative programs are consciously mixed if for no other reason than to deal with the basic conflict between the variation in the world and the generalization and rigidity of rules. But differences in degree are important, and one of the significant reasons for the failure to achieve justice is the lack of appreciation of basic differences in the structure of client/agency relations. There are important differences between an income-maintenance office or a pension office, and schools, hospitals, social services, and a variety of other professionally oriented agencies.

The decision is not only discretionary, it is also *continuous*. The decision about what to do for the handicapped child ought to last for the school life of that child, if we are serious about the idea that our knowledge must be tentative and experimental. Quite often this does not happen. Evaluations and placements are one-time decisions, forcing the child to remain in one slot until school is over. But this is not how the program is supposed to work. Many relationships with government are characterized by continuity, for example, welfare, health, mental health, a variety of services, licensing, and, of course, a vast array of business relations. In fact, continuity of relation is probably the norm in the modern state.

The reason for emphasizing the continuing relationship between the citizen and the state is not only because of its real life importance but also because the theory and practice of the legal system are at such variance with the needs of the participants. Instead of partnership, there are adversaries; instead of community, there is conflict; instead of continuity, there is discontinuity (Simon 1978).

The basic individual/agency relationship that I will be discussing, then, is characterized by high amounts of discretion and continuity. A lot of choice can be made as to eligibility and the provision of service. What is the meaning of "justice" in this relationship? The idea is simple: by justice, I mean the sharing of power, that both parties (the individual and the official) reach a mutual agreement on the important decisions affecting the individual. This does not necessarily mean a compromise. The individual may agree with the choice of the official, but the individual has to agree as a responsible, autonomous, informed person and not because of domination by the official.

In a way, I am talking about informed consent. There are two ideas in the concept of informed consent. There is the idea of individuality—the autonomous, responsible person. This is at the core of our liberal heritage. Individuality is our most fundamental belief, our basic principle of humanity. The other idea of informed consent is a social relationship, and this is the problem. How can two people be both autonomous and responsible? How can two people be both individuals and bound together in a social relationship? Does not one have to decide for the other? Informed consent, as we shall see, turns out to be a very complicated idea. Historically, liberal political theory has been concerned with the individual; social relations (including the state) are considered only insofar as they serve individual ends; they are instrumental. But how can two people be both ends and means? In other words, there is a theoretical difficulty which liberal political theory does not address satisfactorily.

Most of the thinking and debate about informed consent has taken place in the field of medicine. There are strong theoretical objections and practical difficulties to informed consent in the physician/patient relationship. Many physicians believe that patients are not competent to understand esoteric and uncertain information, that they do not want to deal with uncertainty. Patients want to trust the physician, and it is therapeutically harmful for the patient to try to engage in the informed consent process. The law requires informed consent for much of medical practice, but it works badly. It challenges the concept of professionalism and raises dramatically the distribution question—the imbalance in power between the patient and the physician.

Informed consent, or discretion, in the administrative state raises issues both similar to and different from those in medicine. In the remainder of this chapter, I describe the conditions of discretion in summary form. Ordinarily, this would be the concluding chapter. I present the argument here because of the complexity and length of the analysis. We will consider not only the reasons for the inadequacy of the present system but also a new approach, which involves a synthesis of large bodies of theoretical and empirical materials from implementation analysis, complex organizations, social movement groups, informed consent, and political theory.

The initial chapters set forth the case against adversarial advocacy—why the present system of procedural due process fails to achieve its goals. I am talking about individual clients dealing with individual matters—income maintenance, health, education, social services—as distinguished from businesses dealing with agencies in large, complex regulatory matters. I am primarily concerned with ordinary people—the poor and near poor, but also large portions of the working and lower middle classes.

The familiar reasons for the failure of due process are lack of resources and lack of access. Most ordinary citizens, but especially the lower classes, lack the information and advocacy resources necessary to prosecute their claims. Procedural due process depends on the complaining client—the person who knows that a wrong has been committed, knows that there is a remedy, has the resources to pursue the remedy, and calculates that the benefits of victory will outweigh the costs of trying. All of the conditions are formidable; yet all must be satisfied. If there is a failure of any one of the conditions, the procedural due process remedy will not work (Handler 1966). From the agency's side, there is little or no sympathy with procedural due process, no willingness to make hearing procedures accessible. What process there is—and on the books there is a great deal—has been wrung from the bureaucracy through litigation or imposed by statute and administrative regulation. The empirical evidence demonstrates that in the big agencies the bureaucracy can manipulate the client/

agency relationship to defeat procedural due process. This is especially true in the discretionary situation.

The failures of procedural due process are explored in detail in the context of special education. Procedural rights of handicapped children grew out of the legal rights revolution. The Education for All Handicapped Children Act (P.L. 94–142) was directed primarily at two issues: the apparent failure of the public school system to admit large numbers of handicapped children, and the apparent discrimination against handicapped children who were admitted (Heller 1982). The act mandated that local school districts provide an "appropriate" education for such children. The procedural rights granted to the parents were extensive. There had to be multidisciplinary conferences to assess and decide on individual educational plans for the child, and before each major decision could be taken, informed consent had to be given by the parents. If there was disagreement, there were provisions for two hearings, at the district level and at the state level, with a right to judicial appeal if needed.

P.L. 94–142 can be claimed a success in terms of money now being spent on special education, the number of children in programs, and what is happening today as compared to ten years ago (Clune and Van Pelt 1984). It is not so clear that what is happening in the classroom is that successful (Heller 1982). It is even more apparent that the procedural system is not working as anticipated. There are appeals and court cases, but most are originated by well-to-do parents fighting the school district for expensive services for severely handicapped children. For parents with mildly handicapped children the system does not work well for the familiar reasons—the lack of information and resources and a bureaucracy that is unsympathetic and under severe pressures to process students into slots rather than make deliberative decisions. When parents do protest, they do not do well in the hearing system. The result is the worst of all possible worlds. We have imposed paperwork and excessive legalization on the educational bureaucracy, procedural protection for the well-to-do, and false promises for the ordinary and the poor.

This much is familiar and could be said about other large-scale administrative programs dealing with large numbers of people. What I attempt to do here is to analyze more deeply the reasons for the failure of procedural due process in order to lay the groundwork for the major argument of the book—the conditions necessary for a normatively appropriate discretionary decision.

The main reason for the failure is maldistribution of power. Procedural due process is a formally imposed system that attempts to achieve equality of treatment in a social system with dramatically unequal balances of wealth and power. In this case, the inequality is between the citizen and the agency. Time and again, we are reminded that this effort, with rare exceptions, is doomed to failure. There are dramatic instances where power is equalized, where the weak and downtrodden have been able to resist successfully, but these are the rare cases. Progress will not be made unless the distributional question has been confronted.

The second reason for the failure of procedural due process is that it is conceptually flawed. Procedural due process grows out of our historic liberal traditions; it is founded on the liberal conception of individualism and the relation of the individual to the state. It posits a sharp distinction between the individual and the state, between the public and the private, and provides a procedure to protect the individual from state interference. The argument that I make is that the liberal legal conception of the individual and the state does not describe the reality of the modern social welfare state. In a great many areas, and certainly in the ones that I am talking about, the individual is, of necessity, in continuing relationships with the state. Here, we are not talking about the citizen using the law to prevent state interference with private activity. Rather, we mean procedural systems that are trying to protect citizens in their dealings with government. Thus, instead of having a procedural system that is adversarial, with structures that sharpen conflict and dichotomize the relationship, we need a procedural system that moves in the opposite direction—one that repairs relationships and fosters cooperation.

Moving in this direction, however, immediately raises a number of serious questions. As problematic as adversarial advocacy may be, it at least attempts to provide the weak with some protection. What kinds of protection would there be with an informal, cooperative system? Given the distribution question, would the have-nots be in even worse shape without adversarial advocacy? If I argue that one of the problems of adversarial advocacy is the lack of sympathy (to put it mildly) on the part of the bureaucracy, is it not foolhardy to try and impose a cooperative system? Instead of trying to limit and control administrative discretion, would a cooperative system not increase discretion and subject the citizen to even more arbitrary power (Abel 1982)?

These are serious questions. They have been raised about informal systems of decision making and, on the basis of existing programs, have not been answered. In many respects, informal systems have probably resulted in less rather than more justice for the average citizen. The reasons for these apparent failures of informal systems are analogous to the reasons for the failure of adversarial advocacy: they have been imposed on social systems without changing the underlying reality of the maldistribution of wealth and power, coupled with the power, structures, and incentives of the bureaucracies.

We are thus confronted with what look like insoluble problems. Given the nature and direction of the modern welfare state, the citizen and the state are locked into continuing discretionary relationships. Problems cannot be solved by rules that preserve the sharp distinctions between private and public, between citizen and state, in health care, education, social services, and a variety of other service programs. The citizen cannot establish a wall between himself or herself and the state. Yet, our procedural system has this conception in mind: it sharpens rather than mutes adversarial relationships; it truncates and polarizes rather than heals; it is cross-sectional rather than continuous; it creates winners and losers rather than partners. On the other hand, a cooperative system threatens to lose what few protections and restraints exist, fosters rather than limits discretionary power by government, increases rather than decreases the disparities in wealth and power, and conflicts with the basic values of individualism and liberalism.

Chapters 6 through 9 develop an argument that transcends these dilemmas. It is a theoretical argument that seeks to preserve and enhance the liberal values of autonomy and responsibility in the context of the modern state. It accepts, and indeed welcomes, the exercise of discretion at the local level. At the same time it sets forth ways in which the distribution question can be moderated so that cooperative decision making will work. My argument avoids the pitfalls of imposing an abstract procedural system without regard to power, public policy, administration, and bureaucratic constraints. It is grounded, I believe, in reality or at least the possibility of reality, in the sense that the theory is coherent and complete and has some empirical support. It addresses many of the major objections to liberal political theory.

I begin with an empirical example. The Madison, Wisconsin, School District, for interesting and complicated reasons, arrived at a cooperative decision-making model for special education that is both theoretically coherent and seems to work. By "work," I mean that a lot of decision making appears to be made through bargaining, with a genuine effort to involve parents in the process. I say "seems" because my information is not based on a systematic, scientific examination of the Madison system—that would be an enormous, difficult, and complex task, far beyond the scope of this book. But I have conducted a wide range of interviews with a variety of teachers, administrators, parents, and advocates. They tell a fairly consistent story. They point to weaknesses in the Madison system, but these are not fatal flaws; rather, they appear consistent with the theory and seem amenable to reform. What is happening in Madison is not a blueprint for the rest of the country, but the experience shows that these ideas are possible if they are worked out in a specific context. In Chapter 9, I discuss the issues of utopianism and uncertainty.

What are the Madison ideas? Briefly, the Madison School District, over the years, developed three conceptual moves for decision making in special education. Building on the more general concept of mainstreaming, the district first concluded that parents are part of the solution not the problem. This may seem obvious but it is not—it certainly is not the prevalent practice in most school systems. If the school is going to educate the handicapped student, it needs the understanding *and* the cooperation of the parents. The parents become part of the process, part of the organizational task. Informed consent is an organizational goal, not an obstacle to be overcome by the bureaucracy.

The second move is that the existing state of the technology, evaluations, and programs have to be experimental and flexible. Again, this may seem obvious, but it is not common practice. In addition to being substantively correct, this approach immediately reduces the level of potential conflict and sets the conditions for bargaining and accommodation. Teachers and parents come to understand that decisions are renegotiable, and both will, if necessary, suspend judgment to see what works best for the child. In contrast to the adversary system, the participants do not think in terms of winners and losers. The decision making flows with the school life of the child, rather than fixing rights and liabilities cross-sectionally, thereby truncating the parties.

But how can the parents participate? What about the distributional question? The third conceptual move made by the Madison District involves the role of conflict. In cooperative decision making, conflict is viewed negatively, since it demonstrates a failure of communication between the parties. Madison takes the opposite approach. Conflict is viewed as necessary for communication to reach an understanding. Without understanding by the parties, there cannot be cooperation in the program. But the conflict is not adversarial; it is *communicative conflict*. A variety of techniques are used to enhance the ability of parents to engage in communication, although here, as will be pointed out, is where weaknesses have appeared.

It is out of this example that a theory has been constructed. We must consider four bodies of theory: (1) the implementation of public policy; (2) organizational theory; (3) social movement research; and (4) informed consent. The Madison system grew out of its own traditions and particular circumstances. This is not to say that it was impervious to the world. The school system operates within a dense legal, political, and social environment. It is subject to municipal, state, and federal laws and regulations. As a professionally oriented organization, it is influenced by professional educators, ideologies, licensing requirements, employment laws, and so forth. Nevertheless, within these constraints and influences, there is room to maneuver, to develop and modify styles and patterns of operations, to create and emphasize certain programs. These ideas are developed into what I call a theory of public action.

The theory of public action presents a view of policy formation and implementation. The conventional analysis separates the two. Policy is formulated (by the executive or the legislature, for example), and then it is implemented. The contemporary (and my) view is that the two interact; it is a process rather than a series of discrete actions. This is certainly true of an on-going administrative system such as education. What goes on in the agencies affects what is thought about and decided at the "top," and what is considered there is certainly influenced by what is happening below.

The theory of public action, as illustrated by the Madison example as well as other scholarly literature, focuses on two major points. One is the process by which policies come to be formulated and implemented, and the other is local discretion. The two are inseparable. As to the formation and implementation, the argument is made that much of contemporary policy, particularly in the social welfare area (broadly defined) does not emanate from Washington. Congress and other national policy agencies are, to a great extent, reactive to local influences and pressures. At the state and local levels, there is experimentation, agitation, and the working out of ideas. This is particularly true of programs that historically have been state and local concerns—education, health, welfare, criminal justice, and many other types of services. Elmore (1978; 1979–1980) has argued for a "bottoms up" analysis of public policy. On the other hand, local and state activities are not impervious to broader national influences—the law, expressions of ideology and legitimacy, and economic and financial incentives (Handler and Zatz 1982).

At the local and state levels, a variety of forces are at work, much as we are accustomed to viewing at the national level. Organizations, interest groups, politicians, bureaucrats, and other social actors push and resist programs and policies. These actors in turn seek out allies, sometimes at the state and local levels, but also at the national level. The response at the national level aids some actors and not others.

Once stated, the theory of public action seems fairly obvious, but its most important implications are often resisted. The most important implications have to do with local discretion. Discretion in public policy is inevitable—if the theory of public action is correct—and state and local activities play a significant role in the formation and implementation of public policy. This means that at the field level, public policy is contingent. The idea of local discretion is resisted, particularly by those at the top; their view is that public programs are to be uniform, accountable, orderly, lawful. Discretion is viewed with suspicion and becomes something to be controlled.

The theory of public action takes a different view of discretion. Discretion is seen not only as inevitable but as necessary and desirable. If we are going to try and achieve the kind of administrative justice exemplified (at least in theory) by the Madison School District, then there must be creativity, flexibility, and individuality at the local level. The reasons for this will be discussed shortly. However, to accomplish these objectives, not only must there be discretion, there must be the creative use of discretion. Local actors in the development of public policy need to be encouraged along desired directions—but it must be understood that control and direction will be limited.

A key aspect of the conditions of discretion involves the bureaucracy. I do not believe that justice, in the sense of shared decision making between autonomous, responsible participants, can be accomplished if the bureaucracy is adversarial and hostile. The legal-rights, or liberal legal, approach assumes this posture; procedural due process is an adversarial relation. For a variety of reasons, which I discuss in Chapters 2 and 3, I believe that the ordinary citizen, even with assistance from organizations, will not be able to prevail in the vast majority of situations. Over the long haul, the bureaucracies are simply too powerful (Handler 1966, 1978). The bureaucracy, then, has to go along. In Madison, it was the bureaucracy that led the way.

How, then, are we to look at bureaucracies? What are their characteristics? Under what circumstances can they be induced to change, and in what directions? In Chapter 7, there is a long discussion of organizations, and that only scratches the surface. Theories and empirical studies of organizations are as complex, varied, and confusing as the subject matter itself. Nevertheless, certain generalizations can be made. Organizations are flexible, dynamic, evolving, adaptable. There is often a great deal of internal movement. Bureaucracies are also, in the main, highly responsive to their environments; in fact, some theorists even challenge the idea of organizational boundaries. The conclusion that emerges is that organizations are subject to change; sources of influence in the environment can influence organizational direction.

On the other hand, it does not seem at all predictable as to how organizations will respond to various influences, problems, or pressures. These are complex entities, subject to many cross-currents. Thus, in considering the possibilities of organizational response, one must be aware of both contingency and change. Today's solutions will not necessarily be recognizable tomorrow. The organization literature gives one hope, but with a large amount of caution.

The third condition of discretion attempts to address the distribution question. Social movement groups to help the relatively powerless is an old idea; further, it is an idea that has, at best, a checkered history. Reflecting on the experiences of the last thirty years or so, one sees both gains and failures. Some groups are strong and influential (for example, environmentalists, women), while others seem weak or in disarray (for instance, civil rights, the poor). Yet, there is a body of evidence that, at the local level, there are thousands of active community and neighborhood groups; apparently, the experiences of the 1960s and 1970s are still alive (Boyte 1981).

Social movement groups address the distribution question by reducing the alienation of the parents and by providing them with information, support, and resources (including advocacy, if necessary). The groups are able to collectivize grievances and press for systemic reform. In addition, they act as special interest groups in the theory of public action, that is, they are active in the formation and implementation of special education policy and programs.

How does this come about? How can social movement groups provide both service and advocacy when traditional social group theorists argue that there is conflict between the two? Why would these groups succeed here when groups acting on behalf of the relatively powerless have been unsuccessful in the past? The argument that I develop is that two conditions of discretion—the theory of public action and the role of the bureaucracy—increase the chances of successful social movement group activity. There is the reduced level of conflict. The agency wants parental participation in decision making; the parents are viewed as part of the organizational task. The role, then, of the social movement groups is not to wrest power from a recalcitrant bureaucracy but to be capable of effectively using the power now being offered to them.

A number of consequences follow from the position of the bureaucracy. Groups at the grass roots level have to be encouraged and supported. Without the groups, the parents lack an important capacity to fully participate in the decision-making process. Without the social movement groups, there will not be the desired development of policy and programs. At the same time, the bureaucracy must avoid coopting the social movement groups, which will kill the grass roots activity. These groups must be autonomous but not adversarial. If they are or become adversarial, they eventually will die. In the meantime, they will subordinate individual member interests in order to present a unified and solid front.

Group theory has always been troublesome in liberal political thought because of the potential conflict between the organization and the individual. While the importance of groups has always been recognized in American society, we are uncomfortable with the basic idea of associational political life and representation. The groups that I am arguing for ought to be able to preserve individuality. The end here is not communal life; rather, it is to enhance the capacity of individuals (the parents) in their relationship with the agency. The groups are voluntaristic; parents are free to pursue their interests on their own. There are natural forces of change in membership; parents come and go, and have differing and changing interests depending upon the needs of their children. Unless they serve individual needs, the groups will not be able to deliver, and thus recruit or maintain membership.

The argument for social movement groups is complicated and subtle. It is also problematic. Indeed, this is probably the weakest point in the Madison system. There, teachers and administrators complain that parents have become too complacent despite great efforts to get them and keep them involved. It may be that this process of decline is inevitable. On the other hand, there has not been sufficient understanding at the theoretical level of the importance of social movement group activity to the overall success of the enterprise.

The end of the enterprise is the relationship of the citizen to the state in the context of a discretionary decision. As previously stated, I build on the concept of informed consent as discussed in the field of medicine. It is out of these experiences, and particularly the theoretical development, that one can explore the possibilities of what I call "social autonomy" in special education (and similar situations). We are concerned with autonomy—that is the whole point—but it is autonomy in a social relation.

Social autonomy tracks the definition of community as used by Wolff (1968)—a dialogue where each of the participants is reciprocally aware of the states of consciousness of the other participants. Here, we have two sets of community—between the parents and the agency and among the parents. Between the agency and the parents, the goal is to achieve revelation, understanding, and participation. Wolff describes this as a political community, where individuals and groups seek out common ends. Among the parents, the community is also political in an instrumental sense. At the same time, it is an affective community, "the reciprocal consciousness of a shared culture" (Wolff 1968, p. 187). Community, in the sense of social autonomy, complements or completes individualism.

The arguments of this book confront many of the challenges to liberal political theory. These challenges, which are as old as liberalism itself, have produced a rich and complex literature. Without doing justice, I attempt to sketch out, in the concluding chapter, where the arguments here meet these challenges. The conditions of discretion affirm the centrality of the individual, but they also recognize that the individual exists in social relations. It seeks to develop a theory of the individual and the state, and the individual and the group. The public/private distinction is transcended by the theory of public action. Social groups and individuals are considered to be an integral, necessary part of public policy. Epistemologically, social autonomy denies the subject/object distinction. Individuals must be both ends and means; they cannot treat each other instrumentally as in the liberal state. Social autonomy also denies the fact/value distinction of positivism. Social autonomy is knowledge based on individual values and experience. It can still be rational, but not rationally devoid of that which cannot be measured by our senses. It is subjective, but not necessarily arbitrary. It is what Spragens (1981) calls "practical knowledge," as distinguished from abstract, scientific knowledge.

Are the conditions of discretion utopian? That the reader must judge. The theory is coherent, thus possible. Madison is not a major metropolitan center; but it is not a trivial example. It is also not a blueprint. If we are to take the idea of discretion seriously, then each community must work toward the conditions of discretion in its own way according to its own particular circumstances. Policy, agencies, social groups, and individuals are fluid and subject to constant change. If we are to take individualism seriously, then we must live with uncertainty.

REFERENCES

Abel, Richard L. (ed.). *The Politics of Informal Justice: Volume 1, The American Experience; Volume 2, Comparative Studies.* New York: Academic Press, 1982.

Boyte, Harry C. *The Backyard Revolution: Understanding the New Citizen Movement.* Philadelphia: Temple University Press, 1981.

Clune, William, and Van Pelt, Mark. "A Political Method of Evaluating 94–

142 and the Several Gaps of Gap Analysis." *Law and Contemporary Problems*, December 1984.

Elmore, Richard. "Backward Mapping: Implementation Research and Policy Decisions." *Political Science Quarterly*, 94 (Winter 1979–1980), pp. 601–616.

Elmore, Richard. "Organizational Modes of Social Program Implementation." *Public Policy* (Spring 1978), pp. 185–228.

Galanter, Marc. "Reading the Landscape of Disputes: What We Know and Don't Know (and Think We Know) About Our Allegedly Contentious and Litigious Society." *UCLA Law Review*, 31 (October 1983), pp. 4–71.

Handler, Joel F. "Controlling Official Behavior in Welfare Administration." *California Law Review*, 54 (1966), pp. 479–510.

Handler, Joel F. *Social Movements and the Legal System: A Theory of Law Reform and Social Change*. New York: Academic Press, 1978.

Handler, Joel F., and Zatz, Julie (eds.). *Neither Angels Nor Thieves: Studies in Deinstitutionalization of Status Offenders*. Washington, D.C.: National Academy Press, 1982.

Heller, Kirby A.; Holtzman, Wayne H.; and Messick, Samuel (eds.). *Placing Children in Special Education: A Strategy for Equity*. Washington, D.C.: National Academy Press, 1982.

Reich, Charles. "The New Property." *Yale Law Journal*, 73 (1964), pp. 733–787.

Sabatier, Paul, and Mazmanian, Daniel. "The Implementation of Public Policy: A Framework for Analysis." *Policy Studies Journal*, 8 (Special Issue 2, 4, 1980), pp. 538–560.

Simon, William. "The Ideology of Advocacy: Procedural Justice and Professional Ethics." *Wisconsin Law Review*, 1978 (1978), pp. 29–144.

Spragens, Thomas A. *The Irony of Liberal Reason*. Chicago: University of Chicago Press, 1981.

Trubek, David; Sarat, Austin; Felstiner, William L. F.; Kritzer, Herbert M.; and Grossman, Joel B. "The Costs of Ordinary Litigation." *UCLA Law Review*, 31 (1983), pp. 72–127.

Wolff, Robert Paul. *The Poverty of Liberalism*. Boston: Beacon Press, 1968.

PART I

Critique

· 2 ·

Administrative Due Process

This chapter discusses the conceptual and practical failure of due process. I should state at the outset what I mean by the "failure" of due process and what implications are to be drawn from that indictment. In complex social changes there are never complete successes or complete failures, and this is certainly true of due process. I agree with Thompson (1975) that the development of the rule of law is one of humanity's crowning achievements. Its procedural manifestation—due process—is also a grand achievement, both in ideology and in application. It has changed our conception of the fundamental status of large numbers of people. We look at social relations differently now than three decades ago. There has not only been an ideological change; in application, many have won important substantive rights.

Nonetheless, for large numbers of people the remedy does not work. Moreover, because of the conceptual weakness and the failure to address the maldistribution question, the due process remedy, as a practical matter, cannot be extended to those presently outside. While due process has served important functions, it is fruitless to try to improve it in the manner that would be necessary to achieve justice in the modern state. What is needed is a different form of procedure, one that takes a different conceptual approach and that takes account of context. This does not mean rejection of due process. Rather, as I argue in Chapter 5, due process recedes in importance; it remains in the wings, so to speak, for particular problems, when other remedies and approaches fail. The two systems live side by side, and due process no longer dominates client/agency relations.

The arguments concerning the failure of due process are first developed for the civil system and then applied to administration. In Chapter 3, I focus more specifically on the principal example of the book, special education. Chapter 4 presents an alternative system for decision making in special education—a cooperative form developed in the school district of Madison, Wisconsin. This is the principal empirical example out of which the main theoretical arguments for the new approach are developed. Ordinarily, this chapter would be in Part II, where the theory is developed. It is discussed here as part of the critique to highlight the points of criticism by drawing attention to the alternatives. This prepares the reader for Chapter 5, which draws together the theoretical arguments against the liberal legal approach and addresses the question of the proper place of due process in the modern state. Chapter 5 is the transition chapter. It summarizes the case against the old; it is out of the critique that the ground is prepared for the new.

The rise of administrative due process grew out of many concerns. In recent decades, there has been an increase in concern about the exercise of discretion and domination in the relationship between clients and large-scale organizations. In part, this concern grew out of the rise of the modern welfare state. Much of our well-being depends upon the goods and services that large-scale organizations provide. In part, the concern grew out of the civil rights and legal rights revolution. Relationships between people and their government have been recast. The legal conception of clients has changed from beneficiaries of mere privileges to "rights bearing" citizens. Government, when it chooses to act, must act lawfully. Clients of government have rights; they are to be treated fairly and according to law. If one looks broadly at how we view the citizen in relation to the government today as compared to 1950, the change is remarkable.

This transformation has been the work of all principal lawmaking institutions—courts, legislatures, and administrative agencies. Focusing on disputes between clients and welfare agencies, the Supreme Court, in *Goldberg* v. *Kelly*, held that welfare was a valuable statutory entitlement, subject to constitutional due process. The Court rejected the prior view that the relationship between a welfare recipient and the agency was a mere privilege. In that case, the Court imposed a high degree of procedural formality on the agency. Due process remedies would help ensure accuracy in fact-finding and the application of legal rules. The discretion and domination of public agencies was to be checked through the exercise of procedural due process rights.

Goldberg v. *Kelly* struck a responsive chord and was picked up in many statutory and administrative schemes—welfare, Social Security, disability, mental health, education. The early 1970s were the highwater mark of liberal legalism, which relied heavily on procedural due process remedies, such as access, as an important method of achieving a variety of goals (Weisbrod, Handler & Komesar 1978; Handler, Hollingsworth & Erlanger 1978).

Despite its acceptance, shortly after *Goldberg* the Supreme Court drew back. In a series of decisions, the Court emphasized that procedural due process was a flexible concept and that procedures had to be adapted to varying circumstances. The Court sanctioned a cost-benefit analysis. In deciding what procedures were due, one had to weigh three factors: the nature of the interest at stake, the benefits of increased accuracy that would be obtained from more procedural formality, and the cost of the effective operation of the government program (*Mathews* v. *Eldridge*; Mashaw 1973–1974). Very informal hearings were approved (in education suspension cases, *Goss* v. *Lopez*), especially in highly discretionary decisions (academic qualifications, mental health; *Board of Curators* v. *Horowitz, Parham* v. *J.R.*).

What we have, then, is a curious legal situation. Many areas of relationships between clients and agencies are governed by statutory and administrative procedural schemes that were adopted during the *Goldberg* v. *Kelly*, era but are now no longer constitutionally required. This is not to say that these procedural schemes are no longer valid; it is only to point out that in considering procedural remedies, the earlier constitutional strictures have been withdrawn. The Constitution, as articulated by the Supreme Court, no longer defines the policy choices.

The procedural approach emanating from the *Goldberg* era focused on the *hearing* at the administrative level. The law intervened in the client/agency relationship when the agency had decided to withhold or withdraw a benefit or impose other sanctions. At that point in the relationship, the legal system made available to clients the right to invoke the due process procedural system for resolving their conflicts with the agency. There are two clusters of issues with this approach. One is at the point of intervention. Does the law intervene at the right point in the agency–client relationship? Second, when the law does intervene, does it do so appropriately?

Barriers to Hearings

Psychology and Culture

The due process system relies on the complaining client. With rare exceptions, the legal system is not a proactive force, seeking out errors or injustice and instituting corrective actions. Rather, it assumes that regulation is satisfactory unless there are complaints. This is consistent with the liberal view of the individual and the sharp distinction between the public and the private. It assumes a knowing, alert citizenry jealous of its independence and possessive of its right. This approach is pervasive in both public and private law.

There are a great many problems with this method of correcting wrongs in private dealings, but with public regulation, and especially with relationships between individual and large-scale public agencies, reliance on the complaining client is virtually fatal. In order for the due process system to be invoked, the following conditions have to be met: clients have to be aware that an injury has occurred; they have to think that the agency is at fault; they have to be aware of the existence of a remedy; they have to have the resources with which to pursue that remedy; and finally, they have to make a calculation that the benefits of pursuing the remedy outweigh its costs. Two things must be noted about these conditions. All of them have to be satisfied if the due process procedures are to be utilized; if there is a failure in any one of them, the process will not be used. And, each and every one of the conditions is a difficult hurdle to negotiate for the average person dealing with a large-scale public organization (Handler 1966).

Most encounters between field-level officials and clients never give rise to dispute. In many instances, clients may be perfectly satisfied with a decision; in other instances, perhaps only moderately satisfied; and in still other instances, perhaps greatly dissatisfied, but still not enough to do anything. In a recent paper called "The Emergence and Transformation of Disputes: Naming, Blaming, and Claiming . . . ," Felstiner, Abel, and Sarat (1980–1981) analyzed the steps necessary to transform an experience or encounter into a dispute. In real life, there is a substantial capacity for people to tolerate considerable distress and even injustice. The tolerance may be due to a lack of awareness or perception that something wrong is happening to them. Lack of perception may be self-induced or the result of external manipulation. One of the examples given by the authors concerns shipworkers suffering from asbestosis. It was only after they stopped taking for granted that they would have trouble breathing after ten years that they would perceive a particular experience as injurious.

People may become aware of an injury, but a dispute may still not arise. The injured person has to blame someone else (the injured person may blame him- or herself), and even when the injured person has blamed someone else, another step is required—that of making a claim or an official appeal to rectify the wrong.

A dispute arises when the claim is rejected. The claim may be rejected outright, or it may simply not be acted upon. At this point, again, nothing more may happen. Clients, for a variety of reasons, may decide to drop the complaint. Or they may decide to pursue whatever remedy is available, for example, a hearing or a civil lawsuit. In administrative systems, the case and statutory law and administrative regulations give aggrieved clients the right to a hearing (sometimes called a "fair hearing") to challenge the agency decision. The hearings are mostly at the administrative level, and usually involve an adversarial presentation before a disinterested hearing officer. As previously stated, the degree of procedural formality may vary. In most cases, there is a right to judicial review.

Felstiner, Abel, and Sarat argue that the antecedents of the formalized disputes at the hearing level are critically important. A great many factors serve to hide the existence of wrongs and injustices or to chill exercises of claims or modify and alter the form of the claims. A variety of actors—the initial field-level official who made the decision, the advocates who may or may not include professionals, and the listeners, or adjudicators (for example, immediate supervisors) all serve to filter, discourage, encourage, and alter grievances. Important, too, is the effect of ideology, including changes in the law. Changes in perceptions of rights—"you *can* fight city hall"—remove an important barrier. On the whole, deep ideological currents serve to justify the status quo, the position of the person in society, the authority and legitimacy of the state, the bureaucracy, and the law (Gordon 1982). It seems self-evident that the poor, minorities, the poorly educated, the newcomer, the frightened, the mentally ill, the sick, and other disadvantaged are not only more likely to suffer distress and injustice than those better off, but are also less likely to negotiate the antecedents of disputes (Bumiller 1985).

People suffering the same wrongs react differently. Some will recognize the injury, others will not. Some who are aware of the injury will blame, others will not. Some will claim while others do nothing. What explains these differences in reaction to similar events? Coates and Penrod (1980–1981) use psychological theory and research to explain what leads people to name, blame, and claim. Although the authors focus primarily on private law disputes (for example, consumer complaints), much of what they say would appear to apply to client interactions with large-scale public organizations.

Coates and Penrod discuss naming, blaming, and claiming in terms of relative deprivation, equity, attribution, and control. People will perceive an injury if they have suffered a *relative* deprivation, when they are treated less favorably than in the past, or in relation to what others are getting. When people feel that they are getting less than others whom they regard as less deserving, they will feel that there is an equity issue, a violation of entitlement. A relative outcome is more important than an absolute outcome. Coates and Penrod use the classic research of Stouffer (1949) which showed that despite the fact that airmen were much more likely to be promoted than military police, the airmen were more dissatisfied with the promotion system. Other research has shown the importance of temporal and social comparisons to occupational satisfaction. Comparisons are important, the authors claim, in understanding why some people become dissatisfied and not others who may, in fact, be having similar experiences. If it is relative outcomes and equity that are important, then it is not necessarily true that scarce resources will lead to increases in conflict, as long as perceptions of relative fairness are maintained.

Even if people perceive a deprivation, they will not necessarily take the next step, blaming. Coates and Penrod draw on attribution theory to explain why two people experiencing the same event draw different conclusions as to the cause—they can either blame themselves or blame others. Self-blame is apparently a forceful human tendency. "Despite all the human tendencies toward pinning the blame on someone 'out there,' an even stronger tendency toward accepting the blame ourselves seems to exist." (Coates and Penrod 1980–1981, p. 665). Studies have shown that the victims of accidents, rape, and spousal violence blame themselves for their misfortunes. There is even self-blame in the face of clearly contrary evidence.

When the evidence is ambiguous, people will either tend to forget about the misfortune or reach some kind of explanation through the systematic selection of evidence and personal theories; and in these situations, an important systematic bias is that of blaming oneself rather than others. Once made, attributions tend to have staying power. There is a tendency to stop searching for alternative explanations and new information, and instead people seek out information that confirms the initial bias.

Victims get help in their drive toward self-blame. Coates and Penrod report "there is evidence that both harm-doers and uninvolved observers will often distort available information in order to convince themselves that victims of negative events are in some way responsible for those events" (1980–1981, p. 671). Perpetrators will do this for self-justification; observers do so to convince themselves that somehow they will not suffer the same fate. Both friends and adversaries serve to reinforce the bias of the victim, that the victim is somehow responsible for the misfortune.

Why is self-blame so important? It is the desire to assert some control over events. "[W]hen problems threaten people's perceived control and sense of future safety, they may find self-blame more comforting than the alternative belief that they have little power over their own lives" (Coates and Penrod 1980–1981, p. 671).

Nevertheless, people who do suffer injury do not always blame themselves. People may attribute causation to external events, but still not take any other steps. Only certain kinds of external attributions will lead to claiming. If the external cause is considered to be transitory, it is likely that no steps will be taken. The harm (for example, loud street noise) will disappear rather quickly. Even if the external cause is considered to be long-lasting, there will still be no action. The victim will feel helpless and will become apathetic, depressed, or seek to escape. People will be more likely to intervene in moderately stable situations, that is, where the harm would continue without some intervention, but there is the possibility that intervention will be successful.

Blaming and claiming, then, depend on combinations of attribution and perceived control. Attribution theory is fairly well documented, but evidence concerning control is less clear. One would think, for example, that claiming would be income-related, since the higher the income, the more likely one would perceive the ability to control. People who suffer from discrimination are less likely to claim than other kinds of victims. Victims of discrimination are usually less well-off members of society, but research has shown that income alone is not a good predictor of claims (Miller and Sarat 1980–1981). Perceived control has not been directly measured in the research, and it may be, as Coates and Penrod argue, that other measures of control are more relevant than income. Discrimination, for example, would seem to present far different issues of naming, blaming, and claiming than the average consumer complaint. One would guess that the tendencies for self-blame would be stronger, the role of the harm-doers and neutral observers in blaming the victim would be more potent, and the likelihood of successful intervention would be far less in discrimination than in the average consumer complaint. Even if the internal and external tendencies toward self-blame were not stronger, clearly the effectiveness of a remedy in discrimination is much more problematic than in consumer complaints, and this, by itself, would lead to more resignation and inaction (Bumiller 1985).

The state of legal culture bears on the issue of perceived control. The legal system has been very active in the past two to three decades in creating entitlements, defining rights, and granting remedies. However, perceptions of these rights depend upon experience, word-of-mouth, social organization, the availability of legal services, and a variety of other matters. During periods of urban unrest and welfare rights activities, the welfare poor were galvanized into action; at least in certain parts of the country, there was naming, blaming, and claiming on the part of the disadvantaged. But in other localities, there was no activity. Law and language help order the facts as well as invoke the norms (Mather and Yngvesson 1980–1981), but the diffusion of the legal rights culture is uneven within and between social classes; it varies by locality, and even by program. Differences in perceptions will lead to differences in naming, blaming, and claiming. Special education and mental health, for example, probably present a different order of problems than, say, welfare or housing. In the former, it would seem that the potential for self-blame would be greater, and information more ambiguous, than in the latter.

Professionals and Other Helpers

Changes in legal culture have resulted not only in new definitions of rights and procedural remedies but also in the increased availability of professional and nonprofessional advocates. Resources with which to pursue the remedy are one of the conditions that claimants must negotiate. In addition to one's own time and resources—emotional as well as monetary—there is also the need for more professional services. A variety of advocacy services has grown up during the legal rights revolution. The Legal Services Corporation, with its Neighborhood Legal Services offices scattered throughout the country, is the most visible service, but there are also other professional and nonprofessional organizations, including various pro bono efforts of the organized bar, programs of lay advocates, ombudsmen, government offices (for example, consumer complaints divisions), hot lines, and so forth (Handler, Hollingsworth & Erlanger 1978).

Felstiner, Abel, and Sarat (1980–1981) argue that these actors play an important role in the naming, blaming, and claiming process. These helpers do in fact help clients in the process; they provide the necessary resources to pursue their clients' claims. A great deal has been accomplished by these programs and their resources (Handler, Hollingsworth & Erlanger 1978). On the other hand, there is great variation in the availability of these resources both in terms of locality and types of clients and cases served; and these differences are being accentuated with the recent budget declines. Thus, even though a Neighborhood Legal Services office may be in a community, it may now be able only to refer welfare or consumer cases rather than litigate them. Whatever the problems were of meeting unmet needs before the Reagan administration, surely those problems have increased dramatically.

When helpers are available, they play a complicated role in the process. Coates and Penrod (1980–1981) point out the importance of both wrongdoers and neutral observers in the process of self-blame. These could well include initial field-level officials, the helpers, supporters, advocates, listeners, or even adjudicators. Drawing on anthropological and other research, Mather and Yngvesson (1980–1981) note that third parties, including supporters and advocates, shape disputes to make them acceptable to their own interests. Others have also noted the role of professional supporters as either "potstirrers" or "peacemakers" (Fitzgerald and Dickens 1980–1981). In other words, when clients come to third parties, even if they are advocates for the clients, the clients pay the price. The third parties exercise a powerful filtering and shaping role. The clients need advocacy resources, but the advocates, facing their own organizational pressures, have to pick and choose in terms of their own needs. As a result of the interaction, clients may become intimidated, frustrated, or combative.

It would seem that the needs of the advocacy organization would be more pronounced vis-à-vis the client the farther down the socioeconomic scale of the client. With the less advantaged client, it is more likely that the advocate is supported by public or charitable funds, which are growing smaller in absolute terms as well as in relation to need. When it is hard for the advocate to do more than office consultation or referral, it becomes easier to rationalize that the client's problem can be solved by self-help, with a little office advice, or that it is less deserving than other, more pressing matters.

The Benefit-Cost Calculation

The final step in the process of invoking due process is to calculate whether the benefits of pursuing the remedy outweigh the costs. Some of the costs have already been discussed—the time and energy of the complaint and the costs of seeking help. Another cost deals with the relationship between the victim and the harm-doer. Naming, blaming, and claiming are hostile acts. This is particularly so if the claim is made in a formal setting such as a court or administrative hearing with professional advocacy help. With most tort matters, the negative effects of claiming on the relationship are not important since the parties are strangers and the victim probably has less than kind feelings toward the tortfeasor anyway. The relationship may vary with consumer complaints. With large retailers, the harm-doer and victim are strangers; each transaction is an isolated, impersonal event. Sears has no interest in whether the customer is a crank or an innocent victim; the fact has no bearing on future purchases. The situation would be different in small communities, in disputes between local merchants and neighbors. There the relation is *continuing*, and disgruntled customers have to weigh the potential future damage as part of the cost of blaming and claiming. Macaulay (1963) has pointed out that businessmen who want to keep doing business with each other rarely if ever resort to the law to settle contract disputes. If they want to preserve their relationship, they work things out; they negotiate present disagreements with a keen sense of the importance of tomorrow.

Findings and Conclusions

While most of the research discussed above has been concerned with private law—for example, consumer complaints, landlord/tenant disputes—a great deal of the theory and empirical findings apply to client relationships with large-scale organizations, and especially those relationships that are the concern of this book. In some of these agencies, the clientele represents a broad socioeconomic spectrum; the middle class, for example, is deeply involved in special education issues. But for most of these agencies, the vast majority of the clients are at the lower end of the socioeconomic ladder; they are either on welfare or pretty close to it. A great many are minorities; many are recent immigrants. The socio-psychological, educational, language, and health problems of the poor, the near poor, and minorities have to be kept in mind in considering the feasibility of naming, blaming, and claiming against public agencies.

There is considerable evidence that naming is a significant issue; people who deal with these public agencies are often unaware of the availability of benefits, and to what they are entitled. They often do not realize that rules and regulations have been misapplied to their situation (Briar 1966; Handler and Hollingsworth 1971). While a great deal of publicity has been generated about the large numbers of appeals in social welfare programs (for example, Friendly 1975), in fact this has been true only in a few selected parts of the country.

Overall, appeal rates, as compared to the size of the programs, seem to be quite low. As noted, there may be many reasons why clients do not appeal, but one important reason is lack of awareness that they have been injured or knowledge of what to do about their grievances. (Handler 1966; Mashaw 1971). When third-party resources are supplied—for example, public mediators or negotiators—appeal rates go up (Hammer and Hartley 1978).

Lack of knowledge seems to be a pervasive problem. In the Supplemental Security Income (SSI) program, the federal program for the aged poor, the effort was to redesign the program to make it less stigmatic, and more encouraging. Yet, only about half of the expected enrollment materialized. Some proportion of nonparticipants are near the top of the eligibility standard, and the small amount of benefit is not worth the cost. Others have never been on welfare and do not want to participate. But there is also a great deal of ignorance about the program. In an extensive study by the Social Security Administration it was found that 90 percent of all welfare documents required an eighth grade reading level. Yet, the mean level of education for the aged poor is 7.5 years; and more than 20 percent of the SSI nonparticipants had less than five years of schooling, the amount considered to be functionally literate. More than 20 percent were foreign born, so that English as a second language might be a problem. In other words, along with the normal decline of sensory skills, there could well be poor reading and interpretive skills. The study concluded that outreach for this population is not a simple task (Urban Systems Research & Engineering 1981).

There are problems of participation with the elderly in other programs as well. Energy and other special needs programs are particularly troublesome, often resulting in genuine suffering and occasional death. Here, the problem is not only a lack of information but also stigma. Studies in England, where great efforts were made to get the elderly poor to apply for extra heating grants (which would then be given virtually automatically), showed that many of the elderly poor felt that they had to get along on the standard welfare rate (Handler and Sosin 1983). People who suffer shame about public welfare benefits or who lack a welfare experience are not likely to know much about the programs, and when they do enter them they are probably not going to be "rights bearing" citizens.

As the Social Security Administration study of SSI participation shows, information about social welfare programs is not readily available to the consumers. From their perspective, given educational levels and language skills, communication is difficult. One also has to consider social and psychological factors. Contrary to popular belief, many of the poor are not in the "welfare culture"; they do not enjoy being on welfare, they leave welfare after an average stay of about two years (although many return), and they do not think well of other welfare recipients. In short, they would rather be on their own, like most people. The decision to apply for welfare, for most, is thus not a happy, easily taken step; it is usually done after failing to make a go of it after a crisis—loss of a job, break-up of the home, or some other personal disaster. In this situation, the applicant is worried about surviving and getting accepted into the program; he or she is not interested in legal rights, or the finer aspects of entitlements (Handler and Hollingsworth 1971). And while the basic income-maintenance programs—Aid to Families with Dependent Children, Food Stamps, SSI, and Social Security—are difficult enough to fathom, health, mental health, social service, general assistance, emergency assistance, and special needs programs are far more difficult to understand. The latter programs are more technical, more discretionary, less rule-bound, less well-known, and therefore far more obscure and opaque as far as potential clients are concerned.

People approach these programs, then, in a vulnerable personal situation, and are confronted with ambiguous information. At this point, they face a hostile government bureaucracy—waiting rooms, offices, receptionists, officials, paper, forms, questions. No doubt this experience varies from sympathetic, supportive intake workers to the cold, vaguely hostile, impersonal stereotypical agency (Lipsky 1980). In some of the programs the applicant also has to confront the professional. The normally authoritative government official speaks in a technical language that is beyond even most educated lay people. We are familiar with the middle class experiences dealing with professionals in the private world—the complaints that doctors do not communicate, that professionals rather than clients make the decisions, the mystification of the relationship, the feeling of helplessness. The dominating relationship is not solely the doing of the professional. Professionals who try to increase patient or client involvement in the decision-making process report extreme difficulty in getting the patient or client involved. Under the pressure of the workload, all but the most resolute professionals cannot resist telling the client what they think is really the best course of action (Wexler 1970; Katz 1984).

In public agencies, the tendency to dominate on the part of officials and professionals would seem to be overwhelming. Added to the normal propensities of officials and professionals to dominate are the differences in social class and work setting. The pressure of time alone would seem to preclude a leisurely exploration of the client's problems and wishes. It would seem that the tendencies that Coates and Penrod and Mather and Yngvesson discuss would be far stronger in these bureaucratic settings. If victims of accidents tend to engage in self-blame, how much stronger would this tendency be for clients of large-scale public agencies who are unhealthy, or emotionally disturbed, or have a child in academic or disciplinary trouble in school, or are having trouble with a spouse or with children, or have lost a job, or have suffered some other social or economic disaster?

There are also the costs of claiming when dealing with public agencies. For some types of decisions, there is no relationship to speak of and the potential benefits of claiming will outweigh the costs— for example, when applicants are denied entry to an income-maintenance program or when eligibility has been terminated. In many other situations there are continuing relationships and considerable potential for at least the fear, if not the fact, of retaliation. This would be true in education and special education, in fact in all cases where the client still has to deal with the program. Even in the income-maintenance programs many decisions are not clearly limited to being in or out of the program. Here, we would expect fewer appeals from decisions, because of the continuing relationships, than for denials or terminations, and the research confirms this (Handler 1969; Hammer and Hartley 1978).

Hearing Procedures

When all of the above hurdles have been negotiated and a claim is made and rejected, then procedural law comes into play. What decision-making procedures does due process require? *Goldberg* v. *Kelly* specified a high degree of process. This was a case where welfare benefits were terminated. The Court held that the client had to have a hearing before the grant was terminated. It went on to specify what the requirements of the due process hearing were: (1) the right to timely and adequate notice detailing the reasons for the proposed termination; (2) the opportunity to present orally evidence and arguments in opposition to the proposed termination; (3) the right to confront and cross-examine the witness relied on by the welfare department; (4) the right to be represented by an attorney at the hearing, if desired; (5) the right to an impartial decision maker's conclusion as to the evidence adduced at the hearing.

Goldberg involved an administrative hearing claim; yet, the procedures which the Court said were constitutionally required strongly resemble the ideal type of a standard civil or criminal trial. This is the starting point of the legal profession when it thinks of due process—the adversary elements of a standard civil or criminal trial. The ideology goes to the fundamental basis of the relationship between citizens and the state. In the oft-quoted words of Mr. Justice Frankfurter:

> The heart of the matter is that democracy implies a respect for the elementary rights of men, however suspect or untrustworthy; a democratic government must therefore practice fairness; and fairness can rarely be obtained by secret, one-sided determination of facts decisive to rights [O'Neil 1970, p. 161].

In discussing the *Goldberg* case, O'Neil articulated the values served by the elements of the trial-type hearing. These values are lofty as well as plentiful: accuracy and fairness, accountability, consistency, integrity, and credibility. How does all of this come about? If the process is accurate, it will be fair, and "at base, only a hearing—probably only an adversarial hearing—can prevent or correct errors of fact" (O'Neil 1970, p. 161). Personal participation is necessary because the parties themselves usually know more about the facts concerning themselves than anyone else. There must not only be participation but also confrontation to expose mistakes and falsehoods. Requiring the decision to be based on the evidence and arguments adduced at the hearing allows for accountability and consistency, and helps ensure the integrity of the process. When decisions are open, accurate, and consistent, they are entitled to respect.

At the time he wrote (1970), O'Neil had a right to be sanguine. As noted, *Goldberg* was the highwater mark of liberal legalism, the idea that individual rights in the administrative state could be protected by procedural due process modeled after the conception of the trial-type hearing in civil and criminal courts. Lawyers believe that this is a time-tested model; when properly functioning, it does approach ideals of accuracy and fairness, or at least it does so better than any other decision-making procedure. It is the standard by which to judge the fairness of adjudication.

Hearings in Context

 The model due process procedure carries with it certain assumptions about the social position of the actors. In its ideal form, it views the proceedings in isolation from the world, as if free of time, space, and social setting. It is an autonomous proceeding. No mention, for example, is made of who the parties are and what resources they have. Are they organizations? Or individuals? Are they rich or poor? The judge is part of a bureaucracy, but it is very decentralized and she has a great deal of autonomy. In the discussions of the values of the adversary system, for example, is there mention of caseload? Rather, discussions of the characteristics and values of due process are abstract; distribution of income and the problems of bureaucracy are ignored. Due process assumes that parties have adequate resources and that the judge is independent, contemplative, and deliberative.

Of course, the implicit assumptions about civil and criminal trials are far from the truth. Because of that, there has always been considerable concern about the accuracy and fairness of civil and criminal trials. The real-life departure from the ideal is most obvious in the criminal trial. There is a great disparity between the resources of the state and those of the vast majority of the accused. This is so obvious and so unjust that it is now constitutionally required that the state supply legal services to any accused who faces a jail term (*Argersinger* v. *Hamlin*). But even with assigned counsel and public defenders, great disparities exist. The court, too, is far from a disinterested adjudicative body. Instead, it is one part of the criminal justice system, where people are rapidly and perfunctorily processed rather than tried, where, as Feeley (1979) has said, "the process is the punishment."

While the influence of social systems is obvious and dominant in the criminal justice system, it is no less present in civil litigation. Again, the starting point is the difference in the social positions of the parties. Not surprisingly, it is the rich and powerful who can take advantage of access to the law, not the poor and weak. The equality of procedure does not take account of the inequality of resources, and as Galanter (1974) has pointed out, there is a difference between "one shot" players and "repeat" players. The classic example is the small claims court. This was a reform designed to equalize resources; it was a mini-court, with a simple procedure often barring lawyers, where people with small claims could seek redress (Harrington 1982). Instead, these courts have become collection agencies for large retailers. It is the institutional litigants, the repeat players, who appear in these courts day after day, and who have trained lay experts. The one-shot players are at a decided disadvantage (Galanter 1974; Lazerson 1982).

The civil justice system is plagued with the problems of the rich against the poor, and as a result there have been considerable efforts to try to redress the balance. Legal aid for the poor has been a continuing effort since the nineteenth century; its current manifestation is the embattled Legal Services Corporation. The public interest law movement, supported by charitable organizations, represents interests not represented in the free market of legal services. There have also been arrangements to award counsel fees in certain circumstances (for example, rights, employment discrimination) to help redress the balance (Handler, Hollingsworth & Erlanger 1978).

While this is not the place to evaluate the civil and criminal justice system, it does seem evident that it is a system that has fallen short of its ideals. It is a system that assumes a relationship between the citizen and the state that is largely invalid, with efforts to mitigate the maldistribution of wealth and power that are ineffective. When courts are considered in context, they are largely inaccessible because of the social position of the ordinary person.

Administrative Hearings

How much more important is that context when considering adjudication by administrative agencies? Administrative hearing procedures are integral parts of bureaucratic systems. These systems have specific tasks to perform: they regulate, distribute benefits, run programs, and do all of the other things that public agencies do. The programs are the main task, and the hearings, while important to the individual, are incidental. It is important to keep this in mind. The raison d'être of the civil and criminal courts is to adjudicate. This is not true for agencies. They view their hearing system as just one piece of the whole.

Agencies, then, will attempt to alter the due process model to fit their institutional goals. As with courts, agencies have to balance the competing demands of fairness, accuracy, and efficiency, but they view these problems in terms of their own needs. As pointed out, the Supreme Court has given the agencies this flexibility.

An excellent illustration of how the agency hearing systems are molded to the needs of the bureaucracy is provided by Mashaw's studies (1971, 1973–1974, 1982) of the Social Security Disability system. Mashaw's examples show the tensions and conflicts over due process values in a large, complex bureaucratic structure. They make concrete the need for bureaucracies to get the work done. At the same time, there are other important demands that press for consideration: due process values and, with service organizations, the special demands of the healing or service professions.

The complex hearing system of the Social Security Disability program shows the varied roles of the key actors—the bureaucrats, the professionals, the adjudicators, and the clients—and how they affect the operation of the hearing system.

A disabled person is entitled to income maintenance and medical benefits; he or she may be referred to vocational rehabilitation, and may be subject to reevaluation to determine whether the disability has continued. Medical, personal, and vocational criteria are used to determine disability. Disability is initially determined by state agencies (preferably a state vocational rehabilitation agency), with appeal before federal administrative law judges, and judicial review in federal court. Three types of demands on the appeal system, according to Mashaw, produce great stress: (1) decisions should be accurate and efficiently rendered; (2) decisions should take due account of the relevant professional perspectives; and (3) decisions should be fair in light of traditional values for determining individual entitlements. These demands are represented by three models of administrative justice which compete simultaneously in the disability program.

1. *The Bureaucratic Rationality Model.* The goal is accurately to determine claims at the lowest possible cost—"to minimize the sum of error costs and administrative costs" (Mashaw 1981, p. 185). This is best accomplished to the extent that questions for decisions are presented, as near as possible, in factual and technocratic terms that are the least costly way of collecting the relevant facts. This model attempts to exclude, as much as possible, questions of value or preference, or decisions based on intuition or other subjective factors. It is a process that stresses accuracy and costs, clear rules, and hierarchical control.

2. *The Professional Treatment Model.* Since the goal of the professions is to help people, a disability system that is professionally oriented would be client oriented. It would organize the available benefits (income, medical care, vocational rehabilitation, counseling) to further the well-being of the client. As in the bureaucratic model, there are facts to gather and costs to consider, but the professional model emphasizes the distinctiveness of the client and the "ultimately intuitive nature of [clinical] judgment" (Mashaw 1981, p. 186). The task is not necessarily to establish factual accuracy but rather diagnosis and treatment.

3. *The Moral Judgment Model.* Mashaw distinguishes the traditional adjudication from the bureaucratic rationality model: although both are concerned with accurately finding the facts, the bureaucratic model's other function is only the correct application of previously validated norms. The moral judgment model, however, views the decision making as also defining values. The deservedness of the parties quite often enters into traditional adjudication. Civil claims involve not only deciding who did what, but quite often also the reasonableness of the conduct. The "distinctive cast" of this model is that "the deservedness of the parties in the context of events, transactions, or relationship . . . give rise to a claim" (Mashaw 1981, p. 188).

Mashaw points out that there are advantages and disadvantages to each of the models in the disability program. One can argue that the bureaucratic model is the only model suitable to maintaining program integrity. Prior to the adoption of the present system, the judicial system (the moral judgment model) rapidly expanded claims during periods of high unemployment. On the other hand, Congress did build in professional decision making: the medical profession has to make the basic eligibility decision, and decision making was also delegated to state vocational rehabilitation agencies. And it could also be argued that the basic issue in disability involves value conflicts over the distribution of resources; it is not only a matter of skills, impairments, and experience, but whether a particular person with a certain set of characteristics ought to be socially excused from work and to receive benefits. This is the task for the moral judgment model.

Whatever the claims for the competing models, the dominant model selected by the disability program is bureaucratic rationality. The program is primarily interested in the speedy, inexpensive disposition of claims. Selection of the professional model would jeopardize budgetary control, given either a doctor's sympathy for patients or her unwillingness to risk the patient's health. Decision making by vocational rehabilitation specialists would also be risk-averse and would threaten consistency and predictability. The moral judgment approach was also rejected. The Social Security administration has to administer an active program, which means being responsible for gathering sufficient information to decide claims accurately and efficiently; it is not to be a passive arbiter of claims.

Nevertheless, despite these decision-making goals, the program has incorporated elements of the other two models. The initial decision is made by the state rehabilitation agencies, and there are hearings before administrative law judges and judicial review. The scheme is a compromise: the bureaucracy acts first, and then there is a nonadversary hearing for dissatisfied claimants. The hearing officer investigates, conducts an oral hearing, and makes the initial decision. If the claimant is still dissatisfied, there is the option of judicial review.

This is the statutory and administrative scheme. In practice, it has been difficult to reconcile the demands of the competing models. In Mashaw's view, the judges, doctors, and vocational experts undermine the bureaucratic model. The judicial model is used by the independent federal administrative law judges, who are more lenient in granting claims than the state disability officers. The administrative law judges focus on an inclusive definition of disability: in general, they seek to emulate the role of judges, and stoutly resist efforts by the Social Security Administration to impose bureaucratic control on individualized justice.

Protection against the professional treatment model is supposed to be accomplished by a regulation that instructs disability examiners to ignore the opinion of the treating physician concerning the patient's capacity to work; this is supposed to avoid the costs of risk-adverse medical advice. But the problem with this approach, according to Mashaw, is that by limiting the physician's role, the agency lessens its capacity to get the necessary high-quality information that it needs to make accurate decisions.

Similar problems arise concerning the question of whether the claimant should be expected to work. The state vocational rehabilitation professionals, facing scarce resources, also tend to be conservative, like the treating physicians. Here, too, the agency strains, often artificially and unsuccessfully, to avoid delegating decision making to the professionals.

Mashaw argues that the situation described in the disability system is not unique, but that probably in many administrative systems there is competition between at least two, if not three, of the models. Each represents important organizational interests as well as serious claims for achieving administrative justice.

Although special education's mission is different from that of the disability program, these three models also compete in the hearing system of that program. The context of the procedural system is the bureaucratic structure. This structure powerfully shapes the already flexible due process standards.

In addition to the bureaucracy, the social position of the clients affects the hearing procedures. In civil and criminal courts, there are instances when the idealized version of due process is achieved, or at least substantially so. The parties have sufficient resources; the court deliberates and then adjudicates; and there is review. How often the ideals are realized or how often the social position of the parties or other structural features distort the civil and criminal trial is a hotly debated issue. It certainly seems clear that the lower civil and criminal courts in the large urban centers function wide of the mark. The small claims courts, the landlord–tenant courts, the minor and even felony criminal courts bear almost no resemblance to the due process procedure.

A similar situation obtains in the administrative system. For the most part, the due process statutes and regulations are in place, and they are used—from time to time. Public interest lawyers, legal service lawyers, and civil liberties lawyers take important cases, which receive a great deal of publicity (Weisbrod, Handler & Komesar 1978). Middle class parents sue the school and mental health bureaucracies. Criminals, on occasion, fight parole and prison authorities. But how often do these cases occur? How much litigation is there really in view of the massive numbers of decisions that these large public agencies make? Mashaw, after years of studying the disability system, is convinced that the average claimant has very little understanding of what is happening in the process. Studies of public welfare administration reach the same conclusion. The same situation applies to the area of special education. Most of the people who deal with these large agencies are weak, uninformed, minorities, poorly educated, handicapped, disabled. Clients also include the opposite— rights-bearing citizens. Because they (or in rare instances, the downtrodden) can use the procedural system effectively, one should not conclude that the system "works" for all, or for most, or even for many. The societal reasons for the distortions of civil and criminal justice apply with even more force to procedural systems in the bureaucratic setting. Not only is there less of a tradition (and legal compulsion) for procedural due process, but the influence of the bureaucratic setting and the comparative weakness of the client are much more prevalent in the bureaucracy than they are in the judicial setting.

REFERENCES

Briar, Scott. "Welfare from Below: Recipients' Views of the Public Welfare System." *California Law Review*, 54 (1966), pp. 370–385.

Brodkin, Evelyn, and Lipsky, Michael. "Quality Control as Administrative Strategy." *Social Service Review*, 57 (March 1983), pp. 1–34.

Bumiller, Kristin. "Anti-Discrimination Law and the Enslavement of the Victim: The Denial of Self-Respect by Victims Without a Cause." Disputes Processing Research Program, Working Paper 1984–6. University of Wisconsin at Madison, 1985.

Coates, Dan, and Penrod, Steven. "Social Psychology and the Emergence of Disputes." *Law and Society Review*, 15, 3–4 (1980–1981), pp. 655–680.

Feeley, Malcolm. *The Process of Punishment: Handling Cases in a Lower Criminal Court.* New York: Russell Sage Foundation, 1979.

Felstiner, William F.; Abel, Richard L.; and Sarat, Austin. "The Emergence and Transformation of Disputes: Naming, Blaming, Claiming . . . ," *Law and Society Review*, 15, 3–4 (1980–1981), pp. 631–654.

Fitzgerald, Jeffrey, and Dickens, Richard. "Disputing in Legal and Nonlegal Contexts: Some Questions for Sociologists of the Law." *Law and Society Review*, 15, 3–4 (1980–1981), pp. 681–706.

Friendly, Henry. "Some Kind of Hearing." *University of Pennsylvania Law Review*, 123 (1975), pp. 1267–1317.

Galanter, Marc. "Why the 'Haves' Come Out Ahead: Speculations on the Limits of Legal Change." *Law and Society Review*, 9, 1 (Fall 1974), pp. 95–151.

Gordon, Robert. "New Developments in Legal Theory." In David Kairys (ed.), *The Politics of Law: A Progressive Critique*. New York: Pantheon Books, 1982.

Hammer, Ronald P., and Hartley, Joseph M. "Procedural Due Process and the Welfare Recipient: A Statistical Study of AFDC Fair Hearings in Wisconsin." *Wisconsin Law Review*, 1978, 1 (1978), pp. 145–251.

Handler, Joel F. "Controlling Official Behavior in Welfare Administration." *California Law Review*, 54 (1966), pp. 479–510.

Handler, Joel F., and Hollingsworth, Ellen Jane. *The Deserving Poor: A Study of Welfare Administration*. Chicago: Markham Publishing Company, 1971.

Handler, Joel F. "Justice for the Welfare Recipient: Fair Hearings in AFDC, The Wisconsin Experience," *Social Service Review*, 43 (1969), pp. 12–34.

Handler, Joel F., and Sosin, Michael. *Last Resorts: Emergency Assistance and Special Needs Programs in Public Welfare*. New York: Academic Press, 1983.

Handler, Joel F., Hollingsworth, Ellen Jane; and Erlanger, Howard. *Lawyers and the Pursuit of Legal Rights*. New York: Academic Press, 1978.

Handler, Joel F. *Protecting the Social Service Client: Legal and Structural Controls on Official Discretion*. New York: Academic Press, 1979.

Handler, Joel F. *Social Movements and the Legal System: A Theory of Law Reform and Social Change*. New York: Academic Press, 1978.

Harrington, Christine. "Delegalization Reform Movements: A Historical Analysis." In Richard Abel (ed.), *The Politics of Informal Justice: Volume 1, The American Experience*. New York: Academic Press, 1982.

Katz, Jay. *The Silent World of Doctor and Patient*. New York: Free Press, 1984.

Lazerson, Mark H. "In the Halls of Justice, the only Justice Is in the Halls." In Richard Abel (ed.), *The Politics of Informal Justice: Volume 1, The American Experience*. New York: Academic Press, 1982.

Lipsky, Michael. *Street-Level Bureaucracy: Dilemmas of the Individual in Public Services*. New York: Russell Sage Foundation, 1980.

Macaulay, Stewart. "Non-Contractual Relations in Business: A Preliminary Study." *American Sociological Review*, 28 (1963), pp. 55–67.

Mashaw, Jerry L. "Administering Due Process: The Quest for a Dignitary Theory." *Boston University Law Review*, 61 (1981), pp. 885–931.

Mashaw, Jerry L. "Conflict and Compromise Among Models of Administrative Justice." *Duke Law Journal*, 1981, 2 (April 1982), pp. 181–212.

Mashaw, Jerry L. "The Management Side of Due Process: Some Theoretical and Litigation Notes on the Assurance of Accuracy, Fairness and

Timeliness in the Adjudication of Social Welfare Claims." *Cornell Law Review*, 59 (1973–1974), pp. 772–824.

Mashaw, Jerry L. "Welfare Reform and Local Administration of Aid to Families with Dependent Children in Virginia." *Virginia Law Review*, 57 (1971), pp. 818–839.

Mather, Lynn, and Yngvesson, Barbara. "Language, Audience, and the Transformation of Disputes." *Law and Society Review*, 15, 3–4 (1980–1981), pp. 775–822.

Miller, Richard E., and Sarat, Austin. "Grievances, Claims, and Disputes: Assessing the Adversary Culture." *Law and Society Review*, 15, 3–4 (1980–1981), pp. 525–566.

O'Neil, Robert. "Of Justice Delayed and Justice Denied: The Welfare Prior Hearing Cases." *The Supreme Court Review* (1970), pp. 161–214.

Stouffer, Samuel A.; Suchman, Edward A.; De Vinney, Leland C.; Star, Shirley A.; and Williams, Robin M., Jr. *The American Soldier: Adjustment During Army Life*, 1, Princeton, N.J.: Princeton University Press, 1949.

Thompson, E. P. *Whigs and Hunters: the Origin of the Black Act*. New York: Pantheon Books, 1975.

Urban Systems Research and Engineering, Inc. *SSI: A Pilot Study of Eligibility and Participation in the Supplemental Security Income Program*. Prepared for the Office of Research and Statistics, Social Security Administration, Department of Health and Human Services, Washington, D.C., September 1981.

Weatherley, Richard, and Lipsky, Michael. "Street-Level Bureaucrats and Institutional Innovation: Implementing Special Education Reform." *Harvard Educational Review*, 47, 2 (May 1977), pp. 171–197.

Weisbrod, Burton A.; Handler, Joel F.; and Komesar, Neil K. *Public Interest Law: An Economic and Institutional Analysis*. Berkeley: University of California Press, 1978.

Wexler, Steven. "Practicing Law for Poor People." *Yale Law Journal* 79 (1970), pp. 1049–1067.

CASES

Argersinger v. *Hamlin*, 407 U.S. 25 (1977).

Board of Curators of the University of Missouri v. *Horowitz*, 435 U.S. 78 (1977).

Goldberg v. *Kelly*, 397 U.S. 254 (1970).

Goss v. *Lopez*, 419 U.S. 565 (1975).

Mathews v. *Eldridge*, 424 U.S. 319 (1976).

Parham, Commissioner, Department of Human Resources of Georgia, et al. v. *J. R., et al.*, 442 U.S. 584 (1978).

· 3 ·

Special Education and Adversarial Advocacy

Appropriate decision-making procedures have two characteristics: one is the ability to facilitate deciding substantive issues in a reasonably accurate and efficient manner; the other is the ability to determine whether there has been revelation and participation by the parties involved (Michelman 1977). In order to make an evaluation as to the appropriateness of the procedure or to make a persuasive case for an alternative, one must understand fully both the substantive questions at issue and the context within which these issues arise. A major criticism of the ideology of the adversary system is the failure to appreciate the social context within which the decisions are made and how that context fatally undermines the procedure. The substantive questions are also of crucial importance. The adversary system works well when there is joinder of issues, when factual questions need to be decided (for example, who did what, where, when, and to whom?) and when legal norms or claims of right can be enforced. The model of the adversary system contemplates a definitive decision that either ends the controversy or alters it significantly. Liability is established; damages are fixed; the defendant is aquitted or convicted; the tenant stays or is evicted.

In real life, relationships may not be ended with formal adjudication, and indeed, that is one of the major criticisms of the formal adversary system—it is inappropriate when relationships are continuous, as in community disputes, family matters, or minor criminal charges. The formal adversary system, it is charged, takes a cross-sectional approach to the problems; it often exacerbates rather than settles; it tends to cut off what is needed most, namely, ongoing communication.

Special education decisions present the worst possible conditions for the functioning of the adversary system. The substantive questions for each case are: (1) What is the nature of the problem with the child; and (2) What should be done? Both of these questions are complicated, and the existing state of knowledge is uncertain. These two questions are the factual predicates for the legal norm—a handicapped child has the right to an "appropriate education." In view of the ambiguity and uncertainty as to the causes and cures for poor academic performace, how does one decide what is "appropriate"? Thus, the legal standard is also indeterminate. In this chapter, I discuss what it means to enforce a legal right when both the facts and the standards are indeterminate.

The context of decision making has two aspects—the social position of the parties and the bureaucratic context of the forum. The ideology of the adversary system assumes at least a rough equality in social position and a free-standing court or courtlike forum. Neither of these conditions obtains in special education.

The parents of handicapped children are spread across the full socioeconomic range; in this respect, special education is different from many social welfare programs, which draw primarily or exclusively from the low income classes. The barriers to procedural rights, discussed in Chapter 2, apply to all, but of course, they are much more difficult to negotiate for the poor, minorities, and other disadvantaged people. Special education, then, will show how much better the middle and upper income parents are able to use the procedural system as compared to the less well-off.

Confronting the parents is the bureaucracy. The bureaucratic context not only includes the local school and school district but also the network of constraints and incentives that operates from the state and federal governments. All bear in various ways on the discretionary decisions made in the individual cases. The bureaucratic context is more than just a setting; it affects integrally the decisions themselves.

The first section of this chapter discusses the indeterminacy of the substantive decisions in special education, the bureaucratic context, and the social position of the clients. The second section describes and analyzes the incentives and constraints that shape special education decisions. The third section looks at the decision-making procedures that are mandated by the Education for All Handicapped Children Act (P.L. 94–142), and compares these procedures with the three models of decision making developed by Mashaw (1981). The fourth section looks at the empirical results of due process decision making in special education.

Substantive Criteria: Eligibility, Treatment, and Discretion

The law looks at discretion as an issue of control. Discretion is choice, the power of the official to select from more than one option. Does the law allow this? If more than one option is allowed, are the correct criteria used or is the official decision "arbitrary"? Due process adjudication is a way of challenging the exercise of discretion. The complaining party contests the official decision, claiming either that the law does not permit the choice or that the wrong criteria were selected. There are other ways in which discretion can be created and controlled. The enabling legislation and administrative rules can broaden or narrow discretion. The characteristics of the bureaucracy can go either way—a bureaucracy short of resources and facing high volume will limit discretion through rationing and routinization (Lipsky 1980). One with sufficient levels of resources will tend to be expansive.

What does the substantive law provide? How is eligibility for special education defined? Are the official choices narrowly or broadly prescribed? "Mild mental retardation" is the principal label given to most students in special education programs; yet, what constitutes mild mental retardation is less a matter of objective biological properties than a status determined by the needs of the education system.

"[M]ild mental retardation is largely a political invention. . . . It reflects a society's expectations regarding intellectual performances, and is subject to modification as values change" (Shonkoff 1982, p. 64). The definitions of handicap depend on the needs of the school system, and thus fluctuate over time. According to Shonkoff, the label mild mental retardation is rarely applied before school age, grows in frequency during elementary school where it peaks, begins to subside in frequency during high school, and then generally disappears in general society. If nothing else, the age-relatedness of the label indicates its strong link to the school system. In addition to age differences, higher proportions of minorities and boys are in special education, again indicating a system-oriented definition (Shonkoff 1982, p. 26).

States are free to adopt their own definitions of mental retardation, and therefore there is considerable variation throughout the country. According to a recently published National Academy of Sciences study, the most commonly used definition of mental retardation is that of the American Association of Mental Deficiency (AAMD), which defines mental retardation as "significantly subaverage general intellectual functioning existing concurrently with deficits in adaptive behavior and manifested during the developmental period" (Heller et al. 1982, p. 24). "Significantly subaverage" is up to two standard deviations below the IQ mean (70 with a mean IQ of 100). This definition was adopted in 1959, and, as a result, many children previously considered mentally retarded are now part of the normal population. In any event, school districts vary in the cutoffs they use so that children with identical IQ scores may or may not be in special education classes.

There is great controversy over what the IQ test measures and its relevance for special education. IQ is correlated with poor school performance, but since candidates for special education are initially selected on the basis of poor school performance, it is claimed that the IQ test validates what is already known. More important, the IQ test does not help in specifying what should be done about the school performance, and what kind of instruction (other than continuing present practice) would be effective. The crucial issue, according to the National Academy, is whether the IQ test tells the school anything about what to do for the low-IQ child to improve performance. The Academy is of the opinion that as far as instructional programs are concerned, low-IQ children are not different from other children who are having academic difficulties, and therefore the IQ has limited usefulness in making education decisions.[1]

Mental deficiency is also defined in terms of "deficits in adaptive behavior." The AAMD defines adaptive behavior as "the effectiveness or degree to which the individual meets the standards of personal independence and social responsibility expected of his age or cultural group" (Heller et al. 1982, p. 65). Because of the breadth of the definition, a wide variety of measuring instruments is used, but they generally seem to focus on common or typical behavior; they are descriptive and they are usually based on reports by teachers or parents (or parent substitutes) rather than on direct observation.

The other commonly used test—Adaptive Behavior Inventory for Children (ABIC)—has 242 items, each referring to a specific behavior or practical or social skill. Examples include taking telephone messages, crossing streets with traffic lights, and visiting friends. The mother (or substitute) fills out the instrument.

In addition to mental retardation, eligibility for special education may also be based on the category "learning disability" (LD). These are children who have specific learning or perceptual problems, for example, in reading (dyslexia) or in simple arithmetic, but who are otherwise within the normal intelligence range. The LD category, which is growing in importance, is being used in schools to select students with low or normal intelligence mental ability and poor school performance. However, since poor school performance is also

---

[1] The National Academy's conclusion is as follows: "The IQ test remains the most widely used, most influential (in terms of its effect on placement decisions), and most controversial of current measures. Much of the controversy centers on the adequacy of the tests as measures of innate capacity or learning potential, but this has little bearing on their adequacy as measures of developed cognitive abilities. We have also found reason to doubt that scientific resolution of the nature–nurture issue, even were it possible, would dictate or justify different educational treatment of children with IQs in the EMR range. We have found little evidence for test bias, in the technical sense of the term, but we recognize that this null conclusion does not address many concerns about bias as the term is used in public discussion. The IQ test's claim to validity rests heavily on its predictive power. We find that prediction alone, however, is insufficient evidence of the test's educational utility. What is needed is evidence that children with scores in the EMR placement range will learn more effectively in a special program or placement. . . . [W]e doubt that such evidence exists. Although we are not prepared, as a panel, to advocate discontinuation of IQ testing, we feel that the burden of justification lies with its proponents to show that in particular cases the tests have been used in a manner that contributes to the effectiveness of instruction for the children in question" (Heller et al. 1982, p. 61).

used to select EMR children, in practice it is difficult to distinguish between the two groups.

To complicate matters further, there is another group of children who, while they do not receive special education labels, receive special treatment in "compensatory education" programs. These children are selected on the basis of low family income and poor performance on achievement tests. Although coming from a different program, they seem to benefit from the same kind of instruction that has proved effective for the EMRs and the LDs (Heller et al. 1982, p. 87).

In discussions of special education children, attention is usually centered on mental or learning-related causes, but candidates for special education come to the attention of the classroom teacher (the principal source of referral) primarily because of poor academic performance or behavior problems, and a great many factors, singly or in combination, can produce these behaviors. Examples include physical problems such as poor vision or hearing, lack of proper food, emotional disturbances, deprivation in the early stages of life, and lack of relevant academic preparation. Screening for these causes can be complicated; often a variety of specialized tests is needed to pinpoint the exact difficulty. In addition, learning deficiencies, arising from any one of these causes, in the early years can accumulate, causing continuing poor academic performance.

Social and environmental conditions can also produce these behaviors. Home and family environments may contribute to poor performance. Broader historical and cultural contexts also may contribute. The curricula and values of the school system reflect mainstream American culture, which may present problems for minorities and children from various subgroups.

The point is by now obvious. It is a complicated and difficult matter to determine what factors cause poor school performance or misbehavior. Historically, the IQ test was and still is the primary instrument used for determining eligibility. P.L. 94–142 and the implementing regulations require that the assessment of the child not be based on "a single general intelligence quotient" but must also include measures of "specific areas of educational need." The regulations also prohibit the use of any single procedure. In addition, tests must be used to reflect aptitude and achievement rather than only "impaired sensory or speaking skills." A child must be assessed in "all areas related to suspected disability."

The above considerations focus on the individual child in an effort to explain poor school performance or maladaptive behavior in terms of individual deficits. But another issue, which the National Academy emphasizes, is whether the student's behavioral symptoms are due not to individual failures but to failures in the school system. Special education is a construction of the school system designed to separate those students who do not conform to bureaucratic expectations. It may well be that failure to live up to these expectations is caused by inappropriate instruction. An inappropriate curriculum or instructional technique could produce misbehavior, and this may be especially true for children with backgrounds different from mainstream America. The Academy suggests that the following should be looked into: whether the curriculum is effective for the various ethnic, linguistic, and socioeconomic groups actually served by the school; whether the teacher in question has implemented the curriculum effectively for the particular student in question; whether there is objective evidence that the child has not learned what was in fact taught; and finally, when problems have been detected, whether systematic efforts are made to try various educational techniques to correct the problems. All of these steps should be taken, argues the Academy, *before* the child is singled out as a candidate for special education. Its basic position is that a significant portion of children can be treated effectively through improved instruction.

The last point raises the second question to be decided in a special education decision: what education should be given to this child who is not performing well or is misbehaving? This, too, is a difficult question to answer. The starting point is that not all children function well under identical educational programs, and the aim is to match the child to a particular program to improve educational performance. But this can occur only if the child is properly identified, and, as we have seen, this is no small matter. Moving beyond this seemingly insuperable obstacle, there remain a number of problems with the state of the art. Some of the problems stem from the fact that methods of instruction are derived from clinical practice with a highly select group of students, based on careful observation and tutorial instruction, methods that have less applicability when applied in the public school setting. Other problems stem from the fact that educational practices are evaluated in terms of the category of mild mental retardation, but this is the label that is given to the population by the school system; it is general and, in fact, encompasses a quite heterogeneous population.

Historically, the big issue in treatment is whether handicapped students should be segregated. From the 1930s to the 1970s, the assumption was that the mildly retarded student needed smaller classes and a special curriculum and that this could best be done separately. During the 1970s, the dominant ideology became "mainstreaming." Special services were provided either by the regular teacher supported by a specialist or by a specialist with whom the special education students would spend part of the day. The research on both kinds of settings is inconclusive.

Similar conclusions apply with regard to social skills. Before 1970 segregation was justified on the theory that mentally retarded children tended to interact poorly with normal children and as a result developed weaker self-concepts and therefore needed special training. Here as well research results are inconclusive.

Nonetheless, there is an important argument against segregated settings. Some educators claim that mentally retarded children suffer educationally because of lower expectations on the part of their instructors—in the jargon of the profession, there is lack of "cognitive press"—and that this tendency is more likely if a teacher is facing a room full of special education students. This would argue in favor of the heterogeneous classroom. On the other hand, in the mainstream classroom, especially if it is large, the mentally retarded child might not receive enough attention. This would argue in favor of some sort of resource room where the special education child could receive special instruction for limited parts of the day.

The data on instruction call into question the conventional labels. Theory discriminates between the mentally retarded and the learning disabled child—the former is viewed as low in all aspects of mental functioning and the latter as being uneven in abilities. But evidence on instructional techniques indicates that the same kind of program may be just as effective for both. The same is true for the third group—those assigned to various "compensatory education" programs. All seem to benefit equally from what the National Academy calls "direct, externally paced and formally monitored instruction in academic content." In its opinion, behaviorally oriented, direct instruction seems to be effective for all three groups of children. Why then, argues the Academy, maintain the traditional system of labeling? Children will have to be identified, but why not identify them in terms of the specific, intensive instruction that seems to work?

The conclusion to be drawn from this discussion is that both questions in the special education decision are indeterminate—why is there poor school performance or misbehavior, and what should be done about it. The two questions are inextricably linked; it is difficult to know what works for a particular student when the causes of the difficulty are not clear. The qualifying labels are incoherent, vague, and subject to changing standards and administrative expediency. They mask a heterogeneous population. Thus, the available programs suit some and not others. Yet, as we shall see in the next section, the availability of the programs is the most important determinate in generating referrals and placements.

The conclusion is that the substantive state of knowledge does not limit discretion. If eligibility for special education was defined in terms of mental retardation, and mental retardation was defined in terms of an objective standard, such as an IQ cutoff, then discretion would be limited. Discretion would also be limited if only particular types of programs were offered for particular students. But neither condition obtains. It may be that in practice there are limiting conditions (in fact, despite P.L. 94–142, the IQ is relied upon quite heavily), but this is not because of the state of scientific knowledge or the law.

The underlying, basic indeterminacy of the questions in special education is of the utmost importance; it goes to the very heart of the procedure. It constitutes a most fundamental objection to the legal rights approach to decision making, but before addressing this issue, we have to consider two more clusters of determinates of decision making in special education.

The Macro-Bureaucratic Context

Although discretion is not limited substantively, it does operate within a bureaucratic context that shapes its exercise. There are two aspects to this context. One is the actual selection and treatment process itself. The other is the overall setting within which the selection and treatment process takes place. Since the latter determines the choices made in the former, we will consider the overall context first.

P.L. 94–142 clearly contemplates that services should be tailored to

need. Exactly the opposite has happened. The most important determinate for the placement of handicapped students is the availability
of programs. The existence of particular programs means that students eligible to fill those slots will be identified, evaluated, and placed
in those slots. If particular slots are not available, then those eligible
for those programs will not be identified, evaluated, and placed. How,
then, do the programs come to be made available? Availability depends on the laws and regulations; the relative influence of the federal, state, and local governments; the financial incentives; and the
dynamics of the school district and schoolroom itself.

Because special education is costly, local jurisdictions have increasingly sought financial help from state and federal governments, but
the manner in which this financial aid is made affects the selection
process and the availability of the programs at the local level.[2] How
fiscal incentives and constraints become manifest is a complicated
process depending on the interaction of federal and state funding
formulas and policies, state and local perceptions, state and local programs and priorities, other related programs, the characteristics of
the school population, the local tax base, and the availability of other
community resources for the handicapped. While all are important,
this part focuses on financial incentives and constraints.

P.L. 94–142 is the most important federal program. For fiscal year
1980, the federal allocation under this statute was $804 million. How-
ever, for the same period, the states spent $3.4 billion; and local
governments bear about half the cost. Thus, the federal dollars are a
relatively small percentage of the cost of special education. P.L. 94–
142 funds are allocated to the states according to the number of
children served.

State educational agencies may use up to 25 percent of the federal
money for administration and the rest for services for handicapped
children who are not being served or not served adequately. Funds
for this purpose (direct services) have to be matched equally by state
funds for the same purpose. The remainder of the federal money is
distributed to local school districts or intermediate units. The school
districts must apply for these funds; if their applications are successful, they are entitled to receive an amount in proportion to the number of handicapped children served in the particular district as com-

---

[2] This section draws heavily on Magnetti (1982).

pared to number of handicapped children served in the whole state.

There are two other programs with some influence: Title I of the Elementary and Secondary Education Act (revised in 1978) and the Bilingual Education Act (1978). Title I is a large program; in fiscal year 1980 more than $3 billion in federal money was allocated to the states. Actually, Title I is a group of programs. The largest is for children of low income families. Other target populations are migrants, children in institutions for delinquents, and children in institutions for the handicapped (and, under certain conditions, handicapped children who have been returned from institutions). Local school districts apply for Title I money in proportion to the number of eligible children in the district. The funds must be used in areas with high concentrations of children from low income families. Title I also provides incentives (by matching funds) for states to provide compensatory education programs.

The Bilingual Education Act, as the name states, provides funds to local school districts for programs for children with limited English proficiency. In fiscal year 1979, federal funds amounted to more than $158 million, and the programs served about 3.6 million students.

Historically, the bulk of the funds for public education have come from the local level, but this has been changing over the years, and now the states, on the average, pay for about half the cost. The same trend of increased state financing applies to special education. Of course, there is wide variation, but taking all the states together, the amount spent for special education in 1980 was about $3.4 billion, a sum vastly exceeding the federal contribution. Before the enactment of P.L. 94–142, most states had some programs for various groups of handicapped children; since the enactment, all the states now have comprehensive special education laws to cover all handicapped children. In addition, over twenty states have some form of compensatory education program and bilingual or bicultural programs. In 1978–1979, the total state amounts spent on these two programs were approximately $700 million and $98.4 million, respectively.

The state role is thus very important in funding special education, and this role is increasing. How the states transfer the money to the local districts influences the shape and content of the programs. States vary in terms of constraints. They may define handicaps loosely or with particularity; they may place limits on the number of children to be served; they may mandate particular services and programs.

Funding formulas that stress resources (for example, units of service or staff costs) may encourage maximizing class size to reduce per pupil costs. However, the state may set limits on class size. If the formulas are based on the unit or teacher of a special class, then mainstreaming is discouraged, but reimbursements could also be based on mainstreaming units and support personnel. Child-based formulas provide incentives to overclassify, and a weighted formula (per type of handicap) would tend to overclassify for those particular categories. A straight sum formula (the same amount of money per child) would tend to result in more children in the general category of mild mental retardation and less children in the more costly categories. The general incentive is to provide children with low-cost program alternatives. The child-based formulas tend to encourage larger class sizes and caseloads. Once programs are in place, child-based formulas discourage the removal of a child from special education since there is little reduction in the cost of the program. But this, too, can vary if the formula is based on the number of children served at any given time; then, there may be an incentive to move children in and out of programs quickly to increase the body count.

Although the federal share of special education is relatively small (probably not more than 15 percent of the total costs), it is by no means trivial. P.L. 94–142 uses a straight-sum funding formula—each state receives a set amount for each child in special education. No distinctions are made for the type of handicap or the cost of particular programs. This formula encourages identification and service, which was the clear purpose of P.L. 94–142. It was thought at the time of enactment that many more children needed to be enrolled. Estimates were that up to 12 percent of the school age population was potentially eligible, and this is the statutory limit for each state. While the federal formula encourages bounty hunting, it also encourages the local districts to provide the least costly programs, which may be consistent with the federal goal of the least restrictive alternative. Of course, the incentives of P.L. 94–142 could be offset by state formulas. For example, the state may encourage particular programs for particular handicaps. The federal compensatory and bilingual programs may overlap and either reinforce or blunt incentives. An often-cited example is the child who is eligible for two or more programs and consequently spends a significant portion of the school day outside of the mainstream classroom.

The funding formulas contain various incentives and constraints but these are rarely clear-cut. Sometimes they operate at cross-purposes. In any event, they operate within a bureaucratic milieu—the local school district, and here, other types of incentives and constraints come into play, all of which affect the availability of programs which, in turn, affect the identification, selection, and placement of the child.

Before the enactment of P.L. 94–142, many states and local school districts had programs for handicapped students. Nevertheless, P.L. 94–142 (and similar state statutes that immediately preceded it) constituted a drastic change in two aspects. First, the new statutes radically altered the decision-making process. Previously, the identification, assessment, and placement of the child was done informally. There was consultation with the specialist, the parents, and perhaps the principal or other supervisors and specialists. The whole process was a rather simple procedure (Weatherley 1979). All this changed under P.L. 94–142, which requires individual assessments, conferences with parents and a variety of specialists, the development of Individual Educational Plans (IEPs), and periodic evaluations. A great deal of formality and paperwork was introduced. Weatherley studied the implementation of the Massachusetts Comprehensive Special Education Law, Chapter 766, which predated P.L. 94–142 (enacted 1972, effective 1974) but which contained similar provisions. He comments on the effects of the procedural formality and paperwork (Weatherley 1979, pp. 48–49):

The requirements of Chapter 766 presented school personnel with an enormous increase in their work load in several ways. There were suddenly many more children to be evaluated. For each evaluation many more individuals had to be involved, and each assessment and education program had to be written in much greater detail, completed faster, and circulated to a wider audience than before. Getting everyone together for a team meeting, when each team member had a unique work schedule and many additional responsibilities, became a major task in itself. Someone, usually the chairperson, had to make provision for a meeting room, frequently a corner of the library or an anteroom in the often-crowded schools. Arrangements had to be made to have parents and team members come; substitutes had to be scheduled so that classroom teachers could attend. An evaluation of a child that might previously have taken two or three people a few hours to complete now took as much as ten to twenty hours for the chairperson and two to six hours for each of the other team members. Time previously spent working with children was now allocated to paperwork and meetings.

The second reason had to do with the political context of the reform. P.L. 94–142 and similar state statutes were reforms imposed from the outside. Although there were sympathetic supporters within the school system, the new special education laws were the result primarily of efforts of parents, advocacy groups, lawyers, and politicians. The school systems not only felt that a vast amount of work had been thrust upon them, that much of it was unnecessary or inappropriate for the school system to provide—for example, social, psychological, and medical services—that the autonomy of the educational professionals was being challenged, but also that all of this was being done in an adversary atmosphere. Life was being conducted in a goldfish bowl, with parents and citizen groups waiting to sue if procedures were not followed or if their demands were rejected (Lynn 1982–1983).

There were other stresses as well. In Massachusetts, resources to fund the new special education law never materialized. The normal, expected difficulties of implementing a new procedure were exacerbated by the budgetary uncertainties. While the Massachusetts legislature may have been particularly irresponsible, it is probably true that in general, resources were both uncertain and tight. The federal government never funded P.L. 94–142 as promised, and, despite its publicity, special education is still only a small part of the total public education budget.

The Massachusetts law attempted to equalize the availability of funds for all of the school districts, but the wealthier districts managed to get a disproportionate share. The funds had to be applied for, and it was the wealthier districts that had the programs, the staff and the expertise, and the know-how necessary to obtain state funds. Despite the intent of the law, the disparities in per pupil expenditures for special education increased.

In Massachusetts, the special education staff was pitted against the regular school staff for scarce resources. Yet, in a complex way there was dependency as well as competition. The special education teachers were dependent on the regular teachers for referrals. There is no special education program for the best performers, only for the poor performers. Therefore, if the teacher is going to get relief, it is the poor performers that get referred. But there are counterpressures. Special education is costly, and the procedures and paperwork act as filters. Pressure is exerted, directly or indirectly, to hold back on referrals when there are backlogs, or when resources are not available, or to make the kinds of referrals for which there are slots. Schools with more special education staff, facilities, and services identify more children needing special education. Districts with only EMR programs identify only EMR children and no other handicaps (Bickel 1982).

There are other constraints. We have seen in the discussion of the substantive issues that a variety of causes of poor academic performance or misbehavior should be considered. P.L. 94–142 states that these nonstudent considerations should be taken into account, but how likely is this? Given the relationship between special and regular education staff, and the marginal status of special education in the school system, it is unlikely that attention will be directly away from the student to the regular teacher to see if there is anything wrong with the way the regular classroom is being conducted. There are constraints against looking at other possible causes or seeking outside resources. The school probably thinks that the parents are part of "the problem" anyway, so why involve them any more than necessary? Community resources, such as mental health clinics or even law enforcement, are areas unfamiliar to the school. Such outside help may be ineffective anyway, given the current state of knowledge. A special education teacher seeking to expand the concerns of the school to help the program is thus likely to meet skepticism, if not hostility, on the part of superiors (Kirp, Buss and Kuriloff 1974, p. 48).

To the extent that there are barriers in the referral process as well as the need to fill available positions, one would expect the development of informal procedures designed to meet individual needs. One would also expect that placements would tend to become permanent. Once the elaborate and laborious steps have been taken and the student is out of the classroom, there is little incentive to return the student. If, as is charged, special education students suffer from low expectations, then the student falls farther and farther behind. The student is regarded as a burden by the regular teacher but, depending on the funding formula, as a resource by the special education teacher.

Finally, we would expect the system to respond to those who know best how to manipulate it—in this case, the better-off, knowledgeable, vocal parents, the ones who, in the main, were responsible for the enactment of the laws and who are watching the school districts. They will make the most demands on the school district (for instance, the expensive private placements). The field-level decision makers will be aware of these demands and threats. Conversely, this will produce greater pressure to ignore students and parents who do not cause trouble or do not otherwise come to the attention of the school system. Handicapped students who are quiet and passive will less likely be referred; when referred the procedural steps will take longer to complete and more corners will be cut; these students will more likely be fitted into existing programs. As Lipsky and others have pointed out, in the face of high workloads and scarce resources, front-line administrators will ration, routinize, redefine goals, control clients, develop informal priorities, and engage in other practices in order to handle their workload somehow (Lipsky 1980; Weatherley 1979).

Local school districts are social institutions with long histories, an established staff, and an accustomed way of doing business. Their main mission is to educate nonhandicapped children, and they have important social and political ties to the local community, which is concerned with their main task. Prior to P.L. 94–142, the school system dealt with handicapped students in their own particular way. Now, all of this has been changed in ways that most school people disagree with. They probably feel that they were doing an adequate job (especially in light of available resources), but that in any event, the new procedural requirements are animated by an unwarranted public hostility and are unnecessary; and that they have had to implement a radical change without sufficient resources or preparation.

P.L. 94–142 Procedures

P.L. 94–142 imposes a series of requirements on recipient states designed to "assure that . . . a free appropriate public education will be available for all handicapped children between the ages of three and eighteen. . . ." Assistance is to be made available to children in private as well as public schools, on an individual basis according to an "individualized educational plan" (IEP). The statute gives parents the right to obtain an independent evaluation; they are entitled to a due process hearing if they object to the IEP, with a right of judicial review (Bersoff 1982).

Once students are identified, the regulations attempt to insure a multidimensional assessment and placement decision, with full parental involvement. In evaluating the student, the regulations specify that validated procedures be used and that a multidisciplinary team (M-Team) composed of at least one teacher or specialist in the disability has to make the assessment. The assessment is to cover "all areas related to the suspected disability"; "no single procedure is to be used as the sole criterion" in placing a child; the assessment must go beyond a "single intelligence quotient" to measures of "specific areas of educational need"; the child's aptitude and achievement are to be tested rather than the "impaired sensory, manual or speaking skills." Tests must be administered in the child's native language and the assessment must be socially and culturally nondiscriminatory.

There are also restrictions on the interpretation of the evaluation data. Multiple data sources must be used in reaching decisions including "aptitude and achievement tests, teacher recommendations, physical condition, social or cultural background, and adaptive behavior." The placement decision is a group decision composed of people "knowledgeable about the child, the meaning of the . . . data, and the placement options."

Every child determined to have special needs has to have an individualized educational plan (IEP). Meetings to develop the IEP must be held within thirty days of the determination that the child needs special education, and the meetings must include the parent(s), the child's teacher, a representative of the placement team, and a representative of the public agency other than the teacher. Additional representatives can be added at the discretion of the parents or the public agency. The school has the duty to inform the parents about the purpose of the meeting, and it has to develop mechanisms to insure parental involvement. The IEP is a written document that is supposed to cover current performance, short-term goals, annual goals, specific services to be provided, a least restrictive environment designation, objective evaluation criteria and procedures, and expected duration of services and provision for annual and three-year reviews. The least restrictive environment requirement is an attempt to insure a "continuum of alternative placements" (Bickel 1982, p. 18).

The due process regulations are extensive. The parents are to receive written notice before the agency initiates any aspect of the placement process or makes any changes in the child's educational status. The notice is to include a full explanation of the procedural safeguards, explain the action to be taken, with reasons and assessments. The notice must be understandable and written in the native language of the parents. The parents have a right of access to all records and documents and the right to obtain an independent evaluation of the child. They have a right to a due process hearing if they disagree with the placement decision, and there is a right to further appeal. In sum, informed parental consent and participation is required throughout the whole process.

The federal statute does not attempt to control the distribution of special education benefits. Substantive provisions in the statute are few—prohibitions on discrimination; a favoring of mainstreaming where "appropriate." The detailed content of eligibility and what services are appropriate are left to the states and the local school district. Instead, the federal direction is a system of procedural safeguards designed to involve parents in the education placement decisions.

P.L. 94–142 codified several important lower federal court decisions and existing state statutes. California and Massachusetts, for example, had similar laws in place before the enactment of P.L. 94–142. As in many other areas of social welfare, the federal government responded to existing trends, but in so doing, it stimulated continuing developments. By the end of the 1970s, forty-nine states were participating in the federal program, which included the procedural system. Nationwide, this was a triumph of due process (Clune 1984). It was an expression of faith that the correct substantive decisions would be worked out through parental participation.

Parental participation procedures in P.L. 94–142 have been called "due process" but it should be recognized that these procedures entail much more than what is normally provided for. Traditionally, due process procedural rights have meant *hearing* rights. An aggrieved client complains against an official decision; the claim is rejected, and the client has a hearing either at the administrative or at the judicial level. It is at the hearing stage that the client participates in the decision; participation is through the adversary process. The P.L. 94–142 procedural protections go much beyond the standard due process right to a hearing. The right of the parents to participate starts at the beginning of the process before any significant decision is made, and this includes the initial decision to evaluate for eligibility. The law is quite clear that the parents are to be involved in the discretionary decision from beginning to end. "Due process" usually connotes the formal adversary hearing process; P.L. 94–142 guarantees this but it also does much more. It also guarantees rights to informal, unstructured decision-making processes. Procedurally, it is much more radical, more far-reaching than customary due process rights.

Procedural protections not only extend deeper into administrative decision making but also combine the three competing models of administrative justice that Mashaw has identified. The moral judgment model is incorporated by use of the entitlement language. The statute speaks in terms of the right to an "appropriate" education in the least restrictive environment. There is a right to participate in all stages of the proceedings and there is the right to judicial review. Hearing and judicial review rights are in the traditional form. They are adversary, the parents can be represented by counsel, there are rights to notice and reasoned explanations. Before the formal hearings, the procedures are nonadversary; they consist of participation, consultation, and informed consent. The parent has the right to bring in other consultants and to get independent evaluations. Decisions are to be holistic, and not based only on professional assessment. At least as far as the law is concerned, evidence as to "deservedness" is relevant since family circumstances and social and psychological factors (for example, attitudes, motivations) as well as objective factors may cause poor academic performance or misbehavior.

The professional treatment model is also used. Not only does there have to be professional evaluation and participation in the assessment and prescription, but the law also contemplates an ongoing assessment, treatment, and evaluation process rather than a single cross-sectional hearing. The professionals are supposed to stay with the case throughout the entire treatment process much as a doctor stays with a patient (Bickel 1982).

The bureaucratic rationality model is implicitly incorporated by virtue of the fact that a large-scale organization has to administer the special education program. As in the disability system, there has to be explicit hierarchical control or informal rules to handle large numbers of cases and to control the costs generated by the competing models.

In special education, then, procedural due process is complex and multifaceted. It penetrates deeply into bureaucratic decision making. It has two different forms—participation and consultation, followed by formal adversarial procedures—and combines three competing models of administrative justice. How does this system work for a highly discretionary decision in an agency relationship that traditionally has been so dominated by the bureaucracy?

Parent–School Interactions

The availability of programs, the backlogs in the referral procedures, and the relationships between the special education staff and the regular teachers set the parameters for the selection, assessment, and placement of handicapped students. Within those parameters, other factors more directly affect the particular interactions between the parents and the school staff.

We spoke before about the political context of the special education reform, how it was imposed from the outside on a suspicious and reluctant school system. The imposition of the due process hearing procedures is likely to accentuate adversary, negative feelings on the part of local officials. No matter what the rhetoric, a due process hearing is a challenge to the decision maker; it requires the decision maker to justify the decision before a disinterested third party. Due process procedures conflict with bureaucratic and professional attitudes toward the client. In the opinion of the bureaucrat, the expert or the professional, not the client, has the competence to make the decision. Therefore, despite formal compliance with due process norms, there is resistance and evasion. Due process hearings are not viewed as welcome ideals or even as signals that something may be amiss at the field level. The prevailing attitude is that clients seek hearings either because of failures in communication or, more probably, because they are malcontents or troublemakers.

Theory would predict that there would even be more resistance in special education than in the standard hearing situation. The due process procedures in special education provide not only for hearings but also for participation in all of the prior major decisions. Participation means explaining, sharing, persuading, and limiting one's discretionary authority. Special educators are used to dealing with parents, students, and fellow teachers and administrators. They have worked out accommodations and arrangements with various interests. Now, they are commanded to share responsibility for decision making with parents. Why should they? The law and the regulations say they must, and procedures are set up for participation. There are sanctions for failure to comply. If there is lack of participation in prior decisions (for example, formulation of the IEP), then there may be trouble at a hearing. It may be easier to comply at earlier stages than go through a costly administrative proceeding. But participation is a subtle thing. The question is how much genuine participation is there?

The reluctance of the officials to generally participate and their ability to thwart the intent of the law, is only one aspect of the problem of meeting due process goals. The other concerns the parents. The special education due process procedures give them the opportunity to participate. Even if the school officials in good faith make available the opportunities, the parents have to have the ability to take advantage. This is a serious issue since the major control mechanism in the system is the due process procedure. The control mechanism depends on the ability of the parents to participate—to recognize that there is a problem, to perceive a remedy, and to pursue that remedy. In the day-to-day dealings with large-scale organizations, these are formidable hurdles.

The special education system makes perception, participation, and protest especially difficult. For a long time, in a great many school districts, nothing, or very little, was done for the handicapped child. Changes in the law change perceptions only if there is adequate communication. Parents have to become aware that benefits are now available. Effective communication would be far from automatic. Parents have to want to do something for their handicapped children, but painful adjustments and accommodations may already have been reached and now the status quo will have to be disturbed. Parents face tremendous conflicts about what to do with handicapped children, and it is not clear at all that many would eagerly seek out change on the basis of a notice in a public place.

Many kinds of mild handicaps are hard to detect—for example, deafness, certain kinds of sight problems, learning disabilities—and there is a great deal of professional and nonprofessional misclassification. Here, then, we have the situation where the parents, even though only moderately satisfied or greatly dissatisfied, still do not do anything about it. As previously discussed, tolerance or lack of action may be due to lack of awareness or perception that something is wrong, which, in turn, may be self-induced or the result of external manipulation.

The context in which P.L. 94–142 procedures are to operate is characterized by substantive indeterminacy, complicated organizational constraints, and incentives operating through federal, state, and local bureaucracies. The context is set ultimately by the interaction of two sets of actors: front-line school staff not overly enthusiastic about the new law and especially the new procedures, and large numbers of parents who are not the knowledgeable, articulate, educated, aggressive ones who spearheaded the reforms.

The Due Process Experience in Special Education

The decision-making process in special education is formally divided into logically sequential steps: identification, screening, and referral; eligibility assessment; placement; and reevaluation. For analytic and descriptive purposes I will follow that format, but in fact, all of the parts interact and affect each other. The availability of placements inevitably affects the identification, selection, and assessment process. Eligibility criteria influence referrals—"awareness of the guidelines colors the way teachers view children as potential special education children" (Bickel 1982, p. 188). Backlogs in the referral system will slow the identification process. Parental pressures affect referrals. In systems with strong parental contact, teachers are sometimes hesitant to make referrals because of parental hostility. On the other hand, active parents are more likely to receive special education services. Children are more likely to get referred if they have severe handicaps or are disruptive, or if their parents bring pressure. Children who have mild handicaps, who are passive, or who do not cause behavior problems, and whose parents are unaware or not aggressive will tend not to get referred (Bickel 1982, p. 220).

Identification and Referral

Despite the total drop in school enrollment, overall there has been a steady and significant increase in the number of children enrolled in special education classes. There has been a growth and diversification of activities for locating handicapped children, but the consensus is that the classroom teacher still remains the major referral source.

The process generally starts with the teacher telling the principal that "he/she is having difficulty teaching the child and needs assistance" (Bickel 1982, p. 187). Despite the central role of the teachers, they are under considerable constraints. Weatherley (1979) found that most teachers feel peripheral to the process and frustrated. There are strong motivations to get the disruptive or hard-to-educate children out of the class, but they also complain about the lack of services for these children and about the delays and backlogs.

A more recent study of special education referrals in Boston noted that referrals to special education keep increasing (Weaver and Sodano 1982). The formally stated reasons for the referrals are for behavioral and/or learning problems, but teachers admit that the real reasons are to make the classes more manageable and less stressful. With budget cuts and large classes (including mainstreamed special education students), teachers feel that special education assignments are the best alternative for students who are difficult to deal with or who have other kinds of problems. The evaluation teams tend to support the teacher recommendations. They know how to manipulate and present the data so that the student will get the placement that the teacher and the team want.

As predicted, informal systems arise from these conflicting pressures. Kirp, Buss, and Kuriloff (1974) describe the California system. When problems arise in the classroom, there is informal consultation with the principal and the teacher. Sometimes special help is given without the use of formal procedures. If the problem persists or escalates, the teacher may request the principal to test the child for placement. How the principal responds depends on a number of factors—willingness or ability to support the teacher, relationships with the special education people, the availability of places. The principal may grant the request, or ask the teacher to try again, or informally transfer the student to another class or school or program. Another option sometimes used is to place the student with a special education teacher on a trial basis. In some schools, this may be advantageous. A problem is quickly solved and the child returns without a lot of bureaucratic red tape and accompanying labels, but in the inner-city schools, the authors report, these ad hoc arrangements tend to become permanent.

If a child is to be tested, the role of the school psychologist becomes crucial, even though other kinds of information are also gathered. Psychologists in special education are seriously overworked (some may serve as many as 5,000 students), but they still view themselves as the most competent to make individual evaluations. Parental consent for testing is required, but the consent is not informed. The consent form is only one of many that the parents are asked to sign. According to Kirp, Buss, and Kuriloff, "From the viewpoint of special personnel, the model parent neither resists nor discusses—he does what the school asks him to do without challenging the rightness of the professional's judgment. Parents who do raise questions or object to school-recommended placements are frequently dismissed as 'nuts' or 'trouble-makers' " (1974, p. 105). A variety of strategies are used to deal with recalcitrant parents. The school will bombard the parents with records of the child's poor performance; they will threaten to leave the child back, or will put the child on reduced-day or home instruction.

Assessment and Eligibility

Federal law requires that a variety of measures be used in the assessment process; that decision makers be professionally qualified; that there has to be regular reevaluation; and that the assessment be appropriate for the individual child, taking into account language, areas needing assessment, the instruments, and the recommended programs. There is to be full parental involvement at every stage. This means notification, consultation, and informed consent at the referral stage, any tests to be used, the assessment process, and the development of the Individual Education Plan (IEP).

Kirp, Buss, and Kuriloff (1974) report that in California, despite these provisions, the consent requirements are only a formality and do not affect the decision-making process. Often, the consent forms are secured before the placement meetings, and in many districts consent is required only for the first placement.

The school district's admission committees make the formal placement decisions. In large districts, the committees spend an average of 2½ minutes per decision. The committees are supposed to rely on the psychologist's reports, the classroom and background information, and pertinent medical data. In several of the districts the decisions are reached through bargaining which takes place before the meetings. Parents have a right to bring an "advisory" representative to the meetings, but they are not so advised and the right is seldom exercised.

Weatherley's findings (1979) in Massachusetts are similar. He studied three local districts. In two of the districts the staff developed the education plans before the core evaluation meetings and usually without the participation of the parents. At the subsequent core meeting, the parents were often presented with the staff recommendation, and the meeting was a "ritualistic certification" (Weatherley 1974, p. 51). The parents, reports Weatherley, were at a great disadvantage. They were outnumbered, they were strangers confronting a group of people who were used to working together and had struck a bargain between them, and the discussion was often in technical jargon with the subtle implication that the child or the parent or both were at fault. These relationships varied with social class or status. The articulate, middle class, knowledgeable parents could hold their own; but for the average lower class or minority parents, their presence only served the symbolic reassurance of procedural fairness.

Although practices vary throughout the country, research has generally found that the patterns do not differ that much from California and Massachusetts. Several studies show that what in fact happens is a two-step process. There is a preplacement meeting to "organize" the data and develop a consensus among the school personnel as to the general disposition of the case, followed by the placement meeting which the parents and possibly other school personnel attend. Instead of reviewing the data and making an eligibility determination, IEPs are signed off and assignments made. The IEPs are drafted before the meeting, and most activity with the parents is designed to get their written permission for the testing, the IEPs, and the assignments. Studies show that parents apparently do not resent the fact that the IEPs are developed before the meetings and without their participation. The IEPs are kept as general as possible to avoid accountability by the special education people. The use of overly technical language hinders communication with parents. Nevertheless, parents are intimidated by the complexity of the process and the IEP becomes a legal formality (Bickel 1982).

If the parents are not involved, how then are the decisions made? In general, there has been a shift away from a single psychologist administering an intelligence test to a multiteam assessment, as required by federal regulations. Still, the decisions seem to be made by one or two staff members. Usually, the most important information is academic achievement and the student's behavioral and social needs. Thus, the teacher's reports of achievement carry considerable weight. At least in states with definite eligibility criteria, the referral is likely to be made with the final placement in mind. "The net effect of these relationships may be to put a student on a rather preconceived track towards a placement prior to the actual evaluation process" (Bickel 1982, p. 210). Since placement decisions are more likely to be a function of teacher discretion and the availability of positions, there is great variation among school districts, with the single exception of the IQ test, which still seems to be relied on quite heavily in the placement decision. What seems to happen, according to Bickel, is that "poor achievement 'nominates' an individual student for assessment and the IQ 'anoints' him or her in a particular classification" (1982, p. 197).

Federal law stipulates that after assessment and eligibility are determined, the school district, again in consultation with the parents, develop an IEP with the Least Restrictive Environment (LRE). In practice, however, all of these determinations are usually collapsed into one or two meetings (Heller et al. 1982, p. 37). In part, this is due to the sheer problem of logistics. There are a lot of cases to process, which causes difficulties in scheduling, producing the necessary documents, and so forth. Another problem has to do with the suspicion or doubts about the concept of the IEPs. Bickel (1982) reports that teachers and administrators are concerned about accountability since the IEPs are required to set forth short- and long-term goals. There is formal compliance with the IEP requirement but there is no specificity concerning evaluation procedures and criteria and no formulation of long-term goals. Important details are omitted; short-term goals are left ambiguous or are left to the special education teacher (Heller et al. 1982, p. 39). The vagueness, in turn, lessens the ability to monitor student progress (Bickel 1982, p. 221).

The conclusion of virtually all the research is that whereas P.L. 94–142 seems to have resulted in more parental *contact* with the school authorities, there has not been much change in parental *involvement* in the actual decision-making processes. Despite the thrust of the law and the best intentions of the school officials, they are under pressure to minimize parent participation. The school officials have a stake in keeping the decisions predictable and orderly; allowing parents and others, such as advocates or advocacy groups, to participate increases uncertainty. At the time of Weatherley's study, decisions such as private placement could cost between $10,000 and $15,000 per year per child; these are decisions that school administrators pay attention to.

This review well illustrates the imposition of due process procedures on a bureaucratic social system. From the perspective of the parents (and the due process perspective of legal policy), participation in decision making is an individual affair. The perspective of the educational bureaucracy is much more complex and subject to multiple constraints and conflicting pressures. The bureaucracy has a task, only one part of which is special education. It has limited resources and a great deal of work to do. It is not persuaded that all due process is desirable or necessary. Bureaucratic habit and professional self-interest do not favor parental participation in a meaningful sense.

For these reasons the process before the formalized hearings may be far more important than the hearings themselves. The prehearing context may effectively filter out many disputes. One of the important assumptions of P.L. 94–142 is that there was a great deal of misclassification, particularly with low income and minority children, and that parents of these children had to be brought in early in the process to help prevent this. In fact, most of the special education disputes are not about misclassification. The parents seem to accept classification decisions. The disputes are generally about private school placements and related services, that is, items that cost the school system large amounts of money. Moreover, parents who do dispute are more likely to be of higher education and income. The fact that low-income parents are less likely to dispute and more likely to accept classification decisions does not necessarily mean that these decisions are correct.

Formal Hearings

A certain number of decisions do go to hearings. The characteristics of the prehearing filtering process, of course, determine the parameters of the hearings. Thus, we find in studies of hearings that disputes tend to involve requests for private school placements. It is primarily the white middle class that uses the hearing system. In a study by Neal and Kirp (1985) the schools were generally represented by six to eight people; half of the parents and half of the schools used attorneys, but the presence of attorneys seemed to make little difference. Average attorney costs were about $900 for both the parents and the schools. In Massachusetts, parents had an even chance of prevailing at the first hearing, but hearing decisions appealed by parents to the state were upheld in 85 percent of the cases. One of the more significant problems in the hearing cases was the increased tension that resulted from the adversarial nature of the hearings.

Another study looked at the hearings that arose out of the decisions in *Pennsylvania Association of Retarded Children* v. *Pennsylvania* (334 F. Supp. 257 [EDPA 1971], 343 F. Supp. 279 [EDPA 1972]) during the years 1972–1976 (Kuriloff 1985). During this period, parents requested 480 hearings, and 172 actually resulted in formal hearings. In contrast to the findings in Massachusetts and in other empirical studies, here parents did protest classification decisions, especially if the classification was the basis for a decision to remove the child from the mainstream. Generally, parents sought one of two remedies: they either wanted their children to stay in the regular curriculum (mildly handicapped) or receive private placement (more severely handicapped). The school districts almost always resisted the more expensive private placements and were more likely to prevail by a substantial margin. It was only with the severely retarded that parents had about a 50/50 chance of winning private placement. Parents were less likely to win if they took administrative appeals—the schools won about 80 percent of the appeals.

How effective was the Pennsylvania hearing system? Kuriloff thinks that there was a substantial amount of due process. The tests he uses are to see whether parents in the hearings are able to use skills and techniques (for example, the use of witnesses), and whether they prevail. He finds that the parents win at least something in about a third of the cases.

A close look at Kuriloff's study, however, does raise doubts. Pennsylvania was one of the early states to be subject to an important and notorious federal court decision; it has been subject to a great deal of national attention. It is hard to evaluate whether 120 hearing requests a year is a lot without knowing much more about the "base"; but given the problems of Pennsylvania, the size of the state, and the activity, it does not give one confidence that the barriers to hearings are not acting as significant filters.

How to evaluate parent wins is also difficult. Kirp and Jensen (1983) match what the parents ask for with the outcome and come to the conclusion that the parents win in only 4 percent of the cases. Kuriloff and others say that the Kirp and Jensen standard—complete victory—is too high. Taking into account compromises, the parents come away with something substantial in about a third of the cases. Yet, if one looks carefully at Kuriloff's analysis of circumstances of parental victories, additional questions arise. Parents tend to win when they have had children in special education, when the handicap is severe, and when they make a large number of costly demands. The question, then, is what exactly parental winning means. With a severely handicapped child, there may be pressure to give the parents something, especially when they are asking for a lot of things. Even under Kuriloff's standards, success rates vary. With the severely handicapped, parents win about half of the time; with classification, in less than 30 percent of the cases.

In any event, even looking at the Pennsylvania experience through Kuriloff's eyes, one is not left with a great deal of confidence in due process. As noted, parents tend to win when they have had prior experience, have skill and resources, and have a lot at stake; in other words, a special type of parent as distinguished from the ordinary person confronting the bureaucracy. Furthermore, these parents win only if the school presents a sloppy case. It is the combination of the parents' good performance *and* the schools' poor performance that produces parent victories.

What does a school have to do to win? According to Kuriloff, the school has to convince the hearing officers that they are acting in good faith and within the law. By this he means that they have to touch the procedural bases, build the record showing that the necessary evaluations have been made and that in classification and program the school was pursuing the most normal setting possible. It is important to understand what this means. Here is where substantive indeterminacy is so important. If knowledge is uncertain as to why a child is misbehaving and what to do for the child, then discretion will remain with the school. This is what Kuriloff is saying: when the school district is incompetent, when it is obvious that it does not exercise its discretion in a reasonable manner, the parents will win (something). But when the school district shows that it is taking the proper steps, when it is acting reasonably in light of its expertise, then the school will win; the hearing officer will not substitute its judgment for that of the district. As we shall see at the conclusion of this chapter, this approach is standard in administrative law. As long as an agency can demonstrate that it is following the procedural steps in the process (and there is no evidence of bad faith), then the substantive decision remains with the agency.

Consider now the burden placed on the parents. The agency listens to the parents, it receives their evidence and their witnesses, it shows them the IEPs, and so forth, but how can the parents show that the agency is not really paying attention to what they are saying? If knowledge and standards are uncertain, how can the parents show that the agency is wrong? They can't, and that is why parents lose when the agency prepares its case. Parents can win only if the agency does not follow the procedures or makes an obvious substantive mistake.

How do parents feel about the hearing process? Most of the research reports negative feelings. Neal and Kirp (1985) say that parents feel blamed by the school district for being either bad parents or troublemakers. The schools feel that the mere request for a hearing impugns their professional judgment. According to the PARC researchers, most of the parents think that the whole system is characterized by poor communication. Only about a third of the parents who went to a hearing said that the evaluations or the placement decisions or the content of the programs were explained to them.

Despite what seems like a paucity of actual hearings and parent victories, it may be that the hearing system does have other kinds of effects. The PARC researchers were of the opinion that even though the districts were likely to prevail at the hearings and on later administrative appeals, the districts did not like to go to hearings and often negotiated to avoid hearings.

The Failure of Due Process

Although there have been some changes as a result of P.L. 94–142 procedures, the changes have been quite modest. The PARC researchers, for example, feel that on the whole, special education is being better distributed than in the past. The Boston researchers reach the same conclusions. Clune and Van Pelt (1984) are even more sanguine about the achievements of P.L. 94–142; they report that almost no children are presently excluded from the public schools and that the number of children inappropriately placed is probably also reduced. If true, these are impressive substantive results, although this is not the view of the National Academy. Its recent report is not complimentary about what is happening in special education (Heller et al. 1982). Whatever the debate about the substantive changes of the law, there seems little doubt that the procedural system is not working. Parents are not participating.

In Chapter 2, I pointed out that in order for due process procedures to work, there have to be complaining clients. Due process requires clients who must recognize and deal with their problems. Instead, we find, all too often, denial or self-blame. People who feel this way are not rights-bearing citizens. They are the ones who sign consent forms without questions.

The general failure of client participation in special education is not surprising. The system set up by P.L. 94–142 lacked sufficient appreciation of how underlying power relationships will subvert procedural remedies. This is a story that has been repeated distressingly often. Formal access is only the first step; without supplying additional resources, the stronger parties will eventually be able to turn the procedural system to their own advantage. We know from civil litigation how the poor and disadvantaged cannot take advantage of access to the civil courts. Administrative procedural systems use the same conceptual approach as the civil system. While they provide less formal and presumably less expensive access than the civil system, the disparity in resources between the complaining client and the large-scale organization is still vast.

The administrative reasons for the failure of the procedural process in special education are compounded by the nature of the substantive question involved. As we have seen, special education decisions are characterized by wide discretion and high amounts of professional judgments. The wider the discretion and the more extensive the use of professional judgment or expertise, the more difficult it will be to use procedural rights.

In special education decisions there is little agreement as to the nature of many mild forms of handicaps. Federal law recognizes this indeterminacy by requiring multiple professionals as evaluators, multiple sources of data, and requiring reevaluations. This increases the burdens on the participating parents in that they now have an even more difficult task to counter the evidence. Participation, to be meaningful, has to be sensible; it has to be documented and to be persuasive. In the analysis of the PARC hearings, the parents presented vague arguments, they had far less documentation, and they tended to present nonprofessional witnesses (for example, neighbors). Other studies pointed out that they were overwhelmed by the complexity of the process, even though structurally the process looks quite simple.

"Appropriate education" also presents problems. The choice may be determined by hidden constraints—the availability of slots, or tradeoffs between officials. The existence of a range makes it harder to focus for the purposes of challenging discretion. The required reevaluation means that decisions are experimental, subject to change. This, too, gives the decision makers leverage. They argue, "Well, we'll try this and see what happens. If it doesn't work out, then we can move the student back." It is easy to see how a determined school district can keep thwarting and parrying the arguments of the parent. When the factual determinations as well as the substantive standards are multiple or ambiguous, it becomes extremely difficult to prepare the case. What will be the determining factors? What will be the governing principles? What *really* will decide the case? Unless one can make a reasonable estimate of the answers, one is forced to cover all the issues, and, of course, most parents are simply not in a position to do this. It is doubtful whether they can even get their own professional evaluation of the child, let alone bring to bear relevant, persuasive data on the other issues that the evaluators and other officials are supposed to consider.

The substantive rules are not only indeterminate; on close examination, they turn out not to be legal rights in any practical sense. Parents are told that handicapped children now have a "right" to special education, and that if their "rights" are denied, they have procedural due process. Hearing rights are supposed to enable people to enforce substantive rights. With special education, this turns out not to be true. Legal rights—substantive legal rights—are rights that are ultimately enforceable in a court of law; otherwise, the client is subject to the discretion of the agency. The agency in its discretion may choose to award the goods or services but these are not obtainable as a matter of legal right.

Legal rights exist only if discretion is minimal *and* if the substantive right is divisible into as many units as there are claimants (Friedman 1969). There are legal rights in most Social Security pension cases. The law is relatively clear, discretion is minimal (as far as these programs go), and the benefit—money—is divisible. If the claimant wins in court, the benefit will be paid. Suppose, however, that the Social Security is for disability, and the disability is not obvious. The claimant argues that the hearing officers did not take sufficient account of various doctors' reports or psychological damage or some other kind of testimonial evidence. If the court does not agree with the claimant, it will *not* order benefits paid to the claimant. Instead, the court will remand the case to the agency for reconsideration. This is because the disability decision is a discretionary one and because discretion has been lodged in the agency.

Benefits must also be divisible. Suppose that a person is illegally denied public housing; the agency, for example, misconstrues or misapplies the financial eligibility criteria and the court determines that the person is clearly eligible. That person will still not get into public housing unless there is an apartment available. Since public housing apartments are not divisible, all that the winning person gets is a position on a waiting list. That may be a valuable right, but that depends on how long the list is, not on the lawfulness of the claim.

Special education involves both discretion and nondivisible benefits. Assume the rare case in which the parent does prosecute the case up to the court system. On occasion, a court might order a child in or out of a special education program, but the most likely result would be to send the case back to the agency for reconsideration, for another exercise of its discretion. All that the parents would get for their trouble is the right to try again. Or, if the court would make a substantive order, then this too would depend on the availability of slots, which are not divisible. As a practical matter, it may be that if the school district is confronted with a parent who is resourceful and tough enough to bring a lawsuit, it would accede to the parent's wishes. But this is a different issue. The parent would be obtaining the substantive result not by virtue of a legal right but by bargaining power. As some of the studies point out, special education benefits will be given to parents who fight. In certain cases, the system responds to the squeaky wheel.

REFERENCES

Bersoff, D. N. "From Courthouse to Schoolhouse: Using the Legal System to Secure the Right to an Appropriate Education." *American Journal of Orthopsychiatry*, 52 (July 1982), pp. 506–517.

Bickel, William E. "Classifying Mentally Retarded Students: A Review of Placement Practices in Special Education." In Kirby A. Heller et al. (eds.), *Placing Children in Special Education: A Strategy for Equity*. Washington, D.C.: National Academy Press, 1982.

Briar, Scott. "Welfare from Below: Recipient's Views of the Public Welfare System." *California Law Review*, 54 (1966), pp. 370–385.

Clune, William E., and Van Pelt, Mark. "A Political Method of Evaluating 94-142 and the Several Gaps of Gap Analysis." *Law and Contemporary Problems*, December 1984.

Friedman, Lawrence. "Social Welfare Legislation: An Introduction." *Stanford Law Review*, 21 (1969), pp. 217–247.

Handler, Joel F. "Controlling Official Behavior in Welfare Administration." *California Law Review*, 54 (1966), pp. 479–510.

Heller, Kirby A.; Holtzman, Wayne H.; and Messick, Samuel (eds.). *Placing Children in Special Education: A Strategy for Equity*. Washington, D.C.: National Academy Press, 1982.

Kirp, David; Buss, William; and Kuriloff, Peter. "Legal Reform of Special Education: Empirical Studies and Procedural Proposals." *California Law Review*, 62 (1974), pp. 40–155.

Kuriloff, Peter J. "Is Justice Served by Due Process? Affecting the Outcome of Special Education Hearings in Pennsylvania." In *Law and Contemporary Problems*, 48 (Winter 1985).

Lipsky, Michael. *Street-Level Bureaucracy: Dilemmas of the Individual in Public Services*. New York: Russell Sage Foundation, 1980.

Lynn, Laurence E., Jr. "The Emerging System for Educating Handicapped Children." *Policy Studies Review*, 2, Special #1 (1982–1983), pp. 21–58.

Macaulay, Stewart. "Non-Contractual Relations in Business: A Preliminary Study." *American Sociological Review*, 28 (1963), pp. 55–67.

Magnetti, Suzanne S. "Some Material Incentives of Special Education Funding Practices." In Kirby A. Heller et al. (eds.), *Placing Children in Special Education: A Strategy for Equity*. Washington, D.C.: National Academy Press, 1982.

Mashaw, Jerry L. "Administering Due Process: The Quest for a Dignitary Theory." *Boston University Law Review*, 61 (1981), pp. 885–931.

Michelman, Frank. "Formal and Associational Aims in Procedural Due Process." In J. Pennock and J. Chapman (eds.), *Due Process*, New York: New York University Press, 1977.

Neal, David, and Kirp, David L. "The Allure of Legalization Reconsidered: The Case of Special Education." *Law and Contemporary Problems*, 48 (Winter 1985), pp. 63–87.

Shonkoff, Jack P. "Biological and Social Factors Contributing to Mild Mental Retardation." In Kirby A. Heller et al. (eds.), *Placing Children in Special Education: A Strategy for Equity*. Washington, D.C.: National Academy Press, 1982.

Tribe, Laurence H. *American Constitutional Law*. New York: Academic Press, 1978.

Weatherley, Richard. *Reforming Special Education: Policy Implementation from State to Street Level*. Cambridge, Mass.: M.I.T. Press, 1979.

Weatherley, Richard, and Lipsky, Michael. "Street-Level Bureaucrats and Institutional Innovation: Implementing Special Education Reform." *Harvard Educational Review*, 47, 2 (May 1977), pp. 171–197.

Weaver, Betsy, and Sodano, David. "Boston Public School's Response to the Disproportionate Placement of Minority Students in Special Education Programs: Over/Under Representation Project." Unpublished ms., 1982.

· 4 ·

Special Education and Cooperative Decision Making

"Our family has never been criticized,
they've never said, 'you're failing him.'
They've encouraged us to allow him to do
more and try more, and not to be afraid.
They've convinced us he can do more than
we think he can do."

Parent

Special education has a procedural system that is based on high ideals, ideals beyond what the Supreme Court would probably have required in its most liberal days; yet, it is a system that only few can take advantage of. The question is whether different structures would increase participation, limit bureaucratic domination, and allow discretion to be exercised through shared decision making. This inquiry assumes little or no change in the socioeconomic conditions of the parents. The parents that I am concerned with belong disproportionately to minorities. It is also extremely doubtful, at least in the short run, that many of the parents will be middle class. And regardless of the changes in economic conditions, there remain the social and psychological characteristics of the client populations—poor education, mental and physical ill health, lack of understanding, fears of mental retardation, and fears of bureaucracies and others in positions of authority. I am concerned with remedies for the poor and minorities and the less well-off in dealing with large-scale organizations. It does these people no good to design a procedural system that only the upper-income classes can take advantage of. In what ways, then, can a procedural system be designed to lessen the deficits of the parents?

In order to address this question, it is first necessary to return to the decision-making processes of special education and examine those processes in light of the substantive requirements. The major criticism of the adversary due process procedure was that it failed to take account of the substantive and environmental contexts. Proposed procedural models should not make that same error.

Then, I will present a case study of the special education program of the Madison (Wisconsin) School District. The Madison program presents an alternative; it is an attempt to provide consensual, cooperative decision making that preserves and enhances the autonomy of parents of handicapped students. While the data are not systematic, they do show that the Madison system is theoretically coherent and seems to be working. That is not to say that there are no weaknesses in the Madison system. The importance of the example, though, is in its theoretical and policy implications. It presents an alternative vision, an idea that confronts and transcends the inadequacies of liberalism in the modern welfare state. The vision is a real-life working experience.

Substantive Issues for Decision and the Need for New Models

The National Academy of Sciences study of special education (Heller et al. 1982) contains a series of recommendations concerning how students' educational needs ought to be assessed, and how these needs should be met by the school system. The proposals seem to be realistic and, indeed, are already being carried out in some states.

The basic position of the Academy is that the need for special education should be demonstrated on an individual basis and that improved education be the final evaluative criterion. The Academy's view is that not all poor academic performance or misbehavior is due to deficits in the student; rather, the problem may lie in the classroom—inappropriate instruction or the failure of particular programs or classes for particular students. Accordingly, before a child is formally referred to the special education process, it is the responsibility of the teachers and the school system to use all available resources within the regular classroom to see if learning can be improved. Only after these alternatives have been exhausted should there be a referral. A child could not be referred until it was demonstrated that effective instruction does not work. This means the development of appropriate measurements not only to test the effectiveness of particular curricula for particular students but also to see that the curriculum has been properly implemented.

Several school districts take this approach. Specially trained school psychologists are called in for in-class observation, consultation, and cooperation with the teacher to design and implement "alternative approaches to instruction following behaviorally-oriented, direct instruction theories" (Heller et al. 1982, p. 96). The Academy reports that only about 20 percent of children in such programs were later referred for special education placement.

Concerning assessment, specialists have the responsibility to employ measures that validly assess the functional needs of the child and that are also related to potentially effective programs. The intervention is justified in terms of improved education. "Functional needs may be classes of academically-relevant skills (e.g., reading, mathematics), cognitive processing skills (e.g., generalization, self-monitoring), adaptive and motivational skills (e.g., impulse control, social skills), or physical problems that hamper learning (e.g., defective vision or hearing)." But these functional needs are relevant only if there are potential remedies. "Thus assessment can be judged only in terms of their *utility* in moving the child toward appropriate educational goals" (Heller et al. 1982, pp. 98–99).

The focus on functional needs, in the Academy's opinion, represents a significant shift away from the use of general labels—such as EMR, ED, and LD—which, the Academy argues, obscure the different needs of children having trouble in school. Similarly, the "use of global IQ scores would be deemphasized in favor of techniques that link assessment more directly to the provision of educational services" (Heller et al. 1982, p. 93). Several districts have abandoned the use of the IQ test and instead use other tests designed to measure specific needs. The Vermont Consulting Teacher Program trains teachers to conduct multiple and continuous measurements of minimum objectives. As a result of these tests, specific programs are prescribed for use in the regular classroom.

The current, generalized labels should be abandoned in favor of labels that are linked to specific educational needs and that are also tied to specific effective educational practices. Because of the potentially serious negative aspects of labeling, all labels ought to be justified by their utility. Several states, including Massachusetts, California, and Vermont, have either instituted functional classification schemes or are in the process of doing so. In participating districts in Vermont, students are identified on the basis of functional needs. With parental permission, and after referral, a consulting teacher (a new staff role) and the regular teacher use criterion-based tests to measure levels of achievement in the problem areas. The IEP is developed for the specific need; the school provides daily monitoring and bi-weekly evaluations. The Academy reports that this model is about $200 per child per school year less than special education by resource teachers or in special classes.

Despite the above recommendations, there are still children who will need special programs, if not special placements. Here, the Academy would put the burden on the school system to demonstrate the need for separate treatment that cannot be provided in the regular classroom, and that the separate treatment is working. Special placement (or the possibility) requires continual justification, which in turn requires systematic observation of both the student and the teacher as well as periodic testing not only to monitor progress but also as a means of informing instruction.

The Academy would require the special education staff to demonstrate at least annually that the student cannot meet specific educational objectives in the regular setting and therefore ought to continue the special education program. Specific exit programs and criteria have to be established to forestall students remaining separated through inertia. In Louisiana, the child is to be placed in the next least restrictive alternative unless special education can show otherwise; and funds are provided to follow a child for one year after decertification from special education.

The Academy proposals are designed to improve the substantive outcomes of special education decisions; however, these proposals significantly increase the difficulties of achieving due process values as traditionally conceived. The proposals increase individualization and discretion by multiple testing for specific needs and by having more actors, more settings (for example, more effort for more programs in the regular classroom), and many more decision points. The effect is a long series of trial-and-error decisions for the student to see what works in what setting. During the whole period, the Academy urges continual monitoring, feedback, consultation, evaluation, and adjustment. The most dramatic illustration of the lengthening of the process is the Louisiana system.

The Academy's case is persuasive, but what are the implications for the P.L. 94–142 procedures? Informed consent is required for all significant decisions. We have seen how most school districts have converted the P.L. 94–142 procedures into formalities; there may be even more pressure to do so under the Academy proposals, since more time and effort are required. But assuming a responsive, willing district, the difficulties of achieving the due process values of revelation and participation are increased considerably. The decisions are continuous and frequent, and this involves the parents in many sessions. Parental participation is low in systems with fewer tests, fewer actors, and fewer alternatives. How can they maintain an increased level of involvement? It may be argued that if decisions are related to the child's needs they would be more understandable, but this is questionable. With the Academy's proposals, there is an increase in both alternatives and expertise, making participation more difficult. With this greater indeterminacy, the enforcement of legal rights through adversarial procedural remedies becomes even more problematic. There is an opportunity for the bureaucracy, consciously and unconsciously, to thwart due process procedures.

In order for revelation and participation to be achieved, there has to be a *reason* for the school system to want them. A different model has been developed in the Madison (Wisconsin) School District.

An Alternative to the Adversary System: The Cooperative Model

Madison, a city of approximately 170,000, serves (as of 1981) about 24,000 students in twenty-seven elementary, eight middle, and four regular high schools.[1] (There are four alternative schools with low

---

[1] This study is based upon interviews conducted with people involved in the Madison special education system during the 1983 school year. An effort was made to include

enrollments.) There are approximately 2,000 special education students. Special education services are administered by the Central Office Department of Specialized Educational Services and by the regular education administrators under the school district concept of "one instructional program, which provides options to meet the needs of all students." The budget for Specialized Educational Services was $7,955,251 for the 1981–1982 academic year, and $1,676,931 for the mental retardation program. The regular education budgets also absorb some of the costs of educating handicapped students. While the special education program in Madison is under the direction of the Director of Specialized Educational Services, the program has enjoyed the support of the School Board and the Superintendent of the Schools (Taylor 1982). In addition, the Department of Studies in Behavioral Disabilities at the University of Wisconsin played a key role in the development of the Madison program, including the training of teachers and curriculum design.

The Statutory and Administrative Structure

In order to qualify for services that supplement or replace regular education, the Wisconsin state statute provides that a child must be found to have a disability and/or a handicapping condition and a need for "exceptional" (special) education. Conditions that may require such services are enumerated in the statute and include: physical, crippling, or orthopedic disability; mental retardation or other developmental disabilities; hearing impairment; visual disability; speech or language disability; emotional disturbance; learning disability; pregnancy (including up to two months after birth or termination of the pregnancy).

The Madison School District offers handicapped students a variety of options ranging from special services in conjunction with regular school programs (for example, a notetaker for a hearing-impaired student) to resource rooms where students go for special education assistance, to self-contained classes (almost complete instruction by

---

the views of the full range of system participants—parents of handicapped children, parent advocates, teachers, representatives of voluntary organizations, school psychologists, social workers, other M-Team members, those involved in the initial development of the program, and senior administrators.

the special education teacher). In addition, seventeen of the forty Madison schools are made accessible to physically handicapped students. These schools are geographically distributed throughout the city and include three high schools, four middle schools, and ten elementary schools. The dispersal of classrooms for special education students reflects a long-standing commitment of the school district to the integration of special education with regular education.

The Madison School District administrative structure incorporates the federal and state law into its own unique informal, cooperative system. First I will describe the structure of the process, using the state regulations and guidelines and the School District manual; then, we will see how the system works, based on interviews with parents, parent advocates, teachers, special education staff, administrators, and voluntary organization staff.

To identify, evaluate, and place students in special education, five procedures are followed: (1) the identification of students with possible special education needs; (2) referral for evaluation; (3) the M-team evaluation; (4) development of the individualized education plan (IEP); and (5) the placement of the student in an appropriate educational program.

Schools are mandated to seek out children with possible handicapping conditions. Perhaps the most important means of identification is the formal screening of all children as they enter the school system. Parental permission is not required in order to screen a child; however, parents may refuse to permit screening as a prerequisite to starting school. In addition to this initial formal screening, schools are also mandated to ensure that informal, ongoing screening continues. This usually involves observations and testing by regular teachers and other school personnel during the course of the school year.

Under state law, certified personnel working in the school system are required to refer a child if they have reason to believe that the child has a special educational need. Any child thought to have various physical, mental, emotional, or learning disabilities, or to be pregnant must be reported to the district. Parents may also make referrals. Regardless of who makes the referral, the parents must be notified that a referral has been made. The referral must state the suspected handicapping condition and the reason why it is suspected.

Once the referral is made, most of the remaining steps in the process must be completed within ninety days—up to and including the placement recommendation. Parental permission must be obtained if the ninety-day period is to be extended.

The District evaluates the child through the multidisciplinary team (M-team), which is composed of a team of experts from different fields in the schools. Teams must be composed of a minimum of two members, and may vary in size. However, there must be at least two members of the M-team who are skilled in assessing and programming for the area of the suspected handicap. One of these members must be certified to teach children with that condition, and if more than one condition is suspected, then the team must include persons certified in each of the conditions. M-teams frequently consist of a teacher certified in the suspected condition, a social worker, a psychologist, and often a speech and language therapist.

Before an actual evaluation can begin, the M-team chairperson must notify the parents in writing that the school intends to evaluate their child. The notice must state the area(s) to be evaluated (intellectual, visual, auditory, etcetera); who will be doing the evaluation (school psychologist, nurse, teacher); the purpose of the evaluation; and the general type of testing instruments that will be used. The notice must inform parents of the procedural safeguards designed to protect the child's rights. The notice must be given to parents each time the school intends to do an evaluation. If the initial evaluation is to be done by the school, parents must give written consent.

Parental Involvement

The District puts a strong emphasis on parental involvement. In addition to the requirement of written permission for an M-team assessment, the District urges that parents be involved throughout the entire process. The M-teams are encouraged to "formulate and share their hypotheses with parents" and "it is *highly recommended* that parents be a source of assessment and programming information" (emphasis in the original). In any event, parents are required to be involved in the development of the program for their child. If no disability or handicapping condition is found, the M-team has to schedule a conference with the parents to discuss these findings.

The same emphasis on parental involvement applies to reassessments. The District's Handbook says that the parents must be involved in the development of the program and must give written permission for any changes or additions to categorical program placements. If the school feels that the child's rights to an appropriate education may be denied by the parents' refusal to allow the evaluation to take place, the school has the right to ask for a hearing on the matter. Written parental consent is not required for any reevaluation of the child.

Once the school receives parental permission to evaluate the child, the M-team reviews all existing information and data that may already exist on the child. If the M-team determines that not enough information is available to make an informed decision, they must perform the necessary tests or observations of the child's performance. Each individual member of the M-team performs the evaluations deemed necessary in his or her area of expertise, and writes a complete report elaborating scores and findings. After the M-team has completed its evaluation of the child and has determined that the child does indeed have a disability and needs special education, the M-team must detail how that handicapping condition interferes with the behavioral and academic functioning of the child in his or her present educational program. The M-team must specify what interventions or modifications may still need to be tried in regular education classes for the child; and it must demonstrate how the essential elements of the proposed individualized program will differ from the child's current program.

If the M-team finds a disability or handicapping condition and a need for special education programs or services, the initial findings are submitted to an Eligibility Review Committee. This committee is also multidisciplinary and includes the program support teachers as well as other appropriate staff. The Eligibility Review Committee applies the categorical program to the M-team findings, but it can also disagree with the findings or make other suggestions. The two committees then try to work out some common solution. If the Eligibility Review Committee concurs, the program goals and objectives of the IEP placement are completed and incorporated into the M-team report and findings, which are submitted in a written report to the director of the District's special education program. Once approved, unless returned to the M-team for further evaluations or corrections of omissions, the school sends the parents a copy of the M-team recommendations for their child, as well as a statement elaborating the reasons for the recommendations. At this point, the school must schedule a conference with the parents to explain the M-team's findings and recommendations. If parents attend the final M-team staff meeting, this conference requirement is considered to be met. The District attempts to meet with parents at least once at this point in the process, and if necessary will arrange additional meetings.

The IEP Programming Team, consisting of the staff that will most likely be delivering the specific special education services, works out the specific goals and objectives of the program. The parents, and the students, when appropriate, are members of this team. The staff that delivers the special education services continues as an annual IEP programming team functioning in an ongoing manner throughout the year. The parents and students continue as members of the team. The District manual states that the parental signature on the annual IEP does not indicate approval or disapproval but only documents involvement in the development of objectives and review of progress.

The initial IEP is intended to be the working plan for the student for one calendar year, although modifications can be made at any time as needed. Special education services cannot begin without written parental permission. The teacher and the parents are to work out a mutually satisfactory plan to monitor progress. Again, the Handbook emphasizes the importance of parent/teacher communication. At the end of the calendar year, a conference is held with the parent to review progress and write a new IEP.

Procedural Rights and Parent Advocates

At the start of the M-team process, the parents are given an *M-Team Parent Handbook* which, in addition to describing in understandable language the legislation, regulations, and process, also gives the parents information as to their procedural rights. In the event that parents disagree with any decisions made by the school, they have the right to express their views and request alternatives. They are told that they can reopen any decision by contacting any of the school staff that have been involved with their child, including the school principal or the special education administrators. They are also advised that they have a right to a "due process hearing." Requests for a hearing must be made in writing to the District Superintendent of Schools, and a hearing and decision will be made no later than forty-five days after receipt of the written request. If the parents are still not satisfied, they may appeal to the State Department of Instruction, and ultimately to a county or circuit court. Parents are also advised about how to appeal on the basis of federal law.

The *Parent Handbook* also contains information on parent advocates. Parent advocates are described as "family members, friends, or people from a parent support organization who may be familiar with the law and the evaluation procedures" or "an individual who is specifically trained to be a 'parent advocate.' " In informing the parents of the availability of parent advocates, the approach of the *Handbook* emphasizes the need for increasing communication, rather than pressing adversarial rights. For example, the introduction to the parent advocacy section reads: "Even though this handbook was prepared to inform you of the multidisciplinary team evaluation process and although school staff are available to answer questions, it is recognized that this may be a new process to you and may be confusing." If the parent feels this way, the *Handbook* encourages the parent to ask a "parent advocate" to participate in the M-team meeting as well as other school meetings.

The functions of the parent advocate are a blend of communication and legal rights advocacy. The *Handbook* states: "[The parent advocate] may help ask the questions of the M-team members or school staff you may forget to ask while at a meeting. The advocate can help you listen to the various M-team members and ask questions in addition to yours which will clarify what people are reporting." The advocate helps communicate the parents' views—"that your message gets across and that the information you provide is understood." The advocate can interpret for parents what was accomplished at the meetings.

As to legal rights, the *Handbook* states: "[The advocate] may assure that the safeguards built into the law for you and your child are adhered to. . . . Although the school will not purposefully disregard parent/child rights, the parent advocate may help you focus more fully on your rights and responsibilities."

The *Handbook* also states what an advocate can and cannot do. Advocates generally do not have the expertise to provide a second professional opinion, although they can help the parents get this information. And, although the advocates will help the parents review the information and recommendations of the school, the parents themselves must make their own decisions.

The approach of the *Handbook* to the use of parent advocates is important. By deemphasizing the requirement of challenge, the *Handbook* intends to *lower* the barriers to seeking help. It tries to do this in a number of ways. It tries to make the parents feel that their possible uncertainty or confusion may be due to their unfamiliarity rather than their personal deficiencies. This is a normal reaction, one that parents can feel comfortable with. It will be recalled that one of the barriers to the exercise of procedural due process is that it is perceived as a challenge; it is a hostile act. In the social context of special education, parents are more likely to feel confusion, guilt, helplessness, stupidity, or other kinds of inadequacies. They are in a continuing relationship with the school; they feel that they need the school for a variety of purposes.

The *Handbook* recognizes this may be the case and urges parents to get help—not necessarily to challenge the school (although that possibility is recognized), but to help them find out what is going on and to clarify their position. The definition of the helper is something of a misnomer. "Advocate" connotes an adversarial relationship. The *Handbook* describes parent advocates as members of the family or friends, as well as specially trained people. It views the advocate's function as an interpreter or communicator. The School District, at least at this stage of the process, is talking about a communicative relationship.

If parents are dissatisfied with a multidisciplinary team assessment or the recommended program, they first contact the school. According to the officials interviewed, the majority of these conferences concern the parents' "emotional difficulty" in accepting the M-team's assessment. This difficulty is particularly acute when the assessment is any degree of mental retardation. One tough problem is the expectations parents have for their children. Although there are many handicapped children in society, it is a relatively rare event in the lives of particular families. For the larger categories of disability (which are too general anyway), there may be about one in fifty children; for the narrowly drawn categories, one in 500 or even one in 1,500 (Streit 1981). There is no basis on which to draw comparisons and develop expectations. The parents may think that their child is hopeless or that the school can and ought to work miracles. At this point, the goal of the parent–teacher M-team interaction is to help the parents "work through" their feelings in order to deal with the assessment and recommendation, and to encourage parental understanding and consent to the school's recommended placement. After these conferences, most parents accept the decision and give their authorization to implement the Individual Educational Program (IEP).

In the event differences are not reconciled, parents then notify the School District Central Office and arrange a conference with the Program Coordinator who is responsible for the child's particular needs. In addition to the parents and the Program Coordinator, teachers, M-team members, and parent advocates may be present at this meeting. This meeting is also intended to be a reconciliation conference; the view of the officials is that the purpose of the conference is to identify the parents' "difficulty" in an effort to resolve the situation in the best interests of the child.

Parents may request an independent evaluation. The school, at this point, has two options. It can agree to pay for the independent evaluation (in which case the school has the right to insist on the same standards used by the school) or the school can request a hearing to see if they do have to pay. If the hearing examiner determines that the school's evaluations were satisfactory, the parents must bear the cost. There are also provisions whereby the State Department of Instruction will pay for independent evaluations if the parents are needy. In any event, the M-team must consider any independent evaluations that are made available to it.

If there is still disagreement, the parents can seek mediation. Mediation, which is not provided for by either federal or state law, consists of the two parties selecting a neutral third party who attempts to negotiate a settlement. The settlement has to be accepted by both parties.

The parents may elect to go to a hearing, with or without mediation. The District can also elect a hearing if the parents refuse to give consent. Under either method, the hearing procedure is the same. The rules governing the hearing procedures are substantially those discussed in Chapter 3; the parents have full due process rights. There is an appeal to the state superintendent for a second administrative hearing, and to the state courts (as well as federal courts) if necessary.

How the System Works

The informal cooperative system developed by the Madison School District is based on an ideology completely different from the adversarial due process system. The Madison School District makes three conceptual moves which form the heart of its system. The first is that *parents are part of the solution, rather than the problem.* The Madison District takes the approach that special education is part of general education. Students receiving special education services are only receiving a range of options on a continuum of services. It is a holistic, integrated concept of the entire education package for the entire student population. Some students receive the standard curriculum; others receive various kinds of support and services as their individual needs dictate.

How, then, do parents fit into this concept? Parents are considered to be an important part of regular education. They are expected to be knowledgeable and supportive of public education; they are invited and encouraged to participate in regular education programs; and they are supposed to take an interest in and provide support for their children's schooling both in school and at home. In Madison, the same concept and expectation apply to parents of children in special education. The Madison special education officials emphasize that special education is part of regular education; just as parents participate in regular education, so too they ought to participate in special education. A senior administrator in the special education program put the matter in these terms:

> The integrated system is critically important, especially for getting the IEPs and assessments done at the individual school level. Parents need longitudinal contact with the same set of people—for assessment and programming. Within this system, the building level is the primary unit, so the parent is already engaged with the primary unit of the school district. Parents with handicapped children are made more like other parents rather than being differentiated. Parents and kids build their identity first as members of the school district rather than as a handicapped child or a parent of a handicapped child.

This is not merely an ideological position. It is also considered essential for the success of the special education program. The school, they point out, has the child for only five or six hours of the day. The rest of the time, the child is at home, and the program for the child is much more likely to succeed if the parents understand and agree with what the school is trying to do, and work with the child at home. The concept is the same with regular education.

It is this first conceptual move that provides the foundation for the *continuing relationship*. Adversarial advocacy works best in a cross-sectional time-frame, the fixing of rights and duties at a particular point in time in the lives of the parties. In special education, as with regular education, the relationship of the parent to the school is to continue through the school life of the child.

The second conceptual move is that *special education programs have to be administered in an individualized, flexible, experimental manner*; in theory and in practice, services and programs have to be based on individual needs and careful evaluation of results.

The individualized, flexible, experimental approach gives substantive content to the continuing relationship with the parents. It means that the relationship ought to continue through the school life of the child because decisions about what the child needs and what services are to be provided are subject to continual reevaluation. If the parents are to be part of the solution, they must continue to be involved as the program changes. This is in sharp contrast to the cross-sectional approach of the adversarial, legal rights position—the fixing of a position at a particular point in time.

There are other important implications of the individualized, flexible approach combined with parental participation. It not only opens up, it encourages the necessity for negotiation and compromise. As long as the technology is uncertain, as long as there is no agreed-upon way of doing things, and as long as there is a commitment to flexibility, reevaluation, and experimentation, there is room to negotiate. If the parents are uneasy about a particular school plan, the school can hold off for a while and try the parents' plan to see how that works. If the parents are convinced that the school is flexible, they can more readily agree to a school plan with the understanding that they can renegotiate. The concept, then, is a *continuous, bargaining* relationship.

The other implication of the individualized, flexible, experimental approach is that it reduces conflict. As long as the parties realize that decisions made today are not carved in stone, that there will be good-faith reevaluation, and that there is a commitment to listen to each other, the relationship is transformed from winners and losers to partners. Decisions are no longer of the zero-sum variety. It lays the foundation for a cooperative relationship.

A cooperative relationship, however, depends upon communication. Specifically, it requires parents who are knowledgeable and who are willing to express their point of view and indeed press their position, even if it means disagreeing with the position of the school. Here, we encounter again the distribution question. How can the Madison School District expect the average parent to communicate effectively with the school? The parent lacks the expertise and resources of the bureaucracy, and may face additional hurdles of guilt over the child, rejection or confusion over the diagnosis, feelings of stupidity in the face of experts and professionals, and intimidation because of the power of the bureaucracy.

The Madison School District recognizes this problem through its use of the parent advocate. In a number of respects, this is also a unique concept. The use of lay advocates, of course, is an old idea, but it is a device that is usually used to strengthen adversarial systems— for example, minor civil disputes, welfare hearings, landlord–tenant hearings, and small claims. It is a mechanism to supplement or, more accurately, to rectify the maldistribution of professional legal services. Lay advocacy is not recommended in cooperative decision making because it assumes conflict; it recognizes the need for additional resources in helping one of the parties in pressing his or her claim. In cooperative, or consensual decision making, conflict is bad, it is something to be suppressed, not encouraged.

The Madison School District takes the opposite view of conflict: *conflict is used to help communication.* This is the third conceptual move that the District has made. Note the language in the Parent Handbook discussed in the previous section. Only one of the functions of the lay advocate concerns legal rights. The other function, and the one that is stressed, is to aid the parent in understanding what the District is trying to say *and* to help the parents in getting their position across.

Use of the parent advocate helps address the distribution question by providing the parents with resources to aid them in their relationship with the school. But this might not be enough. The District also makes an effort to put the parents in contact with local voluntary organizations or other public agencies that can help parents. The Parent Handbook lists a variety of such places with short descriptions of their services.

This is the ideological basis of the Madison School District. What follows is a more detailed description of how the principal actors think the process works—parents, officials, teachers, advocates, and advocacy organizations. The sample is not scientific. Rather, it is purposive. My aim is to show what the Madison School system is trying to do, rather than present an empirical study of whether they are, in fact, accomplishing their purposes. What the interviews show is that Madison believes in its ideas, that it seems to have made considerable and, I think, commendable progress in carrying out these ideas, but that there are difficult problems in maintaining the health and viability of a cooperative decision-making process.

The interviews have a ring of truth primarily for two reasons. First, outsiders who would not normally be coopted by the system, such as children's rights advocates, agree with the description of the system in its essential features. Second, the principal actors themselves recognize the deficiencies and potential problems and weaknesses of the system. While they are proud of what they have accomplished, they are not defensive about the problems of maintaining active parental participation, which they view as a continuing struggle. These impressions are not a substitute for careful empirical investigations, but they nevertheless lend credibility to the case study.

What has been the experience of some of the parents? One of the most active, aggressive parents, Ms. V., had eight children ranging in age from 1½ to sixteen. One of the children, nine-year-old R.M., had been placed in a TMR class in the Madison City schools. In addition, a 3½-year-old had had preliminary screening and was about to be M-teamed. Though V. first suspected a problem when R.M. was two, it was not until the child was four that she was brought into a mental health clinic for examination. She displayed symptoms of autism and was diagnosed as emotionally disturbed. Later, when R.M. entered the public school system, she was M-teamed. By that time, V. was concerned about the labels that were being attached to her daughter. A friend referred her to a parent advocate. The parent advocate assisted V. during the initial M-team process and V. was satisfied with the team's performance. Subsequently, V. felt that her daughter was not responding to the IEP and she contacted the members of the team for their opinions. A second team was formed. At the first meeting, V. was presented with the psychologist's recommendations that the desired changes could not be made. V. asked for an adjournment so that an advocate could be present. The adjournment was granted. It took more than a dozen meetings to finally work out a satisfactory program.

In V.'s judgment, the special education system process can result in the development of appropriate programs only if there is extensive and continuous parental involvement. The IEP development usually does not take as long as it did in her case because most parents are willing to accept professional judgments with limited questioning. For example, V. insisted, and the parties agreed, that other professionals not involved in the M-team should be consulted in the development of the program. For the next year, because of illness in the family, V. could not maintain regular contact with the school. When she was able to resume contact, she found that a number of specialists who were supposed to have been contacted were not. V. herself contacted the Autism Society. The District cooperated fully with an autism specialist in developing a program for R.M.

V. has had fairly extensive contact with voluntary organizations and has found them helpful. She did experience some difficulty in initiating contact. She did not know the organizations, and was afraid that contact would automatically label her child. Over time, the discomfort lessened. The Wisconsin Association for Retarded Children helped her through some difficulties with a diagnostic clinic. She has also made use of RIDE, a voluntary organization that coordinates horseback riding for exceptional children. She reads *Blast*, a monthly District newsletter that provides information on meetings and organizations providing services for exceptional children and their families.

This year, for the first time, V. and her husband were able to attend a parent training workshop sponsored by the State Department of Public Instruction. The annual workshop can handle fifty participants. Workshops are held one night a week for four weeks. Dinner was included and a $40 stipend was given to all participants to cover transportation and babysitting costs. The conference focused on vocational training but also included role-playing with M-teams, assertiveness and advocacy training, and sessions on parents' rights. All participants were given a comprehensive packet of materials. Despite the fact that V. was experienced by this time, she found the sessions valuable and was pleased with them.

In sum, in V.'s opinion, the Madison School District will deliver appropriate services but only if the parents and advocates work closely with the District. She seems less certain as to the appropriateness of the program when parents are less informed and less involved. There is always concern about the effect of parental involvement on the relationship between the child and the teachers, but V. feels that the way to deal with that problem is to develop good communication with the relevant professionals.

The other parents that were interviewed were not as aggressive as Ms. V., but they did show that over the course of their dealings with the schools, there were successes in communication, in working out differences, in bargaining, and in reaching satisfactory solutions. Ms. L., for example, told of two confrontations with the school that were ultimately resolved through negotiation. This family came from another city where the parents felt that the child had had a successful placement. The Madison School District disagreed with the prior recommendation, but because of the strong position of the parents, agreed to their request to start a new M-team evaluation. After a few weeks, when it was evident that the child was not performing well, there were further meetings, and the child was placed with another teacher. In the meantime, at the urging of the teacher and the parents, the M-team process was completed quickly, and a satisfactory placement was worked out. The second confrontation was more of an organized effort. Here, the problem was a systemwide shortage of speech and language services (Ms. L.'s child was at the end of a long waiting list). Ms. L., with other parents, attended school board meetings to protest further cuts, and met with the principals and the Director of Specialized Services, who knew that the parents were threatening to sue.

Ms. J.'s son had poor reading ability and a great deal of trouble with speech and language. In the second grade, she had her son examined at the University Learning Disabilities Clinic, which could not identify any specific learning disability or make any specific recommendations. At Ms. J.'s request, the elementary school principal and an LD teacher attended the conference with the clinic. The LD teacher was not satisfied with the clinic's conclusion and recommended an M-team evaluation, to which Ms. J. agreed. During the course of the evaluation, the LD teacher took the child into her own classroom. Ms. J. said, "It was against the law, but they made an exception for us, they could see he needed it." The M-team diagnosed dyslexia, and at the parents' request the student received speech therapy as well as special assistance in reading. Ms. J. felt that the M-team was very open to her suggestions ("they really wanted my feedback"), and she is sure that if she had requested a change, they would have been flexible and would have tried to accommodate her. She said that they made every effort to involve her actively in the whole process and that since the placement the school has continued these efforts.

Other staff members—teachers, program support teachers, and administrators—told similar stories of how conflicts were worked out. One middle school special education teacher recounted a difficult situation in which the school believed that the parents were not acting in the best interests of the child. Still, an effort was made to compromise, to work things out. The case concerned an eleven-year-old boy who was both physically and mentally handicapped. The parents would not accept the TMR label and did not want to participate in the IEP process. "They had the child at home until he was nine. His mother was licensed to teach and was providing him with some learning. She did not like the role models he would see in the TMR classroom, but we felt that it was important to get this kid into school. We assigned him at the TMR level, but we placed him in EMR to sell the idea of school to Mom. We'll M-team again next year, and hope to convince her at that time to place him in the TMR program. At least we now have the kid in school." The teacher said that they are willing to make compromises "if, in the end, we think it will serve the child."

Another example involved an autistic child. The special education staff thought that although the child could continue to learn in a mainstream setting, he would need a social relationship with a peer group so that he would have support when he entered middle school. This plan, however, required a change of schools that the parents resisted because the child had been doing well in the placement and a particular teacher had been working with the child for three years. The parents finally agreed to the new plan once they were satisfied with the school's assurances that the child would be returned to the original placement if he failed to make progress. The child did establish a peer group and, in the opinion of the staff person, was able to make the transition to middle school.

There were other accounts of parents not accepting M-team evaluations or reevaluations, and considerable efforts were made to explain what the school thought was right. These stories point out the essential features of the Madison cooperative system—the close connection of the parents to the system; the individualized, flexible approach;

and the use of outside resources to aid in the communication process. Negotiations and bargaining take place within a cooperative context.

Why does the School District take this approach? And what are some of the problems it encounters?

The participation of parents in the process is grounded substantively rather than procedurally. By this I mean that the theory behind the idea of participation is not due process or procedurally oriented; it is not based on liberal, legal ideals of individualism under the rule of law. The school district, if asked, would not necessarily reject these ideals. But when it developed its ideals of parental participation, it was thinking of the *substance* of special education, what was required to educate children with handicapping conditions. The ideas and practices of parental participation were worked out, for the most part, before the enactment of P.L. 94–142, and probably before the changes in our legal culture really began to be felt in this area of education. It was necessary for the parents to be involved if the school district was to fulfill its organizational goals.

How Madison arrived at its present position is an interesting story. It illustrates the importance of discretion as an evolving process at the local level; it also shows how procedure should develop out of substantive needs rather than being imposed as an abstract system. When the principal innovators of the Madison system looked at special education, in the 1960s, they found what was true nationwide— handicapped children were segregated into special rooms and even special buildings. There was little or no education, and certainly not much progress. Convinced that as a general proposition, segregated institutions were bad for children, the innovators wanted to try educating handicapped children in regular classrooms—what is known as "mainstreaming." They had no sure knowledge that mainstreaming would work; they only knew that what was presently being tried was failing. But in order to move students into regular classrooms, they felt that they needed parents to go along with the experiment. This was the first example of parent participation in special education.

The second substantive change involved the "birth-to-three" experiment. The law required that special education be provided to children from age three to twenty-one. The innovators came to the conclusion that three was already too late; the handicapped child was too far behind. Rather than picking an arbitrary number, they decided that they should try to work with handicapped children from birth. This decision, of course, required the use of parents to explain the program to new mothers and then to give them encouragement and support.

Then, the innovators began to look at the results of special education. What was happening to children when they left school at age twenty-one? What they found was discouraging; graduates were not functioning in the community as expected, and for the most part, they were institutionalized. The problem was that much of what students learned in school was not appropriate to their needs outside of the school setting. Handicapped students often have trouble transferring what they learn in school to life in the community. Why not, then, provide part of the program outside of the school? This came to be known as the "Post 21 Program." Once education is conceived of as taking place in the community, the role of parents is again important. They have to give the teachers information about performance outside the classroom.

It was out of these ideas that the concept of parental participation grew and became accepted as the normal way to help handicapped children. It is a cooperative venture. It is an exchange. The school system needs the parents and needs parents to help other parents. The term "parent advocate" came into fashion only when the legal rights approach took hold.

There are some other reasons for bringing parents into the process. At the general, community level, parents are an important source of political support. In Madison, parents support the school budget and the school system, and this support is cultivated by the school system. This applies to both regular and special education. We noted in one of the parent interviews the collective effort to protect speech and therapy resources in the school budget.

On the individual level, parents are a source of information to the school system. Parents are included in the initial screening teams; they are used to provide developmental and medical information; they complete various assessment instruments; and they are encouraged to express their views and concerns as to the child's development. Parents aid and support the school's educational program; they encourage the child to take the school seriously; they help in homework and other kinds of school activities. The school needs parental participation to make the program work, and the parents sense this. In one of the most striking testaments to the school system, one of the parents said, "Our family has never been criticized, they've never said, 'you're failing him.' They've encouraged us to allow him to do more and try more, and not to be afraid. They've convinced us he can do more than we think he can do." This quote captures the essential idea of parents being part of the solution.

When the parents participate in the program, the school feels they are more likely to form a more realistic attitude as to the potential and limitations of their child. This also works for the school; parental participation gives them additional nonclassroom information about the school, which helps the school in the evaluation process.

Another important substantive reason for parental involvement is the commitment of the school district to prepare its special education students for young adult life in the community (the Post 21 program). Parents, in the opinion of the school, have to come to the realization that many of the children will not "grow out" of the handicapping condition and that they cannot remain forever dependent on a custodial situation. Therefore, the parents must be involved in developing nonschool skills.

Parental participation gives the parents not only a chance to influence the substance of the decision but also a stake in the outcome. It becomes their program as well; at the same time, it lessens the risk of later rejection, or disagreement with the school. In short, there are a variety of benefits to the school system from active parental participation. This is important, because one of the key ingredients to the success of cooperative decision making is a change on the part of the bureaucracy, and this can come about only if the bureaucracy believes such a change to be in their best interest.

The development of the child's IEP is an example of the role parents play in the special education system. If a decision is made to go ahead with the M-team assessment, not only is parent participation encouraged, but one of the members of the team is assigned the specific responsibility to be the primary source of contact with the parents. This gives the parents at least one person with whom they can establish an ongoing relationship; it also fixes responsibility on one member of the M-team.

After the M-team completes its findings and if a special education need is identified, the IEP is developed. The parents are encouraged to participate (again, along with a parent advocate if desired). As with the M-team meetings, the school attempts to be flexible with scheduling, often holding meetings in the late afternoon so one or both parents can be present. Various devices are used to encourage parental participation in the development of the IEP. Some teachers said they send home blank forms to require the parents to fill in goals and programs themselves. Others draft part of the IEP and leave space for the parents to make additions or deletions at the conference.

In a small empirical study of nine IEP meetings dealing with young handicapped students, it was found that the meetings on average lasted for about 35 minutes. They were attended by an average of 4.4 persons. At least one parent (the mother) was present at every meeting. Discussions at the meetings were substantive. Almost 70 percent of the topics discussed centered on the skills the child was learning or failing to learn and how the child was being taught those skills. The parents accounted for about one quarter of the conversation at the meetings. The researcher reported that while decisions were not made often, when decisions were made, it was jointly by parents and the school people. The study concluded that parental participation was higher for parents of younger children than for those with older children, which is consistent with other research, but that in Madison, parental participation and satisfaction with the level of participation was higher than reported elsewhere (Davis 1983, p. 75).

Nevertheless, teachers report that the IEP conferences are a trouble spot. Too often, many parents will not look over the draft IEP before the conference and will accept what the M-team recommends. Others report that parent interest fluctuates. Interest may run very high at the initial identification stage or during the development of the IEP, but then drop off until some particular issue arises. One teacher said, "The most difficult parents to deal with are those that still have not come to terms with their child's handicap or label, and although they may have the most questions and concerns, they are often the most reluctant to get involved." She said that she tries to identify these parents, and makes a concerted effort to answer their questions, schedule additional conferences, encourage them to visit the school, and refer them to outside professionals and organizations. She cited one example in which the parents were unable to accept the M-team recommendations, and it required a total of seven M-team meetings as well as numerous parent/teacher conferences before the child's placement could be worked out to everyone's satisfaction. "Of course, we're realistic with parents, but we're willing to go some extra distance to be sure they are satisfied and know we've made the best placement possible for that kid." Ironically, but not surprisingly, participation drops off as trust in the system develops. This is consistent with the study findings that parental participation tends to wane as the child grows older.

Nevertheless, despite the problems of getting parents to participate, the overall sense is one of commitment to parental participation on the part of the school. According to the former director of the Wisconsin Coalition for Advocacy, a citizens group, the Madison system of cooperation and informal conferences is highly successful. There is a great feeling of trust between the parents in the community and the special education system. In part, this is due to the local culture; Madison is a community with a long history of citizen participation. But the feeling of trust is also in no small measure due to the leadership of the special education system, and especially the director. The Madison Director of Specialized Educational Services feels that active parental involvement is essential for the progress of the individual student as well as for the overall program. He wants parents to communicate with the school—weekly, daily, in person, or by telephone. In order to develop this kind of communication, it is necessary to bring the parents in early in the process and to grant their requests as long as they are within the range of alternatives. In his view, the best teachers are the ones who really involve parents in the process.

Parent Advocates and Voluntary Organizations

Both the State Department of Instruction and the Madision School District try to make available to parents lists of organizations that might be of help to them. The Department of Instruction, Division for Handicapped Children and Pupil Services, issues a Guide for Parents which lists a local and statewide hotline number, thirteen public agencies (state and regional), and twenty-seven voluntary organizations, including branch offices. Most of the voluntary organizations are for specific handicapping conditions (for example, epilepsy, the blind), others are for more general handicaps (the Association for Retarded Children), and others are general citizen advocacy organizations (Wisconsin Coalition for Advocacy, and the Youth Policy and

Law Center). In addition, the *M-Team Parent Handbook* has a section on parent advocates, including five places to call for help in obtaining one. The voluntary organizations enjoy a good relationship with both state and local educational officials. The organizations put on workshops for parents, prepare and distribute handbooks and other informational guides, and train parent advocates. Often state and local officials will participate in these efforts—for example, in training and workshop sessions and reviewing handbooks.

How active are the voluntary organizations? How much participation is there? Reports are mixed. One parent told of her experiences in the Parent Advisory Group which she attended as a representative of one of the elementary schools. The Advisory Committee met about once a month, published a newsletter, critiqued a handbook designed to help parents, and worked on booklets and programs designed to teach sex education to handicapped children, among other activities. In her opinion, the State Department actively promoted participation in the group; it readily provided information on budgets for special education, school board agendas, and programs. There was joint participation in workshops on special education programs—"the school even paid babysitting so parents could attend."

Groups do not have to be formal or parts of large, structured organizations to be useful. Parents meet other parents of handicapped children in a variety of settings that can provide information and needed support. One parent told how she met parents of other handicapped children through regular parent and school functions and organizations (for example, the Cub Scout troop; social gatherings for teens organized by the school) as well as the Special Olympics. She felt that some of the discussions were "helpful and enlightening—we found out that other kids have problems, too." Overall, she had mixed feelings about parent groups. "There's good and bad to them, some can get to be just gripe sessions, where we get stuck on one thing and can't get off." On the other hand, many discussions have been of great value to the family: "We talk about how to handle kids, we see we all have the same problems, and it helps lessen parents' tensions."

Other parents also have had good experiences with the voluntary organizations, but their criticism is lack of availability. This seems to be the consensus among staff that were interviewed. What the voluntary organizations do is good and worthwhile, but their availability is inconsistent. They would like the organizations to be more active.

One of the senior administrators, who had been in the Madison system for a long time, told how in the early days, "when people were first learning to implement the laws, there seemed to be a number of people within parent coalitions who took the time to understand [their] rights. . . . During this early period there may have been adversarial relationships that developed, mainly due to people not having good information and knowledge (parents and also school staff)." But, it was his opinion that, as the system matured and trust developed, these organizations declined, primarily because it became increasingly more difficult to keep parents involved. "Parents are not involved, especially in a political way. . . . The staff has difficulty getting the message across that they must have a partnership with the parents and that they cannot allow the parents to just passively participate." A staff person from the Wisconsin Association for Retarded Children was of the opinion that parent training sessions were not offered with any regularity not only because of limited resources but also for lack of demand on the part of parents. However, she thought the lack of demand was not based on parental satisfaction. Rather, it was guilt and denial (relief in having the school bus take away the problem every day), the avoidance of stigma or embarrassment, or just not wanting to request anything or cause any trouble.

Administrators and teachers stress the multiple functions of organizations. They think of organizations as much broader than advocacy or special interest groups. While these groups are important, the school people seek the information, support, and communicative uses of more socially and recreationally oriented organizations. One teacher, for example, told how she encouraged parents to get involved in the Special Olympics, the school social club for handicapped students, school-sponsored field trips, and parent support groups that meet at school. These activities provide a supportive network for parents, in addition to speakers, workshops, and other organized informational activities. The school encourages participation through newsletters and individual teacher efforts. Nevertheless, despite the efforts, one teacher complained that "there are probably never more than ten to fifteen parents who come, even though we have close to 70 EMR and TMR kids here."

The parent advocates' experiences are also mixed. While neither the school district nor the State Department of Instruction has any responsibility for parent advocates, they nevertheless make considerable efforts to inform parents of their availability and to lower barriers to their use. Why does the School District make these efforts? According to one experienced parent advocate, past experience has shown that "if a disinterested third person is there, reason will prevail." Parent advocates often have handicapped children themselves and have had experience with the process. Their presence and experience relieves the parents of trying to accomplish the sometimes impossible task of containing their emotions and examining the child's interests rationally. The parent advocate can usually ask better questions because of greater knowledge about the process and the professional bases for the decisions. They are familiar with the jargon and can serve as an interpreter for both sides throughout the process. According to a school psychologist (very much in favor of the parent advocate system), the advocate does not have to worry whether the question is polite. They can cross the "etiquette" barrier. As one advocate said, "I tell parents which cage to rattle." The parent advocate can help the parent better understand what is reasonably possible in light of the evaluation and the available resources. "I help them determine realistic educational and social goals for their kid; I help them rank-order their goals and priorities. I tell them what's possible in the system, and how to relate to it." The same advocate went on to describe sometimes telling parents how to dress and "look more professional at the meetings" (e.g., carry manila folders with all the reports to the conferences).

When the parent advocate succeeds in communicating the school's position to the parent and vice versa, the special education staff feels that it has a far better chance of obtaining genuine consent to the plan. The advocates give the parents reassurance and help the parents realize that they should play a significant role in the M-team process. Sometimes the parents need one more person to consider the evaluation before they will say yes.

The view of the role of the parent advocate by both the advocates and the officials and staff is one of *communicative conflict*. It is conflict since both the advocates and the school people expect the advocate to be aggressive as well as interpretive. The purpose, though, is not primarily to assert and press rights—although this possibility is certainly not excluded. Rather, the idea is that through conflict (at least at this level), better communication and understanding will occur. It must be kept in mind that the advocate performs these functions within a context where conflict is already sharply reduced—where the school wants a continuing, substantive relationship with the parents and where all decisions are supposed to be individualized, flexible, and experimental.

There are at least two problems with the parent advocates. One, understandably, is the lack of clarity of role. What is the position of the parent advocate if it is felt that the parents are being unreasonable? And who determines what is reasonable? Some parent advocates view their job as aiding communication between the parties, and will not argue for a parental position that they think unreasonable. While this ambiguity is not uncommon in the other helping professions, it is somehow disquieting. We lack a conceptual and evaluative framework with which to judge client/professional relationships once we decide on shared decision making.

The other problem with the parent advocates is in their utilization. Since this is not a systematic study of the Madison School system process, there is no way of telling how often parent advocates are used and how effective they are. Very few of the line staff that were interviewed had any direct experience with parent advocates; many had never even remembered the presence of a parent advocate at an M-team meeting. It is clear that the advocates are used. They are certainly known throughout the system, and the parent advocates that were interviewed certainly had cases. Even if a lot more information was available, it still would be difficult to make a judgment as to whether parents were getting enough help or needed more. But the lack of direct experience reported by the teachers does raise the question of utilization.

The issue of utilization is difficult to analyze and assess not only because of the amorphous nature of the parent–school relationship in the cooperative context but also because of the role of other actors. In the classic adversarial relationship—the standard criminal or civil trial—it is easier to conceptualize the role of the advocate—although even here there is sharp debate (Simon 1978)—and one can develop evaluative criteria as to whether a person was adequately represented. It is far more difficult to do this in a cooperative setting, where both sides are interested in communicating information and in trying to reach an understanding. Understanding, trust, and satisfaction are elusive concepts. This issue is taken up more fully in Chapter 9, which deals with informed consent, but anyone familiar with informed consent in medicine knows the conceptual and evaluative difficulties in a dependency relationship.

The other problem is that roles like that of parent advocate are performed by other actors in the system, especially if one views the parent advocate more as a communicative or interpreter advocate than an adversarial advocate. For example, an important part of the duties of the program support teacher is to act as an interpreter between the parent and the teacher. Program support teachers will work on either side—with the teacher or the parent (or both)—to get the communication process going. To the extent that the program support teachers are successful, they are performing the parent advocate role or at least something close to it.

An outside parent advocate may not be necessary. One teacher said that rather than placing emphasis on outside parent advocates, the district should do everything possible to make the process "accessible and inviting to the parents—by reducing the number of forms, giving them information on the system and the law, and just keeping them informed about where they stand. It is also very important not to pressure [the parents]—let them take home the papers to read and discuss before they sign them. We have to simplify the language. . . . If we do these kinds of things, the need for advocates will be almost nil."

One cannot argue that the system "fails" because a parent advocate is not involved in the process. We do not demand this criterion in evaluating other kinds of negotiations. Businessmen can talk to each other without lawyers. Teachers and parents can communicate successfully without advocates or program support teachers. However, we are here concerned with a dependency relationship, where there is a difference in the amount of information, power, and resources on each side. But how then, does one assess the situation where the program support teacher or the special education teacher communicates with the parent, and the parents are satisfied that they have been listened to? Given the lack of conceptualization and evaluative criteria in the area of informed consent, this may be all that can be asked. But the fact that the teachers and the other staff complain about the lack of parental participation and, at least from their perspective, the lack of direct experience with voluntary organizations and parent advocates, is troubling. The paradox is that the apparent success of the Madison School District in bringing parents into the process, in making efforts to listen to them in a partnership relationship, in developing trust, may lead to the very thing that the district is struggling against—paternalistic decisions and uninvolved parents.

Outside Professionals

The District's views on outside professionals follow from their views on parent advocates. If parents feel the need for such assistance, the school will cooperate in helping the parents find the professionals, supplying them with the child's records, scheduling meetings, and the like. One program support teacher said that the outside experts become a part of the M-team and are given as much deference as other team members. The school does not feel challenged or threatened by independent consultation. A special education teacher described an experience with an outside professional as follows: "One parent who had a kid in the EMR program got a psychologist to check our accuracy in the tests and assessment, and he agreed with us. We would encourage uncertain parents to do that. We have faith in our staff's judgment, and sometimes, who knows, maybe outside feedback could help." A senior official said that in situations where outside opinions have been sought they have generally either been consistent with the staff position or would recommend even "a step beyond."

Additional Organizational Considerations

The Madison School District justifies its use of parent advocates, voluntary organizations, and outside consultants in terms of specific substantive organizational goals—to better educate the handicapped child. There are, however, other organizational benefits to the school system. In various ways, they may serve mediating roles with other organizations that are useful to the school district and, in particular, to the State Department of Instruction. The state supports and cooperates with voluntary organizations. The state funds training sessions; they work with parent advocates. This support or connection lends legitimacy and interconnections with the school districts. The state may be represented by separate governmental units, and there may be conflicts between the governmental units, but they speak the same language. There is a shared experience, a community of interests.

This should result in an increased understanding and trust. Parent advocates are described as a mediating influence. Formally, parent advocates are not a disinterested third party; they consider themselves to be representatives of the parents and/or the child, but the school district thinks what they do is beneficial to the school district's interest in communication.

The Absence of Formal Appeals

The Madison School District appears to work hard at getting parents to agree with the program for their particular child. As one indication of their success, there have been very few formal appeals—three since 1973. Could it be, then, that the purpose behind this elaborate effort is to avoid the costly administrative appeal?

In the Madison data, there are no figures on the costs of appeals, but in other districts in other states the figures average around $900 per appeal, which is about the cost of the education of one child per year. This is not a trivial sum. On the other hand, it is likely that if the school district determined it could reduce the cost of the due process hearings, it could increase its efforts to make the prehearing filters finer by discouraging more claims through the various devices that are already in practice—withholding information, increasing barriers of professionalism and expertise, increasing threats of retaliation, obtaining consent forms in advance, delaying parents who want services, and informal and ad hoc placements for troublesome students. In many jurisdictions, these filters are effective, and there is no reason why Madison could not employ them.

Another tactic is to treat the hearings themselves more rigorously, more adversarially. The school district also has little to fear from hearings as long as it takes the hearings seriously. In Chapter 3, the research on the Pennsylvania hearings concluded that parents win when they are well-prepared *and* when the school district is not. The Madison School District could impose its will by preparing well for the hearings. The District has highly professional, skilled services. They know or could very easily learn how to present a reasonable case, and their lawyers would become skilled quickly. And in time, as fewer parents won appeals, there would be fewer appeals. In special education, as in welfare, even under benign or relatively neutral circumstances, clients take relatively few appeals. When an agency takes the opposite tack, appeal rates will soon decline.

There are other, more important costs to the due process hearing that the Madison School District seeks to avoid—the traumatic costs to the parents and the school as a result of a formalized confrontation. There was evidence from other studies that hearings in special education did have this effect; in one study, for example, 45 percent of the parents said they would never go through a hearing again. This is a substantive concern, something that reflects on the quality of the outcome of the entire endeavor. Even if the hearing process did not cost the Madison School District any money, the District would still oppose the formal system because of what it considers to be the negative attitudes and feelings generated by the formalized confrontation as compared to the informal participation conference model.

The Madison system is also less vulnerable to outside criticism. The value of this argument depends, of course, on one's perspective. Bureaucrats do not like to rock the boat. Whether this is good or not depends on whether the system is viewed as primarily coopting parents successfully or as genuinely meeting their interests. From the perspective of the bureaucracy, this an additional incentive to develop an informal, participatory system.

Problems in Maintaining the Cooperative System: Constraints and Conditions

Disincentives to Participate: Parents

The school wants continual parental participation. Parents, though, have other demands on their time. Consequently, it is not surprising that teachers complain that parent interest fluctuates and often falls short of what the school district considers ideal. According to one program support teacher, parents tend to be involved most in three situations. The first, naturally, is when the initial finding comes in on a handicapping condition, especially if that finding is any kind of mental retardation. This is often hard for parents to accept, and most questioning occurs at this stage and continues through the development of the IEP. If the parent is satisfied and develops trust in the system, interest and participation wanes unless or until another change or crisis occurs. The other two periods when interest rises are when the family is moving or the child is approaching age twenty-one.

In part, the lack of parental participation is produced by what the parents see as the high quality of the Madison system and its accessibility. One experienced teacher described the reasons for low participation as follows. She thought the most important reason was that most parents viewed the M-team members as highly trained professionals, who know their job and do it well. "Parents have great faith in the M-team evaluation and placement process, and tell us, 'you're the professionals, so you must know what you're doing.' " She continued, "Since parents know they can have input at any time they really want it, it reassures them, so they do not feel that every decision or step is final. This helps them relax and feel more at ease with it; if something comes up they don't like, they know it can be changed."

Another important factor is the holistic or integrated approach of the Madison system. Since the IEPs are designed to accommodate both the child's strengths and weaknesses, "we mainstream them in their strong areas whenever possible because parents want their child's education to include traditional subject areas if at all possible, but we also provide the special or adaptive classes where appropriate."

It is possible that the very success of the system breeds complacency. One might argue that this is not necessarily a criticism; after all, if things are working well, why should there be complaints? But that, of course, is not what the Madison system of cooperative decision making is about. It is supposed to be shared decision making, not decision making by the professionals and acquiescence by the parents. The satisfaction-complacency issue does raise important problems of incentives, informed consent, paternalism, and professional domination.

Other reasons for lack of parental participation are not based on the apparent success of the system. The distribution question is still a factor. Parents with higher incomes and educational levels ask more questions, have longer and more frequent conferences, and tend to be more involved throughout the child's educational experience. Parents who are poorly educated, have had a poor school experience themselves or with another child, tend to be intimidated or resentful. These parents will be passive to the extent that they blame themselves for their child's handicap or refuse to accept the evaluation.

There is also the problem of lack of knowledge. Despite the efforts of the District and the staff, some parents simply do not understand what is going on. Quite often these are complex, subtle, difficult problems, especially if one seriously believes (as the Madison system does) that there are no easy answers in special education.

Parental participation faces a number of disincentives—lack of knowledge, intimidation, among others. The Director of the Wisconsin Coalition for Advocacy put it colorfully: "the parents are blown away by the coherence of the system." By this he meant that the parents confront a highly professional, concerned staff. They are shown and asked to read a thick file of professional opinions, evaluations, and test results, and what looks like a thoroughly considered, worked-out program for their child, including yearly goals. Again, this is in part due to the success of the system. Over the years, the District has been successful in recruiting an able, dedicated staff with a common training, language, and value system. The Madison program is recognized nationally and internationally. These attitudes pervade their entire structure and, in the opinion of the teachers, constitute barriers for parental participation.

Disincentives for Voluntary Organizations: Outside Professionals

The success of the Madison School program also tends to create disincentives for vigorous voluntary organizational activity. Everybody in the community comes to believe in the system, and this inevitably lessens the feelings that watchdogs are needed. The general impression among the teachers is that although the voluntary organizations are useful, they are not very active in the community. It is their view that few parents actually contact such organizations and become actively involved in them, at least for any considerable period of time. When particular issues arise, parents will tend to seek out an organization or even form a group, but this subsides when the issue gets resolved.

Similar effects are noted with the use of outside experts. As discussed, the official policy of the school is to encourage the parents to use such resources; past experiences have been good. Yet, one of the interviewees estimated that only about one out of fifteen parents contact an outside specialist. Again, it is hard to know whether this is too high or too low or about right without an analysis of the adequacy of the school evaluations, but this teacher felt that the staff attitudes may erect barriers here as well. The staff feels that they know the child best; although they formally welcome outside opinions, they might not really take them seriously enough, and these attitudes might well be conveyed to uncertain parents.

Organizational Disincentives: Teachers

In addition to the above, there are the "normal" bureaucratic disincentives to parental participation. There are constant pressures in any large-scale organization, and a school system is no exception (Clune and Van Pelt 1984). The ideology of the Madison special education program calls for high-quality, patient explorations between parents and professionals. Time and again, both parents and staff emphasized that the heart of the system was the teacher. There could be top-level support, written manuals and guidelines, and a variety of other organizational structures, but in the end, the results depended on the attitudes, commitment, and behavior of the individual teachers.

But just as parents have limited time, so do the teachers. The teachers, not unexpectedly, complain about the paperwork—the seemingly endless forms that are "never read, just filed away." There are also complaints about the legal requirements. "At in-service," said one teacher, "we focus too much on the letter of the law, and how we have to complete the proper forms, and not on the spirit of the law. When you focus on just the legal aspects, all it becomes is an exercise for DPI [State Department of Instruction]."

The staff, inevitably, will cut corners in the face of conflicting pressures. The school district is aware of the problem and tries to make things easier for the teachers. With several people on the M-teams, more time can be spent with dissatisfied or questioning parents. Small class size, aides, and student teachers free up teacher time to meet with parents. The district had made efforts to reduce the paperwork and has stopped sending lengthy questionnaires to parents—"they were helpful for needs evaluation and the M-team, but we realize that we just don't have time to do everything." Despite these efforts, the pressure remains. IEPs are not changed as often as they should be;

the teachers will use informal methods to avoid the paperwork. Finally, the teachers will tend to respond to those parents who demand their attention, who choose to participate, and less time to stimulating participation by passive parents. This tendency, in turn, raises further barriers to parental participation. They know that the teachers are busy and they hesitate to make demands.

Program Resources

In addition to staff resources, there is also the issue of program resources. There is little doubt about the importance of resources to the success of the Madison system. After the M-team determines that a student has a learning disability, the placement can be among a half dozen LD classes where learning proceeds at different rates and where there are different styles of teaching, sensitivity, and talents. A district has to be large enough and have enough resources to offer this kind of individual service. The range of alternatives reduces conflict with the parents. Not only might they be more satisfied with the initial recommendation but, in addition, the initial decision is less of an either/or alternative. Since there is a range of alternatives, it is easier to review decisions so that parents feel the placement is an ongoing process. Even if parents have misgivings about the initial decision, or any other particular decision, they do not feel locked into a situation and can demand a reevaluation at any time.

The problem, though, is that not all programs can offer this kind of flexibility. There are constraints on staff resources, class size, and the availability of aides and substitutes. The Madison program has always been generous, but its resources are limited. There have been controversies in the past about the unavailability of special services for particular students. Moreover, these controversies are likely to increase in the face of tight budgets.

It is difficult to evaluate the effect of levels of resources. In other jurisdictions, we saw that many of the appeals involved disputes over expensive private placements that parents wanted but the school districts rejected. Is one of the conditions, then, of an informal participation system a high level of resources? It would certainly help to have adequate resources, but what are adequate resources? There is no obvious line between adequacy and inadequacy. What might seem to be minimal resources in a surburban district might appear to be plentiful in a rural or inner-city district. Until ten years ago, special education resources were minimal all over. The adequacy of the resources argument speaks to the *expectations* of the parents. If the parents expect more, they will challenge the system and the informal participation system will break down. But this argument will apply whether there are slender or plentiful resources, since there will never be enough for all situations. It might be argued that at least with a plentiful supply, the parents will get something and therefore will be more reasonable and more amenable to compromise. But there is no reason why the same argument would not apply with less resources. One would expect severe pressure on the informal system if there were *declining* resources. But at this stage of research, it is still largely unknown what effect the availability of resources has on the likelihood of success of an informal, participatory scheme.

In a sense, the availability-of-resources argument misses an important point. There are many school districts that have resources but still have an inadequate system of conflict resolution. While we must consider the availability of resources as a possible important condition, it is also important to consider what kind of dispute resolution system to structure when resources are available.

Community Consensus

Another argument is that an informal participation system can function only when there is an underlying consensus, a relatively homogeneous community, rather than a community with a history of sharp conflict (for example, race relations), large bureaucracies, massive school districts, and heterogeneity. This is a serious argument. It would seem that there has to be a certain level of trust and good faith before one would start dealing. There certainly seems to be a lot of trust in the Madison system. On the other hand, the Madison cooperative system is not used in contiguous communities. It may be that community consensus is a necessary but not a sufficient condition.

The community consensus argument is hard to deal with empirically and theoretically. In a large, urban area, with a great deal of heterogeneity and conflict, it may be that parents and the schools are at loggerheads over some issues, but that different sets of actors (on both sides) can work informally on other issues. It may be that those parents who are in the forefront of the major conflicts can still deal with officials who are not involved in the hot controversies. We noted that one of the assumptions of P.L. 94–142 was that minorities felt that they were suffering discrimination in the classification of their children, but the evidence did not bear this out. The more likely case is that minority parents are passive, alienated, or frightened by the bureaucracy. It may be that the level and intensity of negative attitudes are not such as to preclude the development of an informal system.

Conclusions: Cooperative Decision Making and the Constraints of Ideology

The Idea of the Madison System

The cooperative decision-making system developed in the Madison school system challenges the traditional liberal approach to politics, that the citizen is an atomistic individual in an adversarial relationship with the state. The Madison system recognizes that in the modern welfare state, there are also large areas where the citizen and the state have to cooperate, where the citizen and the state are in a continuous relationship.

The Madison system also challenges the idea of a general, uniform procedure designed to cover all manner of situations. In its essential details, the P.L. 94–124 due process requirements, as supplemented by state codes, are very similar to due process requirements in many other administrative systems as well as in civil court procedure. This abstract, uniform approach makes sense in that we believe that there are certain enduring transcendent values in liberalism, that there are matters of basic fairness and autonomy, and that procedural due process is designed to protect those values. On the other hand, as a mechanism for *conflict resolution*, the general, abstract approach makes no sense. We are, in effect, trying to apply a single method of conflict resolution to very different substantive issues.

The argument of this book is that the liberal legal, adversary approach is inappropriate for a continuing, discretionary relationship. Procedure has to do with two things. It has to preserve basic values of freedom and autonomy, but it also has to resolve conflicts. In other words, it has to be substantively grounded. When it fails to do this, it fails altogether, as we have seen.

The interesting thing about the Madison system is that it has addressed both of these problems. It has devised a procedural system that recognizes the discretionary relationship between the citizen and the state *and* it has done this by starting with the substantive problem first, and then constructing the procedural system to make the substantive relationship work. In constructing the cooperative decision-making system, Madison asked: What does it take to improve the life chances of a handicapped child, and what is the role of the school system? It was out of these substantive concerns that a procedural system arose. The Madison procedural system is contextual. It is primarily designed to adjust and enhance substantive relationships. It also happens to preserve basic liberal values of individualism. Autonomy and informed consent are a necessary part of Madison's concept of the substantive relationship.

Dynamic Models

At this point in the research, I think that we have seen the possibilities of a different system, a cooperative system that addresses the problems of the individual and the state in the modern social welfare context. We have a coherent ideology and a variety of sources of information that indicate that the Madison system might very well be working in a reasonably satisfactory way; at the very least, the interview data show that what Madison is trying to do is not utopian. It is a real-life example of people struggling to implement a new and important ideology.

What the data do show, however, are certain problems or weaknesses that are inevitable or inherent in this system. The Madison system has to be renewed constantly. A number of people in the system recognize this problem. The success of the program carries with it the seeds of its own destruction. Trust breeds complacency. The Madison system reinforces parental passiveness. All organizations tend to become routinized, to develop accustomed ways of doing things. The Madison school system is, of course, subject to these tendencies, too. There may be an additional element here, though, by virtue of the great success of the program. The present director of the Madison Coalition for Advocacy thinks that the system has a lot to be proud of (especially in comparison to other systems he confronts), but it also tends to be self-satisfied, to believe too much in the praise that is constantly bestowed upon it.

The belief in the fulfillment of the ideology, then, not only carries the danger of solidifying bureaucratic procedures but also of developing a community-wide form of cooptation, which diminishes the incentives to question, challenge, and support vigorous voluntary organizations. What are new parents to think if the other parents in the social support group tell them how wonderful the special education people are? If they have worries, isn't something the matter with them? And suppose they turn to people in the community. These people have been hearing about the great successes of the Madison special education system, and how much they care about the parents. Isn't something wrong with these parents?

How much of this presently exists in Madison is unknown. What has to be realized is that procedural models must be dynamic. Underlying substantive relationships are changing constantly; what works today will not necessarily work tomorrow. Just as the Madison special education people constantly search for improved techniques for helping handicapped children in school, they must also continue to search for new techniques to maintain and stimulate communicative conflict. This means figuring out new methods of communicating with parents and providing incentives for participation, stimulating the growth and vigor of voluntary organizations, and encouraging a wide variety of informational programs, such as training sessions, workshops, and so forth.

REFERENCES

Bickel, William E. "Classifying Mentally Retarded Students: A Review of Placement Practices in Special Education." In Kirby Heller, Wayne H. Holtzman, and Samuel Messick (eds.), *Placing Children in Special Education: A Strategy for Equity.* Washington D.C.: National Academy Press, 1982.

Brown, Lou; Branston, Mary Beth; Hamre-Nietupski, Susan; Pumpian, Ian; Certo, Nick; and Gruenewald, Lee. "A Strategy for Developing Chronological Age Appropriate and Functional Curricular Content for Severely Handicapped Adolescents and Young Adults." *Journal of Special Education*, 13,1 (1979), pp. 81–90.

Clune, William, and Van Pelt, Mark. "A Political Analysis of 94–142 and the Several Gaps of Gap Analysis." *Law and Contemporary Problems*, December 1984.

Davis, Jacques. "Parental Participation in I.E.P. Process." Unpublished ms., 1983. *The E.E.N. Triangle of Support: A Guide for Parents*, Bulletin #3198, Wisconsin Department of Public Instruction, Herbert J. Grover, State Superintendent of Public Instruction.

Finn, Jeremy D. "Patterns in Special Education Placement as Revealed by the OCR Surveys." In Kirby Heller et al. (eds.), *Placing Children in Special Education: A Strategy for Equity*. Washington, D.C.: National Academy Press, 1982.

Handler, Joel F. "Justice for the Welfare Recipient: Fair Hearings in A.F.D.C., The Wisconsin Experience." *Social Service Review*, 43 (1969), pp. 12–34.

Heller, Kirby A. "Effects of Special Education on Mentally Retarded Children." In Kirby A. Heller et al., *Placing Children in Special Education: A Strategy for Equity*. Washington, D.C.: National Academy, 1982.

Heller, Kirby A., Holtzman, Wayne H., and Samuel Messick (eds.). *Placing Children in Special Education: A Strategy for Equity*. Washington D.C.: National Academy, 1982.

Magnetti, Suzanne S. "Some Potential Incentives of Special Education Funding Practices." In Kirby A. Heller et al. (eds.), *Placing Children in Special Education: A Strategy for Equity*. Washington, D.C.: National Academy Press, 1982.

M-Team Parent Handbook, Madison (Wisc.) Metropolitan School District, Instructional Services Division/Special Education Services, Council on Exceptional Education, October 1979.

The Multidisciplinary Team Process, Madison Metropolitan School, Donald A. Haferman, Superintendent, Instructional Services Division/Special Education Services, September 1981.

Shonkoff, Jack P. "Biological and Social Factors Contributing to Mild Mental Retardation." In Kirby A. Heller et al. (eds.), *Placing Children in Special Education: A Strategy for Equity*. Washington, D.C.: National Academy Press, 1982.

Simon, William H. "The Ideology of Advocacy: Procedural Justice and Professional Ethics." *Wisconsin Law Review* (1978), pp. 29–144.

Streit, Ken. "Now That There's Movement, Do We Know the Long Term Direction?" Wisconsin Coalition for Advocacy Pamphlet, 1981.

Taylor, Steven J. "Madison Metropolitan Public Schools: A Model Integrated Program for Children with Severe Disabilities." Pamphlet in "Human Policy Reports: An ACTION Series." Syracuse University, Special Education Resource Center, March 1982.

Travers, Jeffrey R. "Testing in Educational Placement: Issues and Evidence." In Kirby A. Heller et al. (eds.), *Placing Children in Special Education: A Strategy for Equity*. Washington, D.C.: National Academy Press, 1982.

· 5 ·

Adversarial Advocacy:
Reform or Reconstruction?

It was suggested in previous chapters that the failure of adversarial advocacy is not only a problem of lack of personnel and other resources (which will always be a serious problem) but that adversarial advocacy procedures are flawed conceptually. In this chapter I explore this latter issue more fully and address the next question: Should adversarial advocacy be reformed (is it capable of reformation?) or should different methods be used to achieve due process values in the discretionary continuous relation? Can various combinations of adversarial and nonadversarial procedures be used?

Due Process Values

We are commonly told that "due process of law is the primary and indispensable foundation of individual freedom. It is the basic and essential term of the social compact which defines the rights of the individual and delimits the powers which the state may exercise" (*In re Gault*, 1967, p. 20). Why is this so? What is the "social compact" that charts the boundaries between individualism and state power? The answer lies in the philosophical origins of the liberal state. The problem of the liberal state is to achieve order and peace under a regime of individualism. Liberal theorists would constrain the sovereign by neutral principles of law; the sovereign can only act on individuals through due process of law. This is liberal legalism—the application of neutral law to the sovereign. Since due process guarantees the application of neutral principles of law to the sovereign, it is indispensable to the liberal state. Two ideas are inseparable in the liberal state: individualism and the rule of law (Wood 1969, pp. 18–28).

Despite the fact that liberalism has always been questioned in terms of its coherence and consistency, it remains a powerful ideological force and an energizing source of current policy. Indeed, the legal rights revolution, the most significant change in our legal culture in the last several decades and the basis for much of our substantive and procedural law, flows from liberal legal ideology.

The argument that I am making is that in the course of this cultural change (if not throughout our legal history), there has been a false identification with fundamental notions of liberalism and procedural due process in its adversarial advocacy form. Historically, the core notion of due process (liberal legalism) is the judicial trial (Mashaw 1981a, p. 91; Frankfurter, concurring in *Joint Anti-Fascist Refugee Committee* v. *McGrath*). The liberal state is equated with adversarial advocacy. The latter, and only the latter, is the guarantor of the former. For example, directly after the above quote from the *Gault* decision, Justice Fortas goes on: "As Mr. Justice Frankfurter has said: 'The history of American freedom is, in no small measure, the history of procedure.'" And what procedure does Justice Fortas have in mind? Adversarial advocacy. "[T]he procedural rules which have been fashioned from the generality of due process are our best instruments for the distillation and evaluation of essential facts from the conflicting welter of data that life and our adversary methods present. It is these instruments of due process which enhance the possibility that truth will emerge from the confrontation of opposing versions and conflicting data. Procedure is to law what 'scientific method' is to science" (p. 21).

This quotation is the norm—fully equating adversarial procedures with liberalism. What I have been trying to do is to separate the two, to raise the question whether adversarial procedures do in fact fulfill liberal values in discretionary decisions in the modern welfare state or whether other procedures are more suited.

The fundamental bedrock of individualism is that each person is to be considered a moral and political being; in terms of Kant's categorical imperative, each person is to be treated as an end, never a means. Other commentators have amplified this concept in terms of autonomy, dignity, and responsibility.

But the autonomy principle is not absolute. People do not function as isolated units. They are social beings. And social interaction raises competing values. How does the person function as an end in a social interaction? How does a person, interacting, avoid becoming a means? Can all persons in a social situation function as ends at the same time?

It is the competing values arising out of social interaction that have caused such great difficulties in liberal legalism. The standard procedures of the civil trial—notice, the right to counsel, the right to introduce evidence and to cross-examination, to have a decision based on the record by a disinterested decision maker—ideally reflect the values of autonomy, dignity, and responsibility. These procedures are designed to ensure that people know what decisions the government is planning to make; they also have the opportunity to present their side of the story and question the government's. The requirement of a decision based on the record, with reasons, by a disinterested decision maker is a guarantee that people are listened to and know how to act accordingly in the future (Mashaw 1981a). The ideal civil trial affords autonomy, dignity, and responsibility.

Nonetheless, adversarial advocacy falls far short of the mark. It may come as a surprise to people not schooled in constitutional law to learn that the Supreme Court no longer conceives of due process in terms of the core values of liberal legalism. This is curious in light of the litany that the Court always recites, as in the *Gault* decision, about the fundamental relationship between due process and the social compact, but in the course of its decisions, the Court has in fact decided procedural questions in terms of an instrumental, positive approach. It has focused on the societal aspects of individualism and, in so doing, has lost sight of the individual. Instead of asking: Do the procedures fulfill the core values of individualism? the Court has instead taken two approaches. Mindful of the competing interests of the government in efficiency, the Court has balanced procedural demands of the claimant in terms of the goals of accurate fact-finding as compared with efficiency. Hearings, for example, would be denied if on balance the Court thinks that in that particular administrative program, hearings would not make a significant contribution to the accuracy of results. Under the positive approach, the Court has reasoned that due process only protects entitlements guaranteed by the positive law (statutes, common law, et cetera); moreover, the positive law that creates these entitlements can limit the procedures for deciding whether the rights have been abridged. The most prominent case illustrating this approach, the *Roth* case, involved a teacher whose one-year contract, without a reason, was not renewed. The Court held that since the positive law only guaranteed the one year, Roth was not entitled to *any* procedure to examine whether the contract should be renewed (Mashaw 1981a).

The instrumental, positive, balancing approach of the *Roth* case has been followed by a great many Supreme Court cases and has provoked a scholarly literature arguing for the adoption of dignitary values as a matter of constitutional law. The great value of the dignitary approach is that it returns the debate to the core notions of individualism; this is what the Constitution is about, argue the dignitary theorists, not cost/benefit analysis, instrumentalism, positivism, or rule utilitarianism. The problem with the dignitary approach, as we shall see, is the failure to deal with the conflicts between the individual and society, the basic flaw of liberalism. Either the proponents of a dignitary theory fail to address the issue of competing values and thus are merely assertive, or when they fully address the issue, the procedures to implement dignitary values become minimal indeed. Nevertheless, out of the struggle to establish the constitutional position of dignitary values, the more thoughtful proponents adumbrate an approach that will prove fruitful.

Another Try at Liberalism: The Dignitary Theorists

The basic distinction between a dignitary approach and an instrumental approach centers on the role of process. Tribe (1978) describes the difference as follows: the instrumental approach treats due process as implementing the rule of law rather than expressing it; due process is the means for making sure that facts are accurately found and that rules are consistently applied. What procedures are due, under the instrumental approach, depends on the extent to which those procedures promote the minimization of "the risk of error in the specification and enforcement" of substantive interests. Under the dignitary, or what Tribe calls, the "intrinsic" aspect of due process, the purpose of the process is to give individuals or groups

> an opportunity to express their dignity as persons. . . . [S]uch a hearing represents a valued human interaction in which the affected person experiences at least the satisfaction of participating in the decision that vitally concerns her, and perhaps the separate satisfaction of receiving an explanation of why the decision is being made in a certain way. Both the right to be heard from, and the right to be told why, are analytically distinct from the right to secure a different outcome; these rights to interchange express the elementary idea that to be a *person* rather than a *thing*, is at least to be *consulted* about what is done with one [Tribe 1978, p. 502].

Tribe considers the intrinsic aspects of process as "the very essence of justice." But Tribe is not any more specific about what he means by dignitary values or what procedures would enhance them.

The most thoughtful work so far dealing with dignitary values is by Mashaw (1981a). Mashaw claims that there is an intuitive sense that process matters, that "we *do* distinguish between losing and being treated unfairly. And however fuzzy our articulation of the process characteristics that yield a sense of unfairness, it is commonplace for us to describe process affronts as somehow related to disrespect for our individuality, to our not being taken seriously as persons" (p. 888). He gives the example of voting. Substantively, our personal exclusion can make no difference in the outcome. Yet, somehow it would be "an affront to our self-image as citizens . . . a sense of unfairness from exclusion." This intuitive feeling is the "unifying thread" among the dignitary theorists; a perception that the "effects of process on participants, not just the rationality of substantive results, must be considered in judging the legitimacy of public decision-making" (p. 886).

According to Mashaw, the search for dignity values is fueled by the desire to avoid the Supreme Court position that the liberty or property interests which the due process clause protects are only those interests created by the positive law and that the validity of a particular procedure depends upon its contribution to accurate fact-finding and law application. Mashaw argues that this positive and instrumental view fails to protect the person in the administrative state where government is increasingly relying on general rules (in our terms, discretionary decisions). In this situation, procedural rights are either denied under the positive law or, under the instrumental cost/benefit balancing approach, the interests of the individual too often give way to the competing demands of majoritarian and/or bureaucratic interests. A procedure that is positivist, instrumental, and utilitarian or interest-balancing in its application "wrenches the due process clause from its constitutional context" (p. 898).

This lack of protection has led to the search for an alternative perspective—the dignitary approach. The Bill of Rights is concerned preeminently with the liberal ideal of protection of individual freedom from majoritarian demands. "A dignitary perspective thus holds out the prospect of returning procedural due process to the family of individualistic concerns that are represented by constitutional values such as privacy, free expression and religious freedom. . . . It would . . . reconcile procedural due process analysis with the spirit of the Constitution" (p. 898).

Having said this, which is no more than other proponents have said, Mashaw then goes on to examine more closely what dignitary values are and whether they can be translated into administrative procedural due process practices. The list of values that Mashaw comes up with are *equality;* the cluster of *predictability, transparency,* and *rationality; participation;* and *privacy.* While these values have great intuitive appeal, on close analysis Mashaw concludes that they are vague, too broad, and too thin to provide much procedural protection in the administrative state. Equality, for example, protects the right to vote, but in other forms of decision making it can be satisfied minimally (for example, the right to file a statement) with only modest amounts of self-respect. Dignity and self-respect require meaningful participation in dealings with government. Participation is necessary not only to protect existing rights but also to participate in the development of the *content* of the rights. But does this value extend to all decisions? Does everything have to be decided through popular referenda or adversarial adjudication or negotiation? Privacy—to be let alone, to be respected as an autonomous human being—conflicts with other dignitary values. Rationality, participation, equality imply a sharing of information, self-revelation, communication, collective decision making; privacy concerns may lead to the withholding of this kind of interaction.

The vagueness, thinness, and contradition are not helped by the search for a more rigorous theoretical defense. In Lockean political theory, there is the basic contradiction between individual ownership of property and majoritarianism. Mill's formulation of the inviolability of individual activity that does not harm others emphasizes the dignitary value of privacy, but the line between individual and social action is so indeterminate that the right becomes fragile and is often no more than an interest to be balanced against other interests. Rule utilitarians take a stronger position: certain individual rights or protections are so important that they are rules rather than interests in a social welfare calculation. A favorite example is prohibition of slavery. Another could be wholly arbitrary procedures. But, Mashaw argues, once one moves beyond these few dramatic cases to the more mundane types of procedural issues that one faces in everday life, matters become more uncertain. Bureaucratic interests do not translate into a reign of terror, and one is quickly back into a social welfare calculation which yields no *a priori* support for any particular process value.

The third strand of liberalism, that of Kant and Rawls, is more promising because of its basic moral command that each person be considered an end, never merely a means. The problem, as Mashaw sees it, lies in the conflict between two individuals—if one is to use procedures to fully ensure her ends, then does not the other become a means to that end? Is she also not entitled to privacy and self-respect? Mashaw finds no strong belief in Rawls for process values beyond those necessary for political liberty and the rule of law. And here, the only firm principle, according to Mashaw, is the requirement of reason-giving by officials. But this right does not imply an elaborate set of procedures; it is only a right to have decisions made comprehensible so that affected individuals can act accordingly.

The conclusion that Mashaw draws from his analysis of liberal theory is that only three dignitary process claims can be considered fundamental: (1) equality of voting (majority rule); (2) equal application of the rule of law; and (3) comprehensibility. Other dignitary values, while important, have contradictions. Because of the contradictions, these other dignitary values have to be pursued only in a "prudential" fashion—by weighing them against other values.

What would a prudential approach look like? Mashaw argues that the bedrock, nondebatable rights of equality and comprehensibility would not offer much procedural protection because, as a practical matter, they could be satisfied by very minimal procedures in an unsatisfactory manner. With more elaborate procedures one would quickly get into interest balancing. Mashaw uses the *Roth* case as an example. At issue is the rationality of the process, that is, comprehensibility. Roth, as a person, wants a reason, but this could be satisfied with a minimal reason—a staff reduction is called for, or, in the judgment of the dean, Roth was less qualified than others. These are reasons and they are comprehensible, but they also do not do much for Roth's dignitary values. It is obvious that Roth wants more; he wants a dialogue. He wants what dignitary theorists argue is genuine participation in the development of the content of the rule or standard that will apply to his case, and to develop the facts and argument in context. Out of this exchange a decision would be reached. But it is precisely at this point that one has to ask the question, How much more procedure and at what cost and for what benefits? As procedures become more elaborate, the balancing test has to be used because now Roth's dignitary values come into conflict with the values of others.

The conclusion that Mashaw draws from all of this is that liberal theory does not provide a sufficient basis on which to ground process values. Mashaw says that this is not surprising. It is not surprising because of liberalism's emphasis on individualism and its failure to establish a coherent theory of the individual's social existence (Wolff 1968).

At this point, the proponents of a dignitary theory, seeing no way to develop a meaningful, robust theory of procedural rights out of liberal theory, hint at an alternative vision, one that would view people as social beings rather than as individuals. In a communitarian or fraternal perspective, equality and rationality are "reconceived as promoting an ongoing dialogue in a community of equals." Mashaw believes that, at bottom, it is this communitarian ideal that motivates the quest for dignitary values. Under a communitarian theory, people are not viewed as competitive individuals asserting rights in competition with their adversaries (equally valid moral beings), but rather as living in a community, in association with their fellow beings. But how, asks Mashaw, does this work out specifically? What place, if any, is there for individuality and liberty in a communitarian society?

The conceptual weakness of liberal legalism remains. One person's justice is another's oppression. Liberalism has little to say coherently about the principles of social interaction. The claims of competing individuals conflict and have to be balanced. There are demands of efficiency—life must go on, decisions have to be made, trials have to be decided. There are also privacy claims. In the administrative state, the effects of balancing have been acutely felt, and many of the standard liberal legal elements of adversarial advocacy have disappeared. This is not because the substantive claims of the individuals are unimportant. Rather, as compared to the competing demands of the state, they lose out in the prudential cost/benefit calculation. The conceptual position of liberalism fails to provide a sufficient bulwark against other competing interests. This is especially true when relationships are governed by general standards (discretion).

The failure to develop principles of social interaction similarly causes great difficulties with the dignitary theorists. While decrying the positivist, instrumental, balancing approach of the Supreme Court, the dignitary theorists are either vague or remarkably thin when it comes time to specifying their procedural program. The reason for this is the starting premise—viewing the individual in isolation and in competition with the government agency, the liberal position (Mensch 1982). This is both curious and ironic. While decrying the turn that liberal legalism has taken, dignitary theorists still adhere to the liberal legal paradigm. Individualism, for them, is based on natural law rather than utilitarianism, positivism, or instrumentalism, but the individual is still viewed in isolation and in competitive conflict with the state. The task of constitutional law is to protect the individual from government action through adversarial advocacy. The desire to preserve individualism still results in the failure to develop principles of social interaction, a failure that has now become catastrophic in the modern administrative state.

The Rise and Fall of Liberal Legalism

Looking at the changes in our legal culture in the decades following *Brown* v. *Board of Education,* one would not have guessed that there were any doubts about the efficacy of liberalism to guide the relationships between the individual and the state. That period witnessed the triumph of liberal legalism and adversarial advocacy. There was a great flourishing of substantive entitlements. This was the rise of the "new property"; people not only had civil rights but also rights to welfare, employment, education, mental health treatment, and a variety of other services and relationships (Reich 1964). Procedural due process protections attached to these positive rights; adversarial advocacy reached its highwater mark with *Goldberg* v. *Kelly* in 1970. Simultaneously, there was a rapid expansion of lawyers to take up the causes of protecting these rights. The legal rights revolution was not restricted to the downtrodden or the citizen-victims of government bureaucracy but extended as well to consumers and environmentalists. We are still feeling the effects of this widespread change in our culture.

I have already discussed in Chapter 3 how the legal rights approach was reflected in special education, indeed, how through the mechanism of informed consent, core due process values were extended to the initial decisions to refer for evaluation—the start of the process. There was the faith in procedures not only to check bias and discrimination but also to correct mistakes in professional judgments. This emphasis was on rights and procedures as opposed to professionalism, expertise, and judgment.

In practice, adversarial advocacy has not accomplished its goals in special education. The most generous characterization of the results of P.L. 94–142 procedures is that there is contact, but there is no involvement (Bickel 1982). The basic conditions of informed consent—adequate information and voluntariness—are not present. Instead, there is the withholding of information, mystification through the use of jargon and expertise, and professional domination of the proceedings. Are we only witnessing a failure in implementation, or does the matter go deeper? Are we dealing with an issue of reform or more basic reconstruction?

In addressing the question of reform or reconstruction, I will first explore a current debate as to the role of liberal legalism as ideology.

Ultimately, we must make a judgment as to the value of this ideology in pursuing individualism and social order in the modern welfare state. Next, I will consider more deeply the problems of liberal legalism in the social context of bureaucracy and the distribution of wealth and power. In the concluding half of the chapter, I introduce a way of looking at procedure that enhances individualism in cooperative or consensual relationships, the kind of relationship appropriate for continuous discretionary decisions.

The Rule of Law as Ideology

Thompson (1975) makes the following argument: granted the inadequacies of the adversary system, it nevertheless serves to restrain the dominating classes in their repressive tendencies. At least at the limits, the rule of law is applied to the rich and powerful; the excesses are curbed, and legitimacy is maintained. The problem is one of reform. The counterargument is that while legal form may from time to time restrain the powerful from acting in their unbridled interest, for the most part it serves to maintain the legitimacy of a system of domination. Adversarial advocacy actually strengthens the position of the rulers even though to some extent it thwarts the interests of individual members of that class (Lempert 1980–1981; Spitzer 1982). This position would lead to reconstruction.

Thompson, in a concluding section of *Whigs and Hunters: The Origins of the Black Act,* states the case for the autonomous role of the rule of law. In some ways, this defense of the mediating, moderating role of law comes as a surprise. The Black Act, enacted by the British Parliament in 1723, established at the stroke of the pen over fifty capital offenses. Ostensibly aimed at curbing poaching at night, the act covered a wide variety of offenses designed to suppress civil disorders. Thompson argued that there was no emergency, in the sense of widespread disorder or rebellion in the countryside, to account for the enactment and enforcement of this legislation. Rather, it was an effort of the Whig Hanoverian government of Robert Walpole to consolidate his party's power. It was brute class legislation, the assertion of power of the propertied oligarchy against the lower social classes. The act was not only enforced (several were hung; more suffered lesser but severe penalties); it was twisted and expanded by the judges to cover a wide range of disorders (for example, cheering a mob brought the death penalty). The Black Act thus seemed an apt case of the opposite—law that reflects no more or less than the dominant interests in society.

The implication of this view, according to Thompson, is to make law irrelevant. It is irrelevant as a field of inquiry since everything that can be said about the operation and function of law is only a mirror image of the infrastructure; and if that is known, its characteristics will determine the character of the legal system. The study of law is therefore also irrelevant for policy purposes; it is determined by the base, not the reverse.

Thompson rejects this orthodox Marxian reductionism. He questions the validity of separating law from the whole and placing it in some other superstructure. The legal system, in all its aspects, permeates the entire society. There is also the law's own internal system of logic, rules, and procedures. The conflict that Thompson studied was not simply the propertied class asserting its rights against the nonpropertied; rather, it was also a conflict over competing property rights. The lower classes, when they could obtain the means, fought for their rights by means of the law (they occasionally won a case). The rights of farmers and foresters were based on ancient practices and customs, where the line between formal and informal law disappears. This customary law is inseparable from community norms and values. Law, then, is inextricably bound up with the means of production as well as the culture of the plebians. On both counts, it is false to see law as the tool of the ruling class only.

Eighteenth-century English society was saturated with law. Law was the centralizing, legitimizing ideology. The ruling class worked hard to project the image that it too was subject to the rule of law, and that its legitimacy was based on universal principals of equity.

Thompson argues that structural reductionism ignores the two centuries of struggle in England against royal absolutism where law was the central arena of conflict. In these struggles, it was the law that held back royal or aristocratic power; it was the law that tied together the intricate relations of lands and marriages. But it was in the inherent nature of law that it could not be reserved for one social class.

Thompson is careful not to exaggerate. But he does argue that it is misleading and wrong to consider law as the mere extension of class power. The relationship of law to power is complex and contradictory. There is a significant difference, he urges, between "arbitrary extra-legal power" and the rule of law.

> The rhetoric and the rules of a society are something a great deal more than sham. In the same moment they may modify in profound ways the behavior of the powerful, and mystify the powerless. They may disguise the true realities of power, but, at the same time, they may curb that power and check its intrusions. And it is often from within that very rhetoric that a radical critique of the practices of the society is developed: the reformers of the 1790s appeared, first of all, clothed in the rhetoric of Locke and of Blackstone [Thompson 1975, p. 265].

Thompson concludes with an eloquent plea for the rule of law and reform of law. He is fully cognizant of the uses to which law was put by the ruling class and how law, in other contexts, has been used to extend and justify imperialism and oppression. Nevertheless, he argues that the rule of law, by inhibiting the exercise of power and its use by the citizen to defend against the all-intrusive claims of the powerful, is not only a hard-won achievement, reflecting centuries of struggle, but is today an unqualified human good.

> To deny or belittle this good is, in this dangerous century when the resources and pretentions of power continue to enlarge, a desperate error of intellectual abstraction. More than this, it is a self-fulfilling error, which encourages us to give up the struggle against bad laws and class-bound procedures, and to disarm ourselves before power. It is to throw away a whole inheritance of struggle *about* law, and within the forms of law, whose continuity can never be fractured without bringing men and women into immediate danger [Thompson 1975, p. 266].

I use Thompson's methodology to examine due process in the relationship of the citizen to the bureaucracy. Substituting for farmers and foresters are ordinary citizens, most in the lower social and economic classes. Instead of Hanoverian England, we have the modern bureaucratic hierarchical welfare state. But Thompson's story has rich analogies. A system of law, he reminds us, is inherently suspect when the social order is characterized by great disparities of wealth and power. We look with suspicion at the laws governing the relationship between the citizen and the government in the twentieth-century

United States. On the other hand, just as Thompson's plebians and rules were also the inheritors of a century and a half of constitutional struggle, so too are the bureaucrats and clients in this study the inheritors of American constitutional values, and particularly procedural due process. To what extent does this ideology restrain the rulers and serve, at least occasionally, to defend the citizen against the intrusions of public power? Or, has the ideological heritage become a sham, serving to legitimize and mystify the public power in the administrative state?

The latter argument is raised by Lempert (1980–1981). The very appearance of or claims to universality of the legal system, upon which Thompson relies so much, may be the heart of the difficulty. Legal proceedings, argues Lempert, have a *prima facie* neutrality about them. "All are, in theory, governed by similar strictures, eligible for similar punishments, and able to achieve similar rewards. . . . [A] semblance of equality is maintained by the publicity given the sanctions visited on the rich when they run afoul of the law, by the successes of the poor in avoiding the full rigors of the law, and by the fact that those in power face obvious restraints in achieving desired goals" (p. 712). But the formal neutrality or equality of the legal process ignores the distribution of wealth and power, and the empirical results of the legal process resemble anything but a neutral, equal distribution of rewards and punishments. The appearance of equality is what induces people to extend legitimacy to government. Where legitimacy is extended because of the belief in the universality and neutrality of the law, we have legal domination. The advantages to the rulers are that the rules are stable, since allegiance is owed to an evolving system of rules rather than to tradition or individuals; flexible, since the rules can be changed if necessary; and cheap, in that large bodies of people can be governed by a relatively small use of force. In such a system, the state's rules "carry a strong presumption of validity; and even if the validity of the rules is questioned, the legitimacy of punishing violators often is not" (p. 712).

A great deal of Thompson's analysis (1975) applies to the history of the rule of law in special education. Prior to the legal rights revolution, there would be very little to write about. Ever since public school became compulsory, provisions had to be made for children who did not fit, but no one dreamed of challenging school decisions. This was the era of privileges, not rights.

All of this changed during the legal rights revolution. Valuable relationships with government and employers came to be considered rights, with procedural protections. The federal courts initiated a new language and new concepts, but the ideology soon spread to legislatures and administrative agencies. P.L. 94–142 was a product of this period. In other words, the terms of the debate owe their existence to liberal legalism and the rule of law. The legal rights revolution took standard liberal legal doctrine and applied it to new and different fields of relationships. Government had to act according to the rule of law when interfering with private property. The legal rights revolution extended the rule of law to other kinds of governmental relationships, where important, valuable interests of the individual depended on status with the government—the "new property" of welfare benefits, certain kinds of employment, disability, education, and others. In these new areas, government, too, was constrained by the rule of law.

In Chapter 6, I develop a theory of social change that ties together the major conditions of discretion. Here I want to discuss some of the elements of change to determine the importance of legal ideology, to show that despite the criticism of liberal legalism, Thompson's argument is sound. Change rarely automatically follows court pronouncements. Sometimes change occurs through the activity of political leaders or senior bureaucrats; they order implementation. But usually, the translation of legal or ideological change is much more complex, and for the changes that occurred during the legal rights revolution, there was a variety of interactions between judicial and political pronouncements and social movement activity. It is rare that a significant court or political pronouncement of major importance springs full-blown from the hearts and minds of the judges or political leaders. Rather, these pronouncements are reflections of activists, groups, and interests struggling for social change. The great Supreme Court cases in civil rights, which were the most important stimulants of the ideological change, were part of a fifty-year campaign by the National Association for the Advancement of Colored People and allied organizations attacking racial segregation in the United States. It is important to recognize the complex, interactive process of grass-roots activity, political leadership, elite support, and the role of ideology. The relationships are reciprocal, dynamic, and evolutionary, rather than linear. One determinate of social change does not inevitably lead to another. Rather, the combinations interact in fits and starts. Grass-roots activity sometimes brings about changes on the part of political leaders and sometimes the reverse happens—charismatic leaders stimulate local activity. Pressure groups bring cases, and court decisions in turn lend legitimacy and support to local groups and political leaders, and help mobilize elite support, so critical for the financial lifeblood of any social movement. In the process, ideology and rhetoric are sometimes the catalysts, sometimes the cheerleaders.

It is out of these complex forces that large-scale administrative programs get enacted and implemented. Legislatures and most political institutions are reactive. It took the concerted efforts of citizens and groups who were single-mindedly concerned about the plight of the handicapped child to press their campaign at the local, state, and federal levels. It is vitally important to recognize the state and local aspects of social change. Long before the enactment of P.L. 94–142 there was a history of social change at the state and local levels. Ideas percolate at this level, and eventually receive attention at the national level. At the state and local levels, activists and organizations receive their training, obtain the experience of mobilization, and learn to lobby. Parents of handicapped children and their organizations are not vicarious leaders; they are vitally interested in specific, tangible programs for *their* children in *their* schools and classrooms. When the state enacts the laws, it is these groups that then pressure the state agency and the local school districts, and the local schools eventually do what the parents and the groups have been demanding.

This process continues after the federal government becomes involved. The program still has to be enacted and implemented at the state and local levels. Moneys still have to be appropriated, staff hired, facilities made available, children classified and taught. The importance of the federal level is in part financial and in part ideological. Although federal law often defines rights and standards, one should not make too much of this activity. Federal law in these areas, as we have seen in special education, is rarely translatable into specific, concrete legal commands. Rather, federal law expresses goals and standards, ideals and procedures, that require discretionary interpretation. However, these goals and ideals—the "right" to an "appropriate education"—may be important in lending legitimacy and support to the activists and interest groups that have for so long spearheaded the campaigns. The legal goals and ideals also affect political leaders and administrators. Depending on the issue or jurisdiction, officials are not always distinct from local political culture. Teachers, school administrators, professionals, and politicians can also be counted as members and supporters of special education activists. They, too, draw encouragement and support from higher levels of legal pronouncements (Handler and Zatz 1982).

We have seen an incredible explosion of social movement activity and emphasis on legal rights as the legitimizer and cutting edge of reform. The result has been an extraordinary change in our legal culture. The change is not one of kind—we have always defined social controversies in legalism—but rather of *number and extent* of social issues that have now been cast in this framework. What seems perfectly normal today—that handicapped children have a *right* to an appropriate education—would have been an astonishing idea just two decades ago.

Thompson's analogy thus holds true today. We would not be concerned about the failure of adversarial advocacy to handle special education disputes today if we had not had a profound change in our legal culture. This change was not produced solely by the pronouncements of the official dispensers of rules—the courts, the legislatures, the administrative agencies. Rather, the pronouncements had to be seized upon by local parents, groups, interests, bureaucrats, educators, and politicians who were actively engaged in seeking social justice for their children and the children of their constituents. Just as the rule of law in eighteenth-century England was the product of a century and a half of struggle, so too was the Education for All Handicapped Children Act and its subsequent implementation the result of broadly based struggles by a variety of people pursuing a variety of causes, but united in the common thread of new and expansive concepts of the rule of law.

Procedural Formalism, Implementation, and the Distribution of Wealth and Power

Although the idea of the rule of law provided energizing force for social change, it also carried with it the seeds of its failure. The problem goes back to the basic ideas of liberal legalism—that power will be distributed according to rules, that the rules will be enforced impartially, according to reason, through procedures based on liberal traditions of individualism. The task, then, is to give people legal rights and meaningful access to rule-making and rule-enforcing institutions (principally courts and administrative agencies). These institutions will guarantee the application of the rule of law; they will enforce legal rights.

Liberal legalism's adversarial advocacy fails to accomplish these goals because of a failure to take account of two interrelated factors: the problems of implementation, and the underlying maldistribution of wealth and power. By ignoring these issues, the reformers achieve victories for their own social class and symbolic reassurance that progress is being made, but for the have-nots there is primarily frustration, domination, and alienation.

Reformers all too often believe that at the stroke of the judicial pen or the enactment of a law, the world will change. But in order for this to happen, the rule change has to either settle the matter or be easily monitored. Many of the programs we are concerned with raise serious implementation issues because they do not share the two characteristics described above. A rule or order may not settle the question. In many areas of administration, basic, substantive discretionary decisions have been delegated by law to the administrative agencies. A claimant can appeal an administrative decision, but it is the relatively rare case where the court will substitute its judgment for that of the agency and enter the substantive decision. More typically, the court will hold that the agency did not exercise its judgment properly (for example, failed to consider relevant evidence, or abused its discretion, or misinterpreted a rule of law) and then send the case back to the agency for reconsideration. What the claimant wins, then, is not the substance of the matter, but rather the right to have another hearing before the agency. The agency can take the remand, give the claimant another hearing, reach exactly the same decision, but prepare a better record to justify the exercise of its discretion. Experienced administrative law practitioners and students constantly point to this form of administrative response to a judicial remand.

In special education, we encounter both one-time and long-term problems. In cases where patients are litigating for an expensive outside placement for a severely handicapped child, the decision could well involve little or no monitoring. The court could decide that the child should be placed. It would be open to the school district to relitigate the issue at a subsequent point in time. The district could argue that now they have an improved program (at a lower cost) and the child should be returned (or the school district should not be financially responsible for the outside placement). At the new hearing, conventional wisdom would predict that the parents would now lose, that as long as the school district made an arguable case, the matter would be committed to its discretion (Kuriloff 1985).

The implementation issue is important for two reasons. It illustrates the nature of the continuing struggle in political and administrative terms. The rule of law and the legal procedures are important in these struggles, but they are rarely determinative by themselves. Law may assist in the initial political dialogue, during the policy-formation process, and there may be court orders or subsequent administrative rules, but in ongoing administrative programs, these are only additional factors in the battle. With rare exceptions, rules are not self-enforcing. That is certainly true for discretionary decisions. And if the rules are not clear-cut, then the various actors will have varying interpretations. Or even if the normative standards are relatively clear but the factual predicates are complicated or indeterminate, there will also be varying interpretations.

Many other factors determine the outcome. Perhaps the most important of these "other factors" can be summed up in the words "staying power." This is the second reason why implementation issues are so important—they exacerbate the underlying income distribution issues. I have previously discussed the difficulties that the average parent faces when trying to understand what the school is doing and then dealing with the school; this difficulty of coping with a school district decision has been discussed in terms of evaluation and placement. I took a cross-sectional view of the process. But when the process is continuous, lasting over the school-life of the child, then all of the problems of inadequate resources are magnified. Each time one of the parties—either the parent or the school—wants a change, then the implementation issue arises and there has to be a mobilization of resources.

Social reformers in special education were not completely naïve about implementation issues. They knew that victory was not achieved with the enactment of P.L. 94–142. Programs had to be put in place, or, if already in place, had to be modified and improved to conform to the new law. More than most law reformers, they continued to press for the expansion of local budgets, hire special education staff, and provide additional resources. All this would be necessary if the reformers were to get benefits for their children or the children of their constituents.

But reformers went only part-way. Not enough attention was paid to the problems of ongoing administrative decision making and activity. Because of the maldistribution of wealth, the bureaucracy, on a day-to-day basis, is able to assert its power in the masses of low visibility decisions. The resources and staying power of the bureaucracy become overwhelming.

It is true that the idea of the rule of law changed the character of the debate and raised the consciousness of the society so that people who deal with government in important ways have or ought to have dignity, autonomy, and responsibility; governmental power, in these relationships, is subject to our liberal, legal traditions. The debate, no doubt, had a lot to do with the enactment of P.L. 94−142, which, in form, embodied liberal legal ideals: parents were accorded dignitary values (the right of informed consent), and by the same token governmental power was to be restrained. For some (I would argue a relative handful), the system worked. They are able to challenge governmental acts, have a meaningful dialogue, and, if necessary, prevail in court. But for the vast majority, the system has not worked out that way. In fact, an argument could be made that the average parent may be worse off. The due process procedures have been manipulated by the bureaucracy, and domination continues unabated.

The system also corrupts the bureaucracy. The school system has a primary organizational task—to educate its students, and, as a side line, to do something with the students who do not get along in the system. Its history, tradition, and present incentive structure push toward the bureaucratic rationality model of decision making. As Weatherley (1979) pointed out in his Massachusetts study, the districts are reimbursed on the basis of the number of children placed in particular slots, not on the quality of decision making, let alone the quality of communication with the parents. The one district that tried to take P.L. 94−142 seriously spent more time per conference and proportionately placed fewer children than the other districts.

The bureaucratic rationality model of decision making competes with the professional and moral judgment models, and will drive them out if the incentives are strong enough. Psychologists will have heavy caseloads; meetings will be structured to reach decisions quickly and efficiently. The professional judgment model calls for a mixture of fact investigation, diagnosis, clinical judgment, and experimentation, usually extending over a period of time; the form is continuity and dialogue. The bureaucratic rationality model stresses a cross-sectional approach. It is discontinuous, in the sense that the participants have only one opportunity to participate at one point in time even though the relationship will extend over the school-life of the child. The moral judgment model will also be suppressed for the reasons already stated—the parents lack the resources to communicate effectively, and the incentives militate against the school encouraging a dialogue. The law requires the procedures; yet, the school people complain about the paperwork, the drain on their time, the diversion from their essential basic task of education (they consider themselves teachers and psychologists, not administrators), and the difficulties of changing placements. Parents who question or complain are troublemakers, interfering with the difficult task of getting the work done in the face of scarce resources. The law requires consultation and consent, but the parents are viewed only as means to serve the ends of the agency. The parents either go along or they are obstacles to be overcome.

The Unnecessary Equation of Liberalism with Adversarial Advocacy

What when wrong? At base, it is a conceptual mistake. There is an unnecessary equation of liberalism with adversarial advocacy. Historically, the due process ideals of liberalism have been translated into only one particular decision-making form which, in turn, exacerbates the historic failure of liberalism to deal with equality (Gutmann 1980). Most issues of equality are ignored; only rights and procedures are provided for. In other cases, feeble attempts are made to provide some form of balance, for example, legal services. The result is that there is a failure of liberalism; instead of individualism, treating people as ends not as means, and restraining governmental power by the rule of law, there is domination, as we have seen in the administration of special education. The problem is that adversarial advocacy no longer serves the goals of liberalism when the social relationship is not individualistic, conflictual, competitive, and atomistic. Different procedures are necessary when there is a valuable continuing relationship that the parties want to preserve.

Granted that adversarial advocacy would not preserve a continuing relationship, why does it follow that adversarial advocacy also defeats liberal goals in this situation? The reason is that adversarial advocacy transforms a cooperative relationship into a zero-sum relationship; there is a winner and a loser, a dominant party and a subordinate party, and the loser becomes the means to the ends of the victor. There is, of necessity, a loss of individuality, of autonomy, dignity, and responsibility.

How does this apply to dealings with government—to life in the modern welfare state? In a situation governed by relatively clear rules, or when a person or business wants to be left alone by government, the relationship could be viewed in classic liberal terms—competitive, individualistic, zero-sum. Either the government can or cannot do what it wants. But the cases that I am dealing with are different—highly discretionary and continuous. The continuing relationship is valuable if for no other reason than that it is usually a necessity. In special education, the relationship is continuous, discretionary, and, since the parents for the most part do not have any alternatives, necessary (Hirschman 1970). In the reality of the social situation, the relationship *ought* to be cooperative rather than competitive. If there is a rough equality of resources, then dignitary values can be enhanced through a cooperative relationship. This is the goal of a properly functioning professional model of decision making, which, of course, *can* apply in a governmental setting. What happens when there is conflict? If adversarial advocacy is employed, the cooperative elements of the relationship are destroyed and the relationship is converted, by the process, into one ruled by classical liberalism. The relationship calls for community, but the procedure forces competition. In real life, the relationship has to continue (the child is still in the school), but now it is adversarial. The result is domination and withdrawal.

The judicial adversarial model derives from our historical view that the government is the enemy. There is a lot of truth to that belief. In the revolutionary struggles, the great civil liberties cases, the development of national resources, the problem was not one of preserving continuing relationships with a welfare state but, rather, preventing the government from interfering with individual initiative. In the modern welfare state, this individualistic, adversarial view of governmental relationships has become problematic. It can sometimes work for the rich, although even they are subject to the continuous power of the state in discretionary situations. And certainly this belief is not useful to the average or poor person; it distorts the situation when the citizen is dependent on a cooperative relationship with the government because the ideology posits the conflictual relationship and designs the procedure for the latter rather than the former. We still believe that adversarial advocacy will preserve autonomy, dignity, and responsibility, but it will not. Where the relations between the citizen and the state are discretionary and continuous, adversarial advocacy will increase domination, mystification, and a false legitimacy.

Individualism in Cooperative Relationships

Is there no way out? Can individualism be preserved in a relationship that is discretionary and continuous? Do people always have to be treated as either ends or means? A necessary condition is a rough equality of bargaining power, and in the modern welfare state, there are vast disparities of wealth and power. One solution, of course, is a radical redistribution of resources at a national level which I put aside for now as unrealistic. A more realistic approach is to view the modern relationship with government in terms of community rather than conflict, to try to collapse the means/ends distinctions in the client/ official interaction and to try to achieve modest redistribution at a decentralized level. Because of continuing relationships and the imbalance of power, classic individualism falters in the modern welfare state, and because we cannot make significant headway on national redistribution issues, why not change the way that the parties deal with each other at a local level? In a word, change bureaucratic incentives and the politics of the relationship.

Fanciful? The Madison School District has done it. They use a decision-making process that preserves individualism in a cooperative relationship. Recall the major features of the process. The fundamental attitude of the school district is that it cannot successfully educate a handicapped child unless the parents fully understand and cooperate with the program. In theory, this collapses the means/ends distinction. Parents are means to the bureaucratic task—they have to support and cooperate with the specific program for their child—but by requiring a high degree of informed consent, the school district is treating the parents as ends, as morally responsible, intelligent beings. They are persons with autonomy, dignity, and responsibility.

The remainder of the book builds a normative theory out of the Madison example. The theory is complete, thus complex. It synthesizes theories of implementation, organizations, social movements, and informed consent—all bearing on the conditions of discretion. A theory of cooperative decision making raises many important issues, which will be discussed in detail in Part II. Here, I want to consider a general issue—informalism as a threat to due process—before returning to the original question of due process.

Informalism

The cooperative form of decision making looks quite similar to the informal systems that are in vogue today. There has been a rash of experimentation with neighborhood justice centers, mediation schemes, and a variety of other kinds of informal systems. Many justifications and advantages are urged for these schemes. Informal systems are supposed to be speedy and inexpensive. Formal systems are professionally dominated, cross-sectional in approach, and for these reasons, inappropriate for problems in real life that are continuous, emphasize long-term relationships, and require the active participation of the parties themselves rather than the structured participation that comes through professional representation. The examples given are family and neighborhood disputes, which, it is claimed, are better handled through neighborhood decision-making systems, staffed by skilled people from the community, rather than through the court system. Rather than the assertion of legal rights, the stress is on communication, conciliation, and future relations as distinguished from vindicating past wrongs (Abel 1982).

Not unexpectedly, serious questions have been raised about the claims of informalism. In some neighborhood and family disputes, the parties may be roughly equal, but informal procedures are not so limited. Merchants and consumers, landlords and tenants, government agencies and clients all raise the distribution question. The informal system, it is claimed, blurs the distinction between the citizen and the state or the citizen and dominating capital interests, and by so doing increases the domination of the powerful interests (Santos 1982). Under liberal theory, formal institutions serve to restrain the absolutist state only when law itself becomes absolute. Conduct not specifically proscribed is, in the eyes of the law, free from official interference. If the government does intervene, then the structure encourages conflict, the assertion of rights, and the right of the citizen to call upon the coercive power of the government to enforce those rights (Abel 1982).

Informalism blurs these distinctions by stressing mediation rather than the assertion of rights, denies the existence of conflict (depicted as a failure to communicate), emphasizes persuasion, seeks to diffuse anger, and, to the extent that it is successful, neutralizes conflict and thus inhibits serious challenges to the exercise of state or capital power. At the same time, informalism, insofar as it stresses early intervention and continuity, expands the reach of state power. Finally, informalism may help to legitimize the formal system by distracting the participants. Critics conclude that even though the formal system is not now very accessible, what the less powerful need is a better formal system within which to enforce their rights against their more powerful opponents rather than informalism where it becomes even more difficult to oppose the powerful.

Many of these concerns could well apply to the cooperative decision making that I have been discussing. There are vast disparities in power between the educational establishment and the average parent of my concern. The Madison system stresses communication, understanding, cooperation, and continuity. It seeks early intervention, and by emphasizing that all decisions are in the nature of an ongoing experiment, it can be argued that it discourages serious challenge and increases state power. As the critics of informalism would argue, it is designed for cooptation, and thus increases domination. Even a poorly working formal system would have less mystification.

The intrusion of state power in the education of the handicapped occurs as soon as the classroom teacher decides that something has to be done about the particular student. Whether or not the parent is notified early (as in the Madison system) or late is only an additional aspect of state power; the state is already acting on the child. The argument that informalism represents an expansion of state power usually takes as its example the neighborhood justice center where the system intervenes early in an incipient or festering neighborhood dispute to head off the commission of a crime. This is an expansion of state power; chances are that if a crime is committed it will be dismissed rather quickly in the court system. Thus, there is less state intervention in the lives of people under the formal system. This analogy does not hold when there is an ongoing administrative program, such as special education. There, the state is already intervening. An additional issue is whether the parents are to be brought into the system and how. Madison does seek early contact, and, in a sense, this is an expansion of state power. But does it increase the power that the state is already exercising over the child?

It can be argued that there is an increase in state power. To the extent that the school is successful in socializing the parents to the school's decision, in persuading or manipulating the parents to go along, in subtly threatening them with the unpleasant consequences of more formal procedures, in deflecting their feelings of frustration or hopelessness or inclination to challenge by labeling all decisions as experimental, there is an increase in state power. Whatever rights and powers the parent have under P.L. 94–142 are diminished to the extent that they are coopted by an informal, cooperative system.

This does not describe the Madison system in its attitude toward the parents. The cooptation described above treats the parents as means, not ends. Under the Madison system, the bureaucracy thinks that its goals will be fulfilled better when the parents genuinely understand and agree. There is a difference between shared decision making and cooptation. At least in theory there is a difference, which also comports with our everyday experience. But whether such a difference can be maintained in a bureaucratic setting, in the real world of administration, is another matter. At least in terms of ideology, the Madison system is trying to achieve shared decision making.

The other difference lies in the use of conflict. A major charge against informalism is its approach to conflict as a failure of communication, a form of deviant behavior. In the Madison example, the opposite is true. Conflict is viewed creatively, as an aid to communication and understanding. This use of conflict prevents (or should prevent) cooptation, but at the same time it enhances participation and continuity.

But to what extent is this conflict controlled? What are the limits? It could be that the school authorities permit conflict only for certain issues but not for others; by allowing a certain amount of conflict, mystification, legitimation, and domination are increased even more than under a straight cooptation model. In Madison, it could be argued, the parents are only given more crumbs to discourage the exercise of rights.

A clear answer cannot be given to this objection. Any time there is a negotiated settlement, one could make the cooptation charge. As long as the focus is on the input of the decision-making process, and the test is whether there was formal, vigorous adversary representation following the judicial model, then anything short of that raises the cooptation issue. In the Madison model, one could point to the presence of the parent advocate, but because a formal proceeding was not instituted and concluded, does that mean that conflict was controlled, that there was in fact cooptation? Well, there could have been, just as there could have been professional domination and repression in the formal system. The only empirical solution to these examples would be a reconstruction of the actual decisions. In theory, the Madison model does meet the objections to cooptation and controlled conflict. Whether it actually meets the objections depends upon empirical investigations.

As a theoretical matter, I have posited ways in which informalism can preserve dignitary values. Conflict can be built in and organizational incentives can be changed so that bureaucratic actors want to achieve genuine informed consent. But how can we be sure these results will be achieved? I talk about freedom of contract, autonomy, equality of position, but the social reality is one of dependency. Advocates can help somewhat, but we know that in many situations these are palliatives at best.

How, then, would one know whether these values are being achieved? In the adversarial advocacy process, we *assume* that these values are being achieved by looking at structural characteristics or inputs (Kuriloff 1985). With informal procedures, one could also look at structural characteristics and make similar judgments. For example, one could note the number of conferences, who the decision makers were, the characteristics of the participation by the parties and so forth. One could also reconstruct the decisions. If, for example, in a Madison School District case, we observed a series of conferences, active participation by the parents, experts supplied by the parents, and a change in position by the school, then one could probably conclude that the parents' dignitary values were respected. But what if the school did not change its position and there were no conferences with parent experts and advocates? Dignitary theorists insist that dignitary values are ends in themselves, goals without regard to substantive outcomes. How do we know that they have been fulfilled or violated when the parent or client or litigant loses, or when the parent or client passively accepts the decision?

I do not see any clear answer to this objection, again, except by a careful historical reconstruction of the decision-making process. One could interview the professionals and the parents, but the former's answers may be self-serving and the latter's deficient for reasons discussed earlier. The problem is that there is lack of conceptual clarity as to what exactly the dignitary values are, and, from this gap in theory, it also follows that there are no sensible measures.

The best that we can hope for, given the present state of our knowledge, is to try to create the incentives that will foster the kinds of results that we want. These are the conditions of discretion discussed in Part II. Cooperative decision making is considered in context—the complex structures of decentralization, organizations, social movements, and social autonomy.

Reform or Reconstruction?

I return to our original questions. Can the adversary system be reformed to make it more effective in discretionary decisions? Even if this is not possible, is it still important to maintain adversarial advocacy because of its ideals or symbolic content? Is there a necessary conflict between the cooperative model and the adversary model, or can they exist side by side in a complementary relationship?

The main argument against the utility of reforming adversarial advocacy is that its worldview is at odds with the underlying requirements of cooperative decision making. Cooperative decision making is grounded in the proposition that there is a continuing relationship between the parties and that relationship, of necessity, has to continue. The function of the decision-making procedure is to *improve* that relationship. The fundamental view of adversarial advocacy is that there is an adversarial relationship; it is a contest between winners and losers. While a new relationship may emerge from an adversarial context, such an event would be fortuitous and is in no way a fundamental goal of the procedure. If there is a continuing relationship, adversarial advocacy usually truncates that relationship by its cross-sectional, discontinuous form.

There are other major structural characteristics of adversarial advocacy that make it inappropriate to the discretionary decision. Adversarial advocacy depends on the complaining client, the person who feels aggrieved and asserts a claim. In the situations that I have been discussing, where there is a dependent relationship, one cannot rely on the complaining client. Indeed, one cannot even depend on the client or patient to perform his or her part of the bargain in pursuing informed consent. Independent resources can be made available, such as voluntary organizations and parent advocates, but ultimately, the burden must be placed on the professional or the agency to pursue understanding and cooperation on the part of the client as part of their organizational mission. Moreover, they have to do this in a non-paternalistic manner—no small feat. The approach of adversarial advocacy is the opposite. The dignitary theorists argue that clients have to *extract* these values from a hostile, recalcitrant adversarial bureaucracy—in my view, an impossible task.

Returning to Mashaw's three models of decision making, adversarial advocacy is based on the moral judgment model, the deservedness of the claim, whereas what is usually called for in the discretionary situation is the professional judgment model, a more-or-less continual consultation looking toward experimental, tentative results rather than definitive solutions. It is true that court cases and administrative decisions can continue after judgment, but these are usually awkward. It is not satisfactory to go back to court for the enforcement of orders, and lawyers usually do not welcome continual monitoring. It is one of the difficulties of using adversarial advocacy when long-term implementation is at issue.

There are also different attitudes on other important matters. Adversarial advocacy believes that dignitary values and accuracy will be achieved through conflict. Cooperative decision making is ambivalent about conflict. There is a line of thought that conflict is bad, a failure of communication; but this approach is worrisome to those who are concerned about cooptation and the loss of individualism. The Madison School District example shows that conflict does have an important, creative role to play in cooperative decision making, that it can be used to further communication, and that, if properly done, it will enhance dignitary values. In other words, conflict can achieve the benefits that it achieves in adversarial advocacy but without the costs that are so devastating to continuing relationships.

Both systems, of course, have serious implementation problems. By now we should realize the difficulties of staffing an adversarial system if we are serious about vindicating client rights when dealing with large-scale organizations; we must also be realistic about the costs of providing adequate hearings. But, of course, cooperative decision making is not cheap. We have seen how the informed consent procedures of P.L. 94–142 have become a sham. If informed consent is to be a genuine goal of administration, then serious attention has to be paid to structures as well as attitudes. Exhortation will matter little if there are huge caseloads and dysfunctional incentives.

In my opinion, on both theoretical and practical grounds, adversarial advocacy will not work in the discretionary continuous situation. Moreover, to keep pressing for its use, as was done in P.L. 94–142 as well as similar statutes, may well produce more harm than good. It allows the better off to garner more of the scarce administrative resources because they can use the legal rights approach to advantage. And, because the claims of the better-off are vindicated in court, we have the symbolic reassurance that the system of rights is working.

Nevertheless, despite these objections, there is no denying the fact that adversarial advocacy or, more accurately, the legal rights revolution, has played an important symbolic, ideational role in our civic life. Following Thompson's argument, we would not even be worrying about these issues in the discretionary situation if it were not for the legal rights revolution. At its best, at its core, adversarial advocacy does reflect basic notions of civil liberty. Moreover, this important rhetoric is long-standing, familiar, deep-rooted, and productive, I am convinced, of much social reform. The problem is that we view adversarial advocacy as the only way to achieve justice, and the reform effort becomes misdirected, as in the case of special education. However, by condemning the use of adversarial advocacy in inappropriate situations, one does not have to take the position that it should be abandoned altogether. Its ideals are important; its use in certain situations has been amply demonstrated; the question is whether it fits in the discretionary situation, and if so, how.

In attempting to answer this question, let us return again to the

Madison School District example. The Madison informal procedures, of course, do not disturb the formal, adversarial procedures of P.L. 94–142; the Madison School District cannot repeal federal and state laws and administrative regulations. But the formal procedures are, for all intents and purposes, not used (there have been three appeals in eight years). It could be that good decisions are made at the field level, that is, that there are in fact no grievances. It could also be that parents are manipulated or coopted or somehow led to believe that it would be futile to appeal. There could also be another reason. Available advocates in the community, such as public interest lawyers, legal services, and the private bar, are fully familiar with the administration of the special education program. They understand what the school district is trying to do and they think that they are doing the right thing. In this situation, if a complaining parent comes to them, they very well might be skeptical. Is this a genuine grievance, or is this person a crank? In other words, cooptation may extend further than the immediate parties. This form of cooptation, of course, is not unique to an informal decision-making model. When people complain about injustice suffered at the hands of officials whom we know and respect from prior relationships, it is normal to doubt the complainer. We are constantly surprised to learn that a trusted person has been discovered in a misdeed.

This danger of spreading cooptation is increased under the expanded notion of informed consent in informal decision making. As I have noted, in order to make informed consent work in a dependent relationship, the powerful officials and professionals have to push it (as in the Madison School District), and this would make it even more likely for others to become convinced that the professionals are sincere, dedicated people who would be unlikely to cause injustice.

Moreover, if we believe that adversarial advocacy has been pushed too far into inappropriate situations, then we need a different reform rhetoric, a different political approach. We need symbols that emphasize dignitary values rather than adversarial advocacy symbols and the language of rights. We have to talk in terms of the values of informed consent, participation, autonomy. We also have to talk in terms of cooperation, mutual respect, agreement. But when we eschew the rights approach, the familiar symbols of civil liberty, do we run the danger of paternalism and the abandonment of clients to the bureaucracy now cast in the helping role? This is probably what happened to the juvenile court movement; we successfully convinced the legal profession and society that the juvenile court was there to help children in trouble in a fatherly role and that legal rights were not only inappropriate but also destructive of the community relationship that the wise and kindly judge was trying to foster. And we know what happened in juvenile courts: children and adolescents got the worst of both possible worlds—penalties imposed in proceedings that were neither helpful nor protective of rights.

The informalism that is urged here is not the juvenile court model; informed consent is to enhance autonomy, not paternalism. Nevertheless, the lesson of the juvenile court movement is chilling. By abandoning the rhetoric of rights in the discretionary decision, we may spread cooptation to other segments of society.

The conclusion is that adversarial advocacy should be somehow preserved. I have been focusing on the discretionary continuing relationship, but what happens if the situation breaks down, if the school officials or the parents think that the other side is unreasonable or holds a position harmful to the child? Suppose that the officials do not genuinely pursue informed consent and seek to manipulate the parents. It would seem that there ought to be a fail-safe position. We have struggled too hard to change our legal culture and reconceive the relation of the citizen to the state to throw out these hard-earned gains because adversarial advocacy is not working in the discretionary situation.

The question, then, is whether the two systems can exist side by side. Can there be cooperative, informal decision making in the shadow of the formal procedure? Would the parties, in effect, be subject to procedural blackmail? This, of course, is the present world in all bargaining situations. When businessmen agree to negotiate, they do not repeal the law of contracts. Neighborhood justice centers are in the shadow of the criminal and civil justice system. This is also true with labor and commercial negotiations. Under some arrangements, the parties may agree to have certain issues not subject to the formal system, but for the most part, all negotiation is in the shadow of the law. More than 90 percent of all court cases are negotiated and settled prior to trial, quite often with the active participation of the judge (Trubek 1983).

The omnipresence of the formal system can be functional. It can provide another incentive for the parties to reach agreement, to compromise, rather than face the costly disagreeable judicial system. Advocates in other administrative systems (for example, mental health) report success when they explain to officials that they can either deal with patient grievances in the informal system or face a much more expensive lawsuit. Agencies, of course, can play "hard ball," and really push adversarial advocacy in the administrative and judicial hearings. My guess is that in the overwhelming majority of situations, they would win handily since by law they have been delegated discretion, and in the long run, this approach could be cost effective. That is, once the agencies really got their methodology down and could churn out standardized legal responses and know exactly what kinds of documentation would be successful, they could quickly and easily defeat client claims. This has been the experience in some welfare jurisdictions. But there are other costs as well. Clearly in a situation such as Madison, a formal proceeding, especially one in court, would most likely destroy a large part of what the school officials think is important. My guess is that a great many officials in discretionary situations would feel the same way. Even if they could prevail in the formal proceedings, the effects would be negative for all the parties. And the reactions of parents in special education are the same. The National Academy of Sciences found that large proportions of parents said that they would never go through formal proceedings again. To the extent that these attitudes are salient, the existence of the formal system can encourage cooperative efforts.

The conclusion that I reach is that the adversarial system should be present. It is valuable for its ideals and for the time when the informal system does not work. But it should not dominate. The task, though, is to redirect the reform energy to improving decision making at the discretionary level. We need a different lens to view agency/client relations.

REFERENCES

Abel, Richard L. "The Contradictions of Informal Justice." In Richard L. Abel (ed.), *The Politics of Informal Justice, Volume 1, The American Experience.* New York: Academic Press, 1982.

Beauchamp, Tom L., and Childress, James F. *Principles of Biomedical Ethics.* New York: Oxford University Press, 1983.

Bickel, William E. "Classifying Mentally Retarded Students: A Review of Placement Practices in Special Education." In Kirby Heller, Wayne H.

Holtzman, and Samuel Messick (eds.), *Placing Children in Special Education: A Strategy for Equity.* Washington, D.C.: National Academy Press, 1982.

Edelman, Murray. *Politics as Symbolic Action.* Chicago: Markham Publishing Co., 1971.

Elmore, Richard. "Backward Mapping: Implementation Research and Policy Decisions." *Political Science Quarterly,* 94 (Winter 1979–1980), pp. 601–616.

Feeley, Malcolm. *The Process Is the Punishment: Handling Cases in a Lower Criminal Court.* New York: Russell Sage Foundation, 1979.

Galper, J. *The Politics of Social Sciences.* Englewood Cliffs, N.J.: Prentice-Hall, 1975.

Gordon, Robert W. "New Developments in Legal Theory." In David Kairys (ed.), *The Politics of Law: A Progressive Critique.* New York: Pantheon Books, 1982.

Gutmann, Amy. *Liberal Equality.* Cambridge: At the University Press, 1980.

Handler, Joel F. *Social Movements and the Legal System.* New York: Academic Press, 1978.

Handler, Joel and Zatz, Julie (eds.), *Neither Angels Nor Thieves: Studies in Deinstitutionalization of Status Offenders.* Washington, D.C.: National Academy Press, 1982.

Kairys, David. "Introduction." In David Kairys (ed.), *The Politics of Law: A Progressive Critique.* New York: Pantheon Books, 1982.

Katz, Jay. "Informed Consent—A Fairy Tale? Law's Vision." *University of Pittsburgh Law Review,* 39, 2 (1977), pp. 138–174.

Katz, Jay. *The Silent World of Doctor and Patient.* New York: Free Press, 1984.

Kuriloff, Peter. "Is Justice Served by Due Process? Affecting the Outcome of Special Education Hearings in Pennsylvania." *Law and Contemporary Problems,* 48, Winter 1985.

Lempert, Richard O. "Grievances and Legitimacy: The Beginnings and End of Dispute Settlement." *Law and Society Review,* 15, 3–4 (1980–1981), pp. 707–716.

Macaulay, Stewart. "Non-Contractual Relations and Business: A Preliminary Study." *American Sociological Review,* 28 (1963), pp. 55–67.

Macpherson, C. B. *The Political Theory of Possessive Individualism.* Oxford: Oxford University Press, 1962.

Mashaw, Jerry L. "Administrative Due Process: The Quest for a Dignitary Theory." *Boston University Law Review,* 61 (1981), pp. 885–931.

Mashaw, Jerry L. "Conflict and Compromise Among Models of Administrative Justice." *Duke Law Journal,* 2 (1981), pp. 181–212.

Mensch, Elizabeth. "The History of Mainstream Legal Thought." In David Kairys (ed.), *The Politics of Law: A Progressive Critique.* New York: Pantheon Books, 1982.

President's Comn.ission for the Study of Ethical Problems in Medicine and Biomedical and Behavioral Research. *Making Health Care Decisions,* Vol. 1. Washington D.C.: U.S. Government Printing Office, 1982.

Rabinowitz, Victor. "The Radical Tradition in the Law." In David Kairys (ed.), *The Politics of Law: A Progressive Critique.* New York: Pantheon Books, 1982.

Rappaport, Julian. "In Praise of Paradox: A Social Policy of Empowerment over Prevention." *American Journal of Community Psychology,* 9 (1981), pp. 1–25.

Reich, Charles. "The New Property." *Yale Law Journal,* 73 (1964), pp. 733–787.

Rothman, D. *Conscience and Convenience.* Boston: Little, Brown, 1980.

Santos, Bonaventura de Sousa. "Law and Community: The Changing Nature of State and Power in Late Capitalism." In Richard Abel (ed.), *The Politics of Informal Justice, Volume 1, The American Experience.* New York: Academic Press, 1982.

Simon, William H. "The Ideology of Advocacy: Procedural Justice and Professional Ethics." *Wisconsin Law Review* (1978), pp. 29–144.

Spitzer, Steven. "The Dialectics of Formal and Informal Control." In Richard Abel (ed.), *The Politics of Informal Justice, Volume 1, The American Experience.* New York: Academic Press, 1982.

Streit, Ken. "Now That There's Movement, Do We Know the Long Term Direction?" Manuscript, Wisconsin Coalition for Advocacy, 1981.

Thompson, E. P. *Whigs and Hunters: The Origin of the Black Act.* London: Allan Lane, 1975.

Tribe, Laurence H. *American Constitutional Law.* New York: Foundation Press, 1978.

Trubek, David; Sarat, Austin; Felstiner, William L. F.; Kritzer, Herbert M.; and Grossman, Joel B. "The Costs of Ordinary Litigation." *UCLA Law Review* 31 (1983), pp. 72–127.

Veatch, Robert M. *A Theory of Medical Ethics.* New York: Basic Books, 1981.

Weatherley, Richard. *Reforming Special Education: Policy Implementation from State Level to Street Level,* Cambridge, Mass.: M.I.T. Press, 1979.

Wolff, Robert Paul. *The Poverty of Liberalism.* Boston: Beacon Press, 1968.

Wood, Gordon S. *The Creation of the American Republic, 1776–87.* New York: W.W. Norton & Co., 1969.

CASES

Goldberg v. *Kelly,* 397 U.S. 154 (1970).

In re Gault, 387 U.S. 1 (1967).

Joint Anti-Fascist Refugee Committee v. *McGrath,* 341 U.S. 123 (1951).

Natanson v. *Kline,* 350 P.2d. 1093 (1960).

PART II

CONSTRUCTION

· 6 ·

A Theory of Public Action

In this chapter I discuss discretion in context, how and why discretion is created in most social welfare programs, particularly those that follow the common federal grant-in-aid structure. The example will be the development of the major special education legislation. This example (as well as dozens of others that could be selected) will show the importance of local and state actors, social movement activity, the manner in which the various actors at the three levels of government interact, and how discretion is created out of this process.

There are two reasons for starting this way. First, it is important to realize the inevitability of discretion in these programs. The second reason is normative: given the dynamics of these programs, discretion should be viewed as an opportunity to be creative, flexible, imaginative.

The discussion of discretion sets the stage for the second purpose. Here, I put together in a systematic fashion a theory of public action. I use the term "public action" to combine "policy formulation" and "implementation," the conventional methods for analyzing and describing change in public programs. The conventional distinction is made between the formulation of the policy at the legislative or executive levels of government and the implementation of that policy. The argument is made, and adopted here, that this is a false distinction, that the two facets of public action are constantly interacting with each other, that in the process of implementation, policy continues to be made and that the implementation process, in turn, structures and filters information, and shapes values, perceptions, and goals. The term public action is simply a shortened version of the combination of policy formulation and implementation.

I am also conflating two other analytic distinctions. Policy formulation and implementation analysis usually describes the process in sequential steps. There is the formulation, followed by the implementation. Whether intended or not, the description is static. I wish to emphasize a dynamic model, a world in constant change. The determinates of social change that lead to public action continue to live, to grow, to evolve, to die; and as these determinates change, so too does the shape and content of the public action itself. I am interested not only in how to bring about change but also in how that change continues through time and space. In terms of our case example, we are concerned not only with how a school district can develop a consensual model of decision making for special education but also how we can sustain the proper working of that model. I argue that the conditions necessary to get the model in place are roughly similar to the conditions necessary to keep the model functioning properly. There is no sharp line between policy, implementation, and change. It is all public action.

It is out of the theory of public action that I develop the conditions of discretion. By conditions of discretion, I mean justice, the sharing of power, in the context of the discretionary decision. Neither the characteristics of discretion nor the theory of public action inevitably lead to justice; they only describe the politics of programs. Within that framework, conscious efforts have to be made to achieve liberal values.

Discretion in Context

When confronted with the failure or inappropriateness of adversarial advocacy in discretionary decisions, the response of the legal rights approach is to try to reduce discretion through more tightly drawn rules, more procedural safeguards, and more advocacy resources. In the minds of many, legal entitlements are inconsistent with discretion. For many types of programs, this approach is futile at best and more often than not counterproductive. But my purpose is not only negative. Rather, out of an analysis and understanding of the structure and context of discretion, new approaches can be found that will better accommodate liberal values in the modern state.

We start our discussion with special education. The structural or contextual conditions of discretion in special education have features in common with other social welfare programs, but special education can also be considered atypical in that the discretionary elements are so pronounced. Thus, special education is a common but difficult illustration. Its common features lead to generalization. Its unique features highlight the difficulties of confronting discretion.

The Paradox of Federal Intervention and Increased Local Responsibility

The federal government entered special education in a major way in 1975 with the enactment of the Education for All Handicapped Children Act (P.L. 94–142). The act was hailed as a signal victory for reformers. It has spawned major changes and, predictably, has brought a significant federal presence—detailed regulations, organizations of interest groups, litigants, and lawyers' organizations operating at the federal level, and a great many federal court cases. Viewed from the Potomac, it seems like a federal program, fairly typical of the Great Society. However, as will be demonstrated shortly, this is not where power lies in special education. The most fundamental point is that the crucial decisions in special education are made at the lowest governmental level—by the classroom teachers, the special education staff, and the principals of the schools.

How does this curious result come about? How can federal intervention, even in significant proportions, result in increased state and local power? The popular belief is that the past decades have witnessed a dramatic shift of power out of the states and local communities to the federal government in a variety of social welfare programs. To some extent this is true. There have been major shifts in some of the largest income-maintenance programs (Social Security,

Disability, Food Stamps, Supplemental Security Income). In other important social programs, the intervention of the federal government has caused significant increases in state and local responsibilities. Special education is one such program.

The answer is common but complex. It concerns the nature of the response of public institutions over time to social demands in a state-local and a state-federal context. Changing conditions at local levels generate demands at higher levels of government, but the response of higher levels can either increase or decrease local responsibility. The history and development of special education shows how local responsibility is increased.

As with so many of our social welfare programs, federal intervention in special education took place in the context of a long history at the state and local levels.[1] Handicapped students require at least some degree of special treatment by the school system; as such, they existed from the first day that the first school opened. In the beginning, this meant exclusion.

As schools and the educational establishment and related disciplines became more professionalized and scientific, definitions of handicap became more sophisticated and gave rise to different forms of treatment. Teachers still had the primary responsibility for identifying children who for a variety of reasons did not fit and who burdened or disrupted the normal classroom. By the turn of the century, the schools were providing special classes for these students, but the basic pattern was segregation.

Early patterns of financing also set the stage for later patterns. Education, including special education, was financed primarily through the local tax base; then, as now, this resulted in great variation between local school districts. However, special education was more costly per pupil, and because of the excess burden, the state governments began to get involved. Advocates for special education and the school districts kept putting pressure on state legislatures, and the involvement increased over the years. By 1975, at the time of the enactment of P.L. 94–142, all but two of the states had some kind of mandatory law requiring the education of handicapped children. On average, the state governments were paying half the cost.

The form of state aid is categorical by type of handicap as well as

---

[1] This section draws heavily on Lynn (1982–1983).

program, which produces incentives and disincentives at the local level. With a categorical program, the local school district seeks the pupil-program mix that maximizes state revenues. As discussed in Chapter 4, depending on the formulae, the local districts are either encouraged or discouraged to find students with certain kinds of handicaps, establish separate instructional units or provide special help within the regular classroom, or provide certain kinds of related services.

As might be expected, there was great variation among the states and the school districts as to the types of handicaps covered, the programs that were offered, and the methods of identification, placement, and evaluation. Variety reflected the fact that for the most part the individual classroom teachers were the principal gatekeepers of the programs. They used a wide range of techniques for selection, placement, and evaluation, including test scores and school performance, but also stereotypes with regard to race, sex, social class, ethnic background, and physical appearance. Children placed in special education—still for the most part segregated units—were stigmatized, and the labels seemed to stick throughout their school careers. The main mission of the school—educating normal children (as the school defined them)—dominated the system. Special education, including the special education specialists, were only marginal. And certainly there was no inclination to involve the parents in decisions about what to do with students who were not in the "mainstream."

As Lynn notes, the impetus for change in special education was a part of the social movements of the 1960s and 1970s—the broader concern for civil rights, social entitlements, and citizen participation—which in this case translated into equal educational opportunities, children's rights, the right to treatment, and the right to treatment in the least restrictive environment. Activist parents were angry with the educational establishment. They felt that too many of their children were either receiving no services, or too little services, or the wrong kind of services. Characteristic of that period, social movement activity sought litigation, and a series of state and lower federal court decisions held that due process applied to the decision to segregate and label a child. Social movement activity and litigation in turn led to pressure and legislation at the state level, which in turn was directed at the federal level.

During this period, there had been some federal response, but it had no real impact or control over state and local developments. In 1958 and 1963, funds were provided to train instructors of teachers of the mentally retarded and the deaf. Although not specifically targeted for the handicapped, funds under the Elementary and Secondary Education Act of 1965 were made available in some districts. The late 1960s witnessed further legislation.

The big change came with P.L. 94–142. In response to the legal rights perspective, the new act gave handicapped children the *right* to a free, appropriate education in the least restrictive environment with procedural due process protections for the classification and placement of children in special education. Handicapped children were now to be treated as normal children, they were to be mainstreamed, and the parents would be able to hold the school accountable. The interest groups considered these changes revolutionary. Needless to say, as Lynn reports, a considerable part of the education establishment was skeptical as to whether these large changes in attitudes, behaviors, and practices would in fact come about.

As with other far-reaching social legislation, there were a lot of problems with P.L. 94–142. The federal promises on funding never materialized—it was supposed to increase up to about 40 percent of the cost, but only managed to do a little better than 10 percent. The burden of the significant increase in the number of handicapped children in special education thus fell on the state and local governments.

In addition, there were problems of conceptualization and implementation. P.L. 94–142 is concerned primarily with procedure rather than with substance. How, then, asks Lynn, can one evaluate whether the substantive objectives are being accomplished? There were problems of quotas and targets and funding classifications, which, as before, created inappropriate incentives concerning classification and programs. Despite these problems, there has been a significant change in special education. While enrollment in public education declined since 1975, it has increased in special education. Between 1975 and 1979, state expenditures for special education almost doubled. Just about all of the states have amended their laws to comply with P.L. 94–142, including the procedural due process requirements.

Field Level Discretion: Structure and Context

Despite the overlay of state and federal law, the basic substantive decisions in special education are made in the school districts. Federal and state law is largely procedural, specifying how decisions are made. The substantive provisions of the law—what kinds of handicaps are covered and what programs are authorized—are loosely defined. This means that discretion is in the hands of the front-line officials—the teachers, the special education staff, the principals. They are the ones who identify, place, and evaluate the handicapped students. In this respect, special education is similar to a great many social welfare programs where front-line officials have to exercise discretion. The unique feature about special education, however, is the breadth of that discretion.

Special education is such a discretionary local-level program because of its history, the nature of the substantive task of the program, and the characteristics of our federal, state, and local governmental institutions. Special education programs started at the local level of government—the school districts. This is the front-line or, in Lipsky's terms (1980), the "street level" bureaucracy. This is a normal development. Education, by history and tradition, is a local government responsibility. It is at the local level—in the classroom—that the problems of the handicapped child have to be confronted on a day-to-day basis.

When social conditions begin to change at the local level, pressures will be felt in the front-line bureaucracy. In education, such changes came about from a number of different sources. There was the increased responsibility of the school system. Education became universal and compulsory, and at the same time continuous new waves of immigrant children came to the school door and had to be socialized. There were different perceptions of "the problem" with increases in professionalism and psychological and medical knowledge and, more recently, with changes in perceptions brought about by the legal rights revolution. These changes in the environment of the school system produced new demands on the bureaucracy, and programs began to develop.

The front line is able to handle some of the changes, but when demands increase, it begins to exert pressure on other aspects of its environment—higher levels of government, allied interest groups, elites, or other influential actors. In special education financial aid was sought at the state level.

Before the intervention of the state government, the school district was coping with the new demands in terms of its own discretionary authority and probably with little outside constraint. There were the state and federal constitutions and general state laws governing municipal powers and education, but in the main, it was up to the school districts to decide who was handicapped and what to do for them. Seeking and obtaining state aid, however, changed this picture. State aid is program money; in making the appropriation, the legislature defines the terms and conditions of the grant. This is categorical aid, and the state has to define the categories. At this point there is a potential shift in discretionary authority. If the school district accepts the money, it has to spend the money according to state law. What is the nature of the state response to the local demands? To what extent does the state alter the distribution of discretionary authority as the price of the grant?

In this kind of a situation, where a local problem starts to become unmanageable, the classic response of the legislature is reactive and minimal rather than one of seizing the whole issue and absorbing all of the issues and power. Legislatures are normally reactive institutions. Most of their scarce time is taken up with the chief business of government—the budget. All other issues compete for time on a crowded legislative docket. As an institution, the legislature will tend to handle only problems that it has to handle.

Legislatures also tend to avoid problems that are controversial. Most problems that demand scarce legislative time and have budgetary implications are controversial. Problems that disturb existing jurisdictional lines, such as state aid for education, tend to be controversial; there are jealousies between levels of government and concerns about local control. In special education, interest groups press for better treatment for their clientele. Favoring one group over another will gain both friends and enemies.

The best way in which a legislature can save scarce resources and avoid controversy is to avoid dealing with the problem. When it has to deal with the problem, the next best strategy is to handle the problem minimally; and this means delegating the problem back to its source—in this case, the local school district. If there is a conflict

among interest groups as to which handicaps need support, the preferred technique of the legislature is to authorize expenditures for all
groups and delegate to the school district the power to allocate among
them. The granting of discretion satisfies local jurisdictional interests
and gets the politically controversial problem out of the legislature's
hair. A successful delegation, from the standpoint of the legislature, is
one that stays delegated. The problem is resolved at the local level and
does not rise up and demand more legislative and political capital
(Friedman 1969).

There are other reasons for delegation. Historical traditions play a
large part in education, crime and delinquency, public health, licensing, land use. These are primarily local functions and will remain so
unless great social changes occur. Absent a significant social disrup-
tion, federal intervention will usually not disturb basic allocations of
authority. One such change came about in the Great Depression,
which produced, among other things, a national system of old-age
pensions. Previously, the aged either had to provide for themselves or
go on the dole, which was a state and local function (Handler 1979).

Another important reason for delegation has to do with the nature
of the regulatory problem. If the problem is technically complex, or
requires significant amounts of professional expertise, or if answers
are unknown, then the solution has to be delegated. A blanket legislative or top-level administration rule would be unworkable. Instead,
there have to be step-by-step, trial-and-error decisions. The classic
example is what is considered to be the start of the modern regulatory
state, the Interstate Commerce Commission, where the problem was
regulating railroad rates. It was recognized that a legislative body
could not appropriately set rates with sufficient flexibility.

In short, there can be a variety of reasons for a reactive, minimal
delegation posture on the part of the legislature. Some make sense
administratively (the problem is best handled at a local level); some
are the result of power struggles between different levels of government; and some are for institutional and political reasons.

The same response also characterizes relations between Congress
and the states. Most of our social welfare programs started as state
and local programs. For a variety of reasons, problems are no longer
solved in a satisfactory manner at this level, and demands are made
on the federal government. Congress, a busy, risk-averse institution,
often reacts with the minimalist, delegation approach. This was true

with public assistance when the state programs got into deep financial trouble during the Depression. The federal government responded with money but with minimal federal requirements.

This was the pattern with special education. As costs rose at the local level, state aid was granted, but not with very many conditions. Eventually, there were full, flourishing state and local programs, but they were perceived to be inadequate and demands were made on the federal government. At first, some halting steps were taken; then P.L. 94–142 was enacted, but the structure of that act fit the common pattern. The act provided procedures, but it carefully avoided the substantive questions—the definitions of the handicaps, and what to do for the handicapped students in the school system.

There may be good and sufficient reasons for the federal government not to decide the substantive issues in special education. That is not the point. The important point is that the power and responsibility remain at the local level. The federal as well as the state governments are sources of influence and change, but this influence is variable, subtle, and indirect.

The federal-state-local structure is important for a number of reasons. It is important to fully grasp both the downward flow of discretionary authority in the three-tiered bureaucratic system and the extent of discretionary authority at the lowest levels. The downward flow is a conscious policy and, as stated, has both positive and negative causes. The negative causes stem from the fact that for many issues, the top-level policymakers do not want to deal with the issue and delegate the problem back down. The positive causes lie in the nature of the substantive decision—it may be inherently discretionary, that is, not suitable for solution by a clear rule; it may be technically uncertain; it may require professional expertise. Whatever the reasons, the substantive program choices are made at the lower levels. To be sure, they are made within parameters. School districts, welfare offices, clinics, and other agencies are subject to budgetary constraints; they are bound by constitutional and other basic laws; they have enabling legislation and guidelines. These are constraints, more or less. If there is no money in a school district to pay for certain things, then, in fact, a decision has been made. Certain eligibility definitions are clear-cut. Programs differ in the degree of rule-boundedness. AFDC, a program long in controversy, has more rules than special education, juvenile delinquency, social services, and health. AFDC is somewhat atypical in this respect, although even this program has a great amount of discretion at the front-line office. In the main, a distinguishing characteristic of all of these programs, and especially special education, is the absence of clear rules or, to state the converse, the presence of great amounts of field-level discretion. At the macro-level, the federal- and state-level influence may be manifest, but in the day-to-day decisions between individuals and bureaucrats the discretionary power is at the local level.

A Creative View of Discretion

The structural reasons for lower-level discretion demand a new way of thinking. Discretion is not only a fact of life; it must be viewed as a creative challenge, a positive good, rather than a necessary evil. This view is in contrast to deeply held values. The legal profession, for example, and especially the ideology of the legal rights revolution, views discretion as an evil. Discretion is the opposite of the rule of law. The law, in the liberal state, is to be applied uniformly, openly, equally, objectively; discretion is the opposite—often secret, individualized, taking account of special circumstances, subject to bias. Discretion is subjective justice; rules are formal justice. Discretion is the opposite of legal entitlements; the two cannot co-exist (Kennedy 1976). If discretion exists, then a claimant cannot establish a legal entitlement to a substantive outcome. A claimant may be entitled to a hearing, or the right to submit an application, or the right to overturn a decision if it exceeds the bounds of discretionary authority, but if a front-line decision maker has the legal authority to make a discretionary decision, the claimant does not have a substantive legal right to a particular outcome. The power is in the hands of the official (Handler 1979).

Top-level officials have conflicting views of lower-level discretion. As previously stated, there are important reasons why discretion is delegated downward. But lower-level discretion is a two-edged sword. It becomes uncontrollable from the top. Lower-level officials usually have control over information as well as other resources (Mechanic 1962). If the top level does not want to know what is going on below (which is not uncommon), well and good; but if it does want to know, there are usually great difficulties in obtaining accurate information.

Lower-level discretion conflicts with Weberian ideology, the ideology of the modern state—the view of the efficient, rational bureaucracy governed by rules and procedures emanating from the top, where lower-levels function as cogs in a smooth running, well-oiled machine.

Denial or grudging tolerance of discretion is dysfunctional. This becomes apparent when one considers the problem of change. How can change come about if obedience to rules and commands is problematic? But the top cannot have it both ways. By necessity and desire, discretion below is encouraged, but that means that lower levels of the bureaucracy are free to ignore commands from the top. And indeed, this is the most persistent charge made against bureaucracies—the difficulty of implementing policy changes. Lower levels have it within their power to thwart, disobey, or otherwise sabotage changes from the top (Mechanic 1962).

But organizations do change. In fact, they are constantly changing. The history of the change that came about in special education contains several important suggestions as to how the exercise of discretion can change. Initially, change came about through various changes in the social and political climate which began to affect first the local districts, then the state level, and then the federal level. There are multiple responses at the state and federal levels, each reinforces those pressing for change at the lower levels. Higher-level responses are money, legal and other symbols, technical assistance, and professional interactions. All, in different ways, serve to encourage or discourage forces from below.

Conversely, the higher-level change could also produce a counterreaction at the local level. It may reinforce those who are jealous of local prerogatives, and there are a variety of ways in which they can sabotage the program. Local decision makers can ignore changes in higher-level rules. One of the characteristics of grant-in-aid programs is weak enforcement, and chances are that sanctions will not be imposed. More likely, discretion will be exercised in such a way as to obfuscate the entire matter. A few children with a particular kind of handicap will be served to blunt some of the pressure, or local officials will drag their feet.

An interesting question is why government works at all. We have examined some significant changes in special education. The simple answer is the wrong answer. The federal government did not throw bushels of money at this problem. Quite the opposite. Federal expenditures have been slight, yet there has been a significant increase in the number of children served and the dollars spent. There has been a significant change in the law. There has been a steady growth in the industry.

The forces for change come from many different points in the bureaucracy and the environment. The forces vary—ideas, laws, money, technical assistance. The actors vary—interest groups, officials at various positions and levels, politicians. In the past few decades, courts have been influential. These forces interact continuously in a dynamic, reciprocal relationship. Programs tend to change incrementally; each change creates incentives or disincentives, encouraging certain groups, actors, and activities and discouraging others, which in turn produces different kinds of effects and changes. In special education, this process has been going on ever since schools began.

We are looking at a particular point in time for special education. It has undergone a period of change in response to more general impulses nationally. This makes it interesting not only in its own right but also because many other social welfare programs underwent similar changes responding to similar pressures. These pressures consisted of broadly based social movement activity, the legal rights revolution, and a peculiarly American federalist mixture of state and federal laws and resources.

This chapter focuses on discretion exercised at the field level. This discretion is set in the wider context—the bureaucracies above the school district, up to the federal government and the social and political climate that has produced the change: interest groups; lawyers and advocates; professional organizations; courts; politicians and related units of government; other social welfare programs; as well as other actors. All, in various ways, shape the exercise of field-level discretion; and all have to be taken into account when seeking to direct changes in discretion.

A Theory of Public Action

Characteristics of the System

From what has been described so far, we see that each individual school district is hardly an island unto itself. Starting from the bottom up, each district is a unit of government that is connected vertically through the state at both the executive and legislative levels and up to the federal government. We have discussed the most important piece of federal legislation, P.L. 94–142, but there are many other federal laws and programs that affect the local school district. The school district is part of the tri-partite federal-state-local structure.

There are lateral connections as well. The school district is a public body that affects and is affected by other public and private bodies surrounding it. At the most basic level, it is primarily dependent on the local government unit tax base. Historically, schools were entirely dependent on the local property tax. Over time, increasing proportions of revenue began coming from state and federal sources but the predominant share still comes from the property tax. There are also extensive program relationships. School districts, in varying degrees, have relationships with offices of health, mental health, juvenile justice, social services, legal services, in short, the social support systems that affect the families and students. Many of these community programs are nongovernmental. There are the voluntary organizations—parent groups, charities, special interest groups. Schools are also significantly influenced by professional organizations, labor unions, and civil service personnel requirements. In short, school districts are complex organizations living in complex contexts.

In the aftermath of the New Deal, World War II, and The New Society, the federal government appears as the focal point of social change. The great social movements of the past few decades centered on the federal initiative. So if one is interested in social reform, it would be logical and consistent to start with the federal government. How is policy formulated at the federal level, and how is it implemented? I am starting at this point, too, but to argue the reverse. By examining the characteristics of the public action system in the federal-state-local structure, I will show that the major impulses for change do not come from the federal level but from the local and state levels. Indeed, I go farther: unless the forces that bring about the change at the local level continue to operate, the federal government will be relatively ineffectual. This is not to deny the importance of the federal government; it is to argue the crucial importance of local-level activity. It is easier to clarify this argument by starting with federal-state-local relationships.

Education is still a peculiarly local institution. Even today, there is great controversy about the federal role in this historically local function. Does this mean that I have selected a special case to illustrate the relative importance of local activity in the process of social change? I do not think so. Education is more locally centered than income-maintenance programs. Nevertheless, the points that will be made have general applicability. They will apply to a broad range of social welfare programs.

The thesis that I will demonstrate, then, is descriptively accurate; it is policy relevant in that it specifies the conditions of social change; and it has general applicability across a broad range of social welfare programs.

Federal programs are addressed to the states, the local governments, and other public and private organizations as providers of goods and services. What happens when programs enter this structure? How likely is it that the goods and services will be delivered as intended? Zald (1980), summarizing a wide range of implementation literature, states the following proposition:

> To the extent that the actual delivery of service, goods, contracts, behavior, depends upon an inter-connected, though not well integrated set of groups and authority, to the extent that the various components of the target system [the state and local governments] do not share the same goals, nor share the goals with the implementing agency, and to the extent that the components of the target system are not well coordinated and integrated, implementation will fall short of the mark and target systems will not deliver desired outputs. Where, on the other hand, target objects have unambiguous structures of coordination and well established procedures, or easily established procedures for monitoring actual progress and program compliance, implementation problems decline [p. 67].

In the social welfare programs that are our concern, the basic structural arrangement between the federal and state governments is the grant-in-aid. As the name implies, the federal government gives the state a grant in aid of a state program. The basic format is that the state applies for the money under certain conditions and specifications. If the conditions are satisfied, the money will be granted. Periodically, the state reapplies. The typical arrangement is cost-sharing between the states and the federal government. There is variation across programs as to both the proportionate share of federal support and the nature of the federal conditions. Some programs have higher proportions of federal dollars and/or greater amounts of federal control than others. Others are more state and locally oriented. Moreover, these characteristics change over time. Education, as we have seen, is still quite state and locally oriented. Income-maintenance programs have seen greater shifts toward federal dominance, although even here, this varies across specific income-maintenance programs (Handler 1979).

States are not required to accept the grant-in-aid offer, although all of them eventually do. The degree of implementation at the state and local levels depends on a variety of factors—the characteristics of the mandate or the rules, the characteristics of the relevant agencies, and the particular environments. Quite often several fields are involved. That is, a federal grant-in-aid may ostensibly be in one area (for example, education, mental health), but at the state and local levels, several other programs (public and/or private) may be relevant to the actual delivery of services. Each field has its own traditions, histories, and relationships with the various levels of government and private sectors.

Although there is great variation, some generalizations can be made. It is difficult to overemphasize the importance of the separate bureaucracies within each of the relevant fields. In all of the states, counties, municipalities, and other subdivisions of government there are schools, police departments, courts, child protection agencies, social services, welfare departments, hospitals, clinics, and so forth. These agencies have traditions, structures, alliances with special interest groups; in short, they have their own agendas, which may or may not coincide with the federal mandate. The central mission of the schools is to educate mainstream children who will enhance the survivability of the organization; it is not to educate handicapped children, or deal with children in trouble with the law, or achieve national civil rights or antipoverty goals. The schools may be required to take on these other tasks as a result of federal laws or because of a decision of the state to participate in grant-in-aid programs, but the point to recognize is that these additional tasks then have to compete at the organizational field level for scarce resources in an environment which more often than not is less than enthusiastic about the additional mission. This is not to say that these programs will always fail, that they will be sabotaged at the local level. It is to emphasize that existing bureaucracies are being asked to take on new tasks, and that quite often these new tasks are not within the central mission or goals of the bureaucracy, however broadly they may be defined.

The agencies not only have their separate agendas but also are fairly autonomous within the state. By autonomy, I mean latitude in exercising discretion. The administration of the criminal justice system is largely a local matter. School districts exercise a great deal of autonomy vis-à-vis the state; the independent traditions of the local school system are quite strong and successful in resisting state interference.

Further complicating the picture is the existence of the private and not-for-profit sectors. There has been a significant increase in the public purchase of services, now being called the "privatization of government." Perhaps this trend is more evident in social services and other kinds of public services (for example, garbage collection) than in education. The increased use of purchase of services creates additional autonomous units that have to be bargained with in the implementation process. In the course of time, the suppliers of services become independent forces; they build alliances and become special interest groups.

The federal/state grant-in-aid structure is best characterized as highly decentralized, with problems of information, communication, coordination, and control.

While the relationship between the state government and subordinate units within the state (including private) is extraordinarily complex and diverse, the same basic dimensions apply between the states and the federal government. Between the federal and the state government there is a complex web of relationships built up over the years across many programs and affecting many units of government. There is no state government and no federal government in the sense of a single entity. There may be a single federal contracting agency—for example, a subdivision of the Department of Health and Human Services—and a single grantee at the state level—the state department of health and social services—but there are many other networks of relationships between the levels of government that have an interest in the particular program. What immediately comes to mind are the interested legislators. The presence of an interested delegation from the particular state sitting in the Congress is of great importance, especially when conflicts arise between the federal executive department and the state. Within the executive branch, other departments have an immediate interest in the program. On the federal level, this would be the Office of Management and Budget; on the state level, the equivalent departments of administration.

Casting the net somewhat wider, agencies that have related programs will also be interested in the particular grant-in-aid. If the particular program will have an impact on, say, mental health, then another complex web of agencies, bureaucrats, and special interest groups enters the picture.

In addition to the agencies and units of government, the private and professional groups and organizations that were identified at the state level operate between the state and federal levels. These include professional and union organizations, citizen groups, special interest groups, and charities. Quite often the groups and organizations that are working at the state and local levels are simultaneously working at the federal level.

From the description so far, one might get the impression that the responsible federal granting agency is an inert dispenser of funds only, caught in a buffeting sea of complexity. To some extent, it is valid to emphasize the context, if only to correct the traditional simplified version of an active, purposive, effective single federal government speaking with one voice. The granting agency, the legal and administrative structure of the program, and the funding are of importance; but they are variables rather than fixed determinates.

What usually happens in the grant-in-aid programs is that all federal monies from a large number of programs are received by the state. The state then receives all of the requests for funds from the other state agencies, local government, subdivisions, and private agencies and eventually funds the requests from the various pots of federal and state monies. The point is that there is usually no segregation of federal funds. There is no separate stream of money coming from the U.S. Department of Health and Human Services for a particular mental health program at a county-level agency that is in fact administering that program. Instead, the state agency receives the request from the county program and allocates money to that program. The state pool of money is made up of state and federal monies from a variety of sources.

Further complicating the matter is state practice in shifting money. States receive monies from a particular federal grant-in-aid, but often do not allocate the proportionate share of state money. This is a

common practice, but difficult to pin down because of state accounting practices.

In addition, federal enforcement efforts in general are weak and
uncertain. Information systems are inadequate; rules and standards
are often vague. The politics of enforcement also weaken federal
control. State bureaucracies are powerful agencies with friends in
Congress who are ready to defend state interests against federal au-
ditors. In most really serious confrontations, the states are able to
muster sufficient pressure to force the federal executive agencies to
back down (Handler and Zatz 1982).

In a sense, the role of the federal government is perverse; the
introduction of the federal government paradoxically increases state
and local discretion. The federal government authorizes and pays for
additional or expanded programs, but since the federal government
cannot constrain the states significantly, there is an expansion of state
and local discretion. Clearly this has happened in special education.

Thus far, I have emphasized decentralizing tendencies. There are
centralizing ones as well. Although the regulatory effectiveness of
federal law and administration may be problematic, there are other
sources of federal influence. In some grant-in-aid programs, the federal share is quite significant—for example, more than half in
AFDC—but even in programs where the federal share is only a small
proportion, the additional amount can have considerable influence.
In special education, it allows some states to launch new programs, or
change direction, or expand existing programs. Then, over time,
these new programs develop internal and external constituencies and
become permanent.

Paperwork is also an important influence. The masses of rules,
regulations, bulletins, circulars, reporting requirements, and forms
affect the delivery of services. Teachers will avoid making decisions or
changing decisions once made.

An important centralizing force is the process of social change itself. Again, this presents an apparent paradox. As noted, virtually
without exception all of the major federal social welfare programs
start at the state and local levels. There is a long history of testing,
experimentation, struggle, and change in the local communities. If
federal intervention is reactive to these demands and tends to delegate, how can this process be thought of as centralizing? This is because the groups, organizations, officials, and citizens who have been

pushing at the state and local levels are the ones who are interested in federal standards and support. In special education, they are the ones who claimed that local discretion had led to the systematic exclusion of large numbers of handicapped children from the school system and permitted discrimination against minority and male students. They are the ones who successfully urged the enactment of P.L. 94–142 and kept pushing for the enforcement of federal standards and goals.

These groups draw on a variety of sources of federal support. There is the money, of course, which can fund new positions and mute opposition. Another source of support may be the federal mandates themselves—the statutes, regulations, and court decisions. Law-abidingness and legitimacy will vary from community to community, but in some, the law legitimizes the values of the reformers and gives them moral support. It is hard to pin down the precise effects of legitimacy (Friedman 1969; Hyde 1983), but social reformers think that it is important to have official, legal confirmation of their position. Social reformers use law in a variety of ways. They appeal to legality and the affirmation of values. They use law for litigation and the mobilization of resources. Law helps mold public opinion; it speaks to the media, elites, and sources of support (Handler 1978).

In sum, when we look at the implementation system, we do not see a pyramidal structure, with commands and resources emanating from the top down. Instead, we see arenas of competing jurisdictions, both public and private. Programs have long historical traditions at the state and local levels. There are multiple layers of agencies and organizations, with their own perceptions, values, and traditions. There are interest groups, advocates, and professional organizations. Some are vigorously defending state and local interests; others are seeking federal sources of support and influence. It is a system of interaction and reciprocity.

A Theory of Public Action

Given the complexity and diversity of the social system, how then does change come about?

Zald 1980, in a paper setting forth a framework for analyzing the deinstitutionalization of status offenders, addresses four issues that bear on the question of change. The first issue concerns the relationship of the beliefs and ideologies of the particular program as social movements to the broader currents and trends in American society. Zald's example, and one that I will use, is the effort to deinstitutionalize status offenders (Handler and Zatz 1982). With regard to status offenders, we would want to know how the broader concerns of institutionalization and deinstitutionalization relate to beliefs and ideologies concerning deviant behavior in general and status offenders in particular. In the 1960s there was a strong and diverse, broadly based growth for deinstitutionalization in general supported by a wide variety of citizen groups, advocacy organizations, professionals, reformers, and public officials. The carriers of the movement varied in terms of composition, strength, and influence. There were variations in terms of clients and institutions. Some favored outright release; others objected to the form of the care and argued for substitute settings and treatment.

The second issue is how these ideas work themselves out at the state and local levels. Scholars note that states vary in terms of structure, political culture, and the ability to innovate. Some states are "leaders," others "laggards," and still others "nonadopters." Within the states, variation in the subsystems is important. Subsystems include the units of government as well as the interest groups. With deinstitutionalization, the juvenile court plays a key role. The court has a high degree of autonomy and therefore the likelihood of innovation depends upon the attitude and organization of this particular subsystem.

The third issue concerns the links between the three levels of government. Federal programs can operate as either constraints or opportunities. Zald stresses the personal and professional links between the various subsystems at all three levels—technical and staff contacts, consultative linkages, regional and national contacts—which may contribute to the diffusion of innovation.

The fourth issue concerns the specific intervention of the federal government in the particular program. Prior to the specific federal move, a great deal was already happening. There had been the changes in ideologies and beliefs, the general trends in deinstitutionalization concerning a wide range of populations, and a more specific trend concerning status offenders. How much had been going on in each particular state and local government varied in terms of the strength and size of the interest groups, the size and scope of the delinquency and status offender population, and the structure and culture of the state and local governments. It is into this variable milieu that the federal government intervenes. It intervenes with multiple voices: statutes, regulations, court opinions, offers of money, technical assistance, as well as other forms of incentives and disincentives. In some states and communities, behaviors seem to change; in others, not. What accounts for the difference?

Zald notes that the traditional method for attempting to answer this question was "impact analysis"—a comparison of changes in behavior (called "outcomes") with the policymakers' intent. Impact analysis was then superseded by "implementation" analysis, which pays more attention to the processes of the entire social system. Implementation analysis more critically examines the explicit and implicit theory concerning the relationship between the policy and the expected outcome. Implementation theorists focus on the characteristics and processes of the various agencies and organizations and the relationships between them.

Sabatier and Mazmanian (1981) have attempted to identify the relevant variables and hypotheses in implementation analysis. Summarizing their major points, they note, first, that problems differ in terms of their solvability. Some problems are more tractable than others. With deinstitutionalization, for example, it is "easier" to close down particular institutions and simply release their populations than to construct alternative facilities and develop alternative forms of care. Success will also depend upon the attention that the policymakers pay to the implementation machinery—whether a structure is established and adequate resources are provided.

Major problems in implementation are also attributed to lack of coherence in the causal theory underlying the statute and conflicting or ambiguous policy objectives. Emphasis is also paid to the structural arrangements between the various agencies in the implementation system; there is a greater chance of success when agencies are hierarchically integrated and actions between them are coordinated. Conversely, when agencies are relatively autonomous, they tend to view policy goals in terms of their own organizational incentives. Other important factors internal to the system are, of course, the adequacy of resources and the rules for administrative decisions.

Factors more or less external to the system include the extent to which other actors (target groups, constituency groups, politicians, officials) can and do participate in the process. All major programs require political support; this is especially true if the system is loosely coupled, thus requiring cooperation between various agencies. But public opinion and political support is variable and unstable. Changes in the environment affect perceptions about the nature and seriousness of the problem. Changes in the relative importance of the constituency will affect political support. The media play an important role in maintaining or changing these perceptions.

Sabatier and Mazmanian think that all of these variables affect the success or failure of implementation: tractability; lack of policy coherence and the ambiguity of goals and objectives; poor coordination; the sufficiency of resources; the lack of flexibility in rules; and variations in media attention and public and political support. Nevertheless, the single most important factors in their judgment are the commitment of the agency leadership *and* their skill in using available resources.

Zald agrees with the importance of this analysis, but would emphasize three additional factors. The specificity of the mandate is important. Vague standards in effect create discretion and invite conflicting interpretations by lower-level officials. The implementing machinery is important. What precise mechanisms does the supervising agency have for gathering information, monitoring performance, and providing incentives and disincentives? The third factor is the variation in what Zald calls the "target objects as social systems." By this he means the difference between implementing systems that have clear coordinating structures and well-established monitoring and compliance procedures as compared to systems that are loosely coupled, do not share the same goals, are not well coordinated, and lack established procedures for the gathering of information and monitoring compliance.

An alternative view of implementation is presented by Elmore (1978). Elmore draws a sharp line between what he calls "forward mapping" and "backward mapping." Conventional implementation analysis is the former. It is the commonsense approach. One starts with an analysis of the policymakers' intent, and then examines the steps taken through the various implementing agencies. The object is to identify and compare the outcomes, the field-level behaviors, as measured against the intent.

Backward mapping is the opposite; it is a bottoms-up approach. It starts at the field level, with the officials and agencies that have responsibility for the delivery of the services, and looks at the problems of change from their perspective. The choice between forward mapping and backward mapping depends on the assumptions that one is willing to make about the ability of the top to control the implementation process. If one assumes that this ability is fairly decisive, then it is logical to use forward mapping. If, on the other hand, one views the efforts of the top as contingent, as one factor among many in the process of social change, then forward mapping will always show a disjuncture between field-level behavior and the policymakers' intent. Backward mapping takes a wider view of the process; it looks at the environment within which the field-level agencies are operating. It assumes a loosely coupled, poorly integrated social system of relatively autonomous agencies with different sources of information, perceptions, and goals. It assumes a decentralized system with large amounts of discretion at the field level. For these reasons, according to Elmore, backward mapping would more accurately describe the implementation process in most social welfare programs.

It would be a mistake to look at the world only from the bottom up. Local units of government do not operate in a vacuum. Even in a basically decentralized system, there are factors that push toward centralization, that attempt to curb discretion in favor of uniformity. State governments, for example, can create or foreclose options through the use of law and funding. The basic statutory framework, the governmental structures, the funding patterns all set the parameters for the exercise of discretion. I have also mentioned other factors in the environment that push toward centralization—technical assistance, professional and organizational linkages, social reform groups. However, none of the centralizing tendencies lessen the importance of looking at implementation at the field level. The central, overarching fact is decentralization, the presence of widespread discretion at the local level, the decisiveness of the local units in the implementation process. Discretion is bounded by its environment, and that environment includes local, state, federal, and private influences. Nonetheless, the most important sources of influence operate at the local level. Ultimately, it is the community that determines the nature and character of the delivery of the services.

An Application

With theory in this state, what can be said about the processes of social change? The best that can be offered are case examples of social systems that roughly share similar characteristics, and to see how change came about. We can then make commonsense estimates for prescription in the situations that we are dealing with. The example that I will use is the deinstitutionalization of status offenders. It shares the characteristics of special education along the following dimensions. Both are essentially state and local matters, in fact, primarily local. There is a federal effort to encourage deinstitutionalization, but as with special education, there was a long history of state and local experimentation and reform effort. Federal intervention is in the form of grant-in-aid.

Both systems are loosely coupled. In fact, juvenile justice is even more decentralized than special education. The most powerful actor in the system is the juvenile court judge, although the court, too, operates in an environment—the police, the institutions, the probation staff, the support services, politicians, social reform groups, professional organizations, citizens.

I have three major purposes in using the deinstitutionalization example. One is to show how different issues present different kinds of implementation problems. The potential success of implementation varies in terms of the specificity of the program. The greater the specificity, the more likely there will be agreement on goals, and the development of techniques for coordination, control, the collection of information, and monitoring. Discretion (at the field level) is the opposite of specificity. Special education is characterized by widespread discretion at the field level. The deinstitutionalization program, as we shall see shortly, was more varied; parts were fairly specific and parts depended on field-level discretion. Thus, by examining what happened in deinstitutionalization, we are able to compare implementation issues and highlight the particular problems of discretion.

The second purpose is to show the interaction between the top and the bottom in the implementation process. That is, while the theory of action developed here places great emphasis on Elmore's backward mapping, it also recognizes the sources of influence from the top and how these are used by the bottom in reciprocal interaction. Much of the social change in deinstitutionalization involved change from the bottom, but it was influenced by the top.

The third purpose is to show the various sources of change at the local level, especially the interaction between leadership and social movement activity. The importance of this interaction lies in the prescriptive aspect of this essay, namely, that the two key elements in bringing about cooperative decision making in special education are bureaucratic change and social movement activity.

There were four elements to the deinstitutionalization of status offenders: (1) the removal of status offenders from the large state institutions; (2) reducing or eliminating the use of secure detention for youths who have been charged with a status offense; (3) diverting youths labeled as status offenders out of the juvenile court; (4) providing alternative care and services for those youths who are diverted. Research on what happened was conducted by the National Academy of Sciences. In addition to looking at a variety of programs, case studies were conducted in seven states (Arizona, Louisiana, Massachusetts, Pennsylvania, Utah, Virginia, and Wisconsin) and two local jurisdictions within each of those states (Handler and Zatz 1982).

The principal findings were that the vast majority of status offenders have been removed from the large state institutions; there has been a decline in the use of secure detention; and fewer youth labeled status offenders are entering the juvenile justice system. It is less clear what is happening to youths who are diverted. The predominant form of placement seems to be group homes or foster care. It is even less clear what is happening to youths who do not enter the juvenile court system or a closely related diversion program. Many think that these people are being ignored altogether.

How did these changes come about, and what accounts for variation? As with special education, concern began long before the issues surfaced at the federal level. The deinstitutionalization of status offenders was part of the broader currents concerned with the institutionalization of other clients groups (particularly the mentally ill), which in turn was part of the broader concerns for civil rights and the changes in our legal culture. The rights and protection of status offenders are part of the same story as the rights and protection of handicapped children.

There was great variety in the states and communities as to perceptions of the issues, remedies, and social movement activity. In some states, the reform impulse was squarely in the liberal, humanist, rehabilitative tradition. Status offenders needed treatment, not punishment, and this treatment was best afforded not in the juvenile justice system, but in a social service system in local communities. Other reformers took a different tack. These youths did not violate any law; they were only having difficulties with their families; and there was no basis for the coercive intervention of the state. Still others approached the problem from a different perspective. Communities were experiencing a rise in criminal activity, and it was felt that too many scarce resources were being devoted to status offenders rather than delinquents. People of this view favored deinstitutionalization, diversion from the juvenile courts, and, like the second group, had no interest in providing alternative services.

The key actor in all of the areas studied was the local juvenile court judge. As expected, there was great variety. In some communities, active, interested judges started programs and played key roles in mobilizing community support for diversion programs and alternative services. In other communities, the judges accomplished at least some of the goals of deinstitutionalization by refusing to deal with status offenders at all in their courts. In at least one other jurisdiction, the judge circumvented a state deinstitutionalization statute by relabeling status offenders as delinquents. And in another jurisdiction, a new judge who disagreed with the philosophy of deinstitutionalization, killed a well-developed, functioning program. The best programs had the judge as a key figure in the mobilization of other groups and actors. Unless the judge went along, it was unlikely that there would be much success, especially in those areas directly under the control of the judge (for example, jurisdiction, diversion as compared to incarceration in the state institutions).

There was great variety in the sources of local or community support. In some communities, there would in effect be a single social activist who was the principal organizer, lobbyist, and fundraiser. In other communities, it would be local community leaders. In still others, it would be relevant officials—for example, staff members from corrections and probation departments. In a few communities, programs were started by police departments.

Patterns and rates of change also varied by community and by state. In some states, there was a slow, piecemeal process of small change. In others, there was a comprehensive revision. In still others, change came through informal practices at the local level well before legislative change. States and communities started differently, proceeded differently, and were at different stages of deinstitutionalization at the time of the study. This variation would follow from differences in perceptions, information, leadership, and political culture.

Before turning to the role of the federal government, it will be useful to analyze the variables that the implementation theorists have identified in the deinstitutionalization story. This exercise will help clarify the circumstances in which backward mapping applies, and point up the central importance of social movement activity in the theory of public action.

Theorists speak of the characteristics of the mandate. The 1974 federal deinstitutionalization statute (Juvenile Justice and Delinquency Prevention Act) had both negative and positive commands. The decarceration part mandated the removal of status offenders from state institutions. Implementation here was most successful. The statement of this rule was relatively clear. It was a negative duty in that officials were told to refrain from doing something rather than take affirmative action. Monitoring was relatively simple in that results could be counted. The mandate also largely circumvented the court, since the court was told not to send status offenders to the institutions. Although there was controversy over the decarceration portion, there was more agreement on this requirement than on the others. Of course, no law is completely airtight, and implementation is never complete. There was some slippage in the definitions of status offenders; no doubt there was some relabeling; but by and large, these youth are no longer in institutions; moreover, there seems to be no inclination to reconsider this policy decision.

Implementation is not as clear with regard to the second requirement—eliminating the use of secure detention for status offenders. This, too, is a relatively clear mandate, a negative command, and one that is relatively easy to monitor. However, there is decidedly less consensus on this issue. Many feel that secure detention is a valuable short-term option for unruly youths. The police, the courts, and the probation staff have particularly strong feelings on this issue. As a result of sustained, intense lobbying efforts from the states, the federal statute has now been amended to allow secure detention under some circumstances.

The other parts of the deinstitutionalization mandate required affirmative actions—diversion and alternative systems of care. Implementation now becomes far more problematic. Here, the autonomy of the juvenile court becomes crucial; there is very little that the federal and state governments can do as long as the courts have initial jurisdiction over the youth brought before them. However, the judges are not completely impervious to their environments. Especially if they want to build programs, they become dependent on other agencies and actors in the community. Judges cannot build alternative facilities; they cannot compel existing facilities in the community to take status offenders. As previously noted, the relevant public and private organizations all have their own agendas and organizational needs. These are older, more difficult children. In some states and local areas, there was a tendency for facilities to reject status offender referrals or discharge them promptly if they misbehaved. There were also reports of difficulties in foster home placements for this group.

Not only were the affirmative duties more difficult to implement because of structural characteristics, but here there was a sharp disagreement over policy. Once policy moved beyond the prohibitions, there was far more conflict and ambiguity. Nevertheless, in several of the states and local communities, diversion programs were established and alternative facilities were created or utilized to deal with status offenders. How did this part of deinstitutionalization come about?

Looking at those states and communities where affirmative action was taken, there were complex interactions between the growth of ideas, the mobilization of social movements, the reception of the ideas at the state and local levels, and the intervention of the federal government (Zald 1980). In most of the states, the reform effort was incremental—a piece here, a piece there—until ultimately, the essential elements of the whole package were in place. Thus, in one state, the initial effort centered on a single issue; in other states, it was a series of measures. When some goals were achieved, the reform groups would then move on to the next stage. The growth and transformation of ideas, the mobilization of resources, the achievement of legislation and organizational reform was a continuous, interactive process evolving over several years. The mobilization of groups on the basis of ideas led to policies and programs which in turn led to the development of new groups, ideas, and further mobilization.

Local leadership, though, is not enough. Problems differ in their tractability. Again, a distinction is made between the negative and positive commands. It is clearly easier to commit "no more" status offenders to state institutions than to provide alternative facilities and care.

Another cluster of factors involves political support and the availability of resources. In all of the states, coalitions tended to fall apart once decarceration and the prohibition on secure detention were achieved. In contrast to diversion and alternative facilities, the negative commands were highly visible issues. There was more of a consensus; once enacted, the participation of other actors was not needed; and significant resources were not required for implementation. None of this was true for diversion and alternative facilities— except if diversion is taken to mean ignoring status offenders altogether, which has happened in some jurisdictions. But if new programs are to come into being, then mobilization efforts and coalition and institution building have to continue; resources have to be found. Again, in several communities this happened; but in others, deinstitutionalization faltered at this stage. In some of the communities where not much happened in the development of programs, it was lack of resources rather than lack of social movement activity. Status offenders are not the most popular group; nor, given scarce resources, could they claim to be the most in need—as compared to handicapped children, for example. Deinstitutionalization, in general and for status offenders, was undertaken in part on the promise that it would save money. When this promise did not materialize, it is not surprising that additional resources were not being made available for noninstitutional services.

Generalizing from the deinstitutionalization case studies, implementation worked best when there was strong local leadership, supported by social movement groups and agencies, resources, sustained public opinion, and agreement on certain goals. When some of this support subsided over time, progress became uncertain and programs began to falter. There was variability in all aspects, in all of the states, and in all of the local communities. The reality of experience reflects the uncertainty and unpredictability of the theory; it comports with the reality of discretion at the local level.

The normative prescription, then, of the theory of public action is to accept the existence and importance of local-level discretion and to seek social change through these processes. The federal government not only accepted the existence of discretion at the state and local

levels but actually used that discretion to encourage the deinstitutionalization of status offenders. I turn now to the role of the
federal government.

The federal role in the deinstitutionalization of status offenders is
an excellent example of the complexity and subtlety of influence; yet,
because it can be described in a relatively simple program, one can
grasp the main points without a great deal of elaboration. In 1974, the
federal government established its grant-in-aid program—the
Juvenile Justice and Delinquency Prevention Act—under which
monies would be offered to the states if they would meet the goals of
the deinstitutionalization program, as outlined above.

Looking at the array of federal sources of financial support, it was
the opinion of the National Academy of Sciences study that the most
important source was the discretionary funds administered by both
the Law Enforcement Assistance Administration and the Department
of Health, Education, and Welfare (HEW). In most of the states and
local areas where deinstitutionalization projects were successful, one
could find some amounts of HEW or LEAA discretionary money.
There was no single formula. A specific project, for example, a shel-
ter, may have been funded, or staff paid for, or an advocacy group
assisted, or planning money granted. The federal money alone was
not enough, but in many cases, it was the kind of crucial support that
either enabled the project to get off the ground or stabilized it during
an uncertain period (Handler & Zatz 1982).

Federal money of a more general type, that would include status
offenders as parts of larger populations, allowed state and local
groups to obtain discretionary funds at the state level. A good example is Title XX of the Social Security Act, which is in effect reve-
nue-sharing with the states. Local groups and organizations would
apply to the state granting agencies, and while the state agencies had
no specific emphasis on status offenders, they would acknowledge
these youths under more generally defined target populations. The
process was often one of seed money, the formation of a demonstra-
tion project, the building of a constituency, replacing the seed money
with state, local, private, or other kinds of federal money.

Prescriptively, what the analysis of deinstitutionalization means in
social welfare programs that are discretionary and where the major
influence and power lies at the state and local levels, is that if social
change is to come about, the role of the top policymakers is to stimu-

late, encourage, and support social movement activity throughout the entire process, but especially at the local level where the delivery of services takes place.

There is going to be considerable variation at the local level. People in the communities will have different sources of information and different perceptions of problems and remedies. The federal government was most effective when it encouraged and facilitated these differences rather than imposing some notions of uniformity. What this also means is that there will be change and failure. Programs, social movement organizations, and groups evolve over time, grow in strength, and die or simply tread water. So too, particular granting agencies at the state and federal level can lose their capacity to remain flexible and responsive to local perceptions and needs. When this happens, the delivery of services will change as well. Organizations, above all, seek to survive and will shift with the environment; they will evolve as the environment changes. Social change proceeds at an uneven pace. In the deinstitutionalization of status offenders, the federal government played an important, even crucial role; but that role was supportive of local social movement activity. In the final analysis, the local climate had to be right.

Conclusion

I have spent perhaps an inordinate amount of time on the deinstitutionalization story to illustrate the theory of public action in a closely related social welfare program. I believe that the prescriptive implications apply to special education, and indeed more broadly to social welfare programs where discretion in the delivery of services at the local level is seen as a positive good and the aim of public policy is to encourage that discretion and try to channel it along new paths. Uniform commands cannot (and should not) be mandated from the top. Instead, local social movement activity has to be found, supported, and nurtured along the desired paths. Instead of uniformity, there has to be flexibility and diversity. Traditional methods of monitoring performance are inept.

How, then, does this kind of social change come about? It seems to me it depends on two factors. There has to be change on the part of the bureaucracy and there has to be social movement activity, not only in the community, but at all stages of the process. Both are essential to bringing about the desired change. The questions then are: How capable are organizations of changing to adopt this new position? Under what circumstances will organizations change? The other set of questions concerns the role of social movement groups: Is it reasonable to expect social movement groups to assume a creative role in the implementation process? What does it take to encourage and maintain social movement groups in the role that has been specified for them?

The theory of public action incorporates a creative, flexible view of discretion. It does not necessarily prescribe justice between the citizenry and the bureaucracy. The remaining three chapters will discuss what kind of change is necessary in organizations, what the role of social movement groups should be, and what shared decision making means in the context of the discretionary decision.

REFERENCES

Baier, V.; March, J.; and Saetren, H. "Implementation as a Doubtful Metaphor." Unpublished Manuscript, Aug. 1982.

Clune, William H., and Lindquist, R. E. "What 'Implementation' Isn't: Toward a General Framework for Implementation Research." *Wisconsin Law Review* (1981), pp. 1044–1116.

Clune, William H., and Van Pelt, Mark. "A Political Method of Evaluating 94–142 and the Several Gaps of Gap Analysis." *Law and Contemporary Problems*, December 1984.

Elmore, Richard. "Backward Mapping: Implementation Research and Policy Decisions." *Political Science Quarterly*, 94 (1979–1980), pp. 601–616.

Elmore, Richard. "Organizational Models of Social Program Implementation." *Public Policy*, 26 (Spring 1978), pp. 185–228.

Friedman, Lawrence. "Social Welfare Legislation: An Introduction." *Stanford Law Review*, 21 (1969), pp. 217–247.

Furniss, Norman. "The Practical Significance of Decentralization." *The Journal of Politics*, 36, 4 (1974), pp. 958–982.

Haider, Donald. "Intergovernmental Redirection." *The Annals*, 466 (March 1983), pp. 165–178.

Handler, Joel F. *Protecting the Social Service Client: Legal and Structural Controls on Official Discretion.* New York: Academic Press, 1979.

Handler, Joel F. *Reforming the Poor.* New York: Basic Books, 1972.

Handler, Joel F. *Social Movements and the Legal System: A Theory of Law Reform and Social Change.* New York: Academic Press, 1978.

Handler, Joel F., and Zatz, Julie (eds.). *Neither Angels Nor Thieves: Studies in Deinstitutionalization of Status Offenders.* Washington D.C.: National Academy Press, 1982.

Herbert, Adam W. "Management Under Conditions of Decentralization and Citizen Participation." *Public Administrative Review,* 32 (1972), pp. 622–637.

Hirschman, Albert O. *Exit, Voice, and Loyalty.* Cambridge, Mass.: Harvard University Press, 1970.

Hyde, Alan. "The Concept of Legitimation in the Sociology of Law." *Wisconsin Law Review* (1983), pp. 379–426.

Kennedy, Duncan. "Form and Substance in Private Law Adjudication." *Harvard Law Review,* 89 (1976), pp. 1685–1778.

Levy, Francis, and Truman, Edwin. "Toward a Rational Theory of Decentralization." *American Political Science Review,* 65 (1971), pp. 172–179.

Kochen, Manfred, and Deutsch, Karl W. *Decentralization: Sketches Toward a Rational Theory.* Cambridge, Mass.: Oelgeschlager, Gunn & Hain, 1980.

Lipsky, Michael. *Street-Level Bureaucracy: Dilemmas of the Individual in Public Services.* New York: Russell Sage Foundation, 1980.

Lynn, Laurence E. Jr. "The Emerging System for Educating Handicapped Children." *Policy Studies Review,* 2, Special #1 (1982–1983), pp. 21–58.

Mechanic, David. "Sources of Power of Lawyer Participants in Complex Organizations." *Administrative Science Quarterly,* 7 (1962), pp. 349–364.

Nathan, Richard. "State and Local Governments Under Federal Grants: Toward a Predictive Theory." *Political Science Quarterly,* 98,1 (Spring 1983), pp. 47–57.

Ostrom, Vincent. "Nonhierarchical Approaches to the Organization of Public Activity." *The Annals,* 466 (March 1983), pp. 135–147.

Rounds, J. "Information and Ambiguity in Organizational Change." In *Advances in Information Processing in Organizations,* Vol. 1. Greenwich, Conn.: J.A.I. Press, 1984.

Sabatier, Paul A. "Legal and Political Mechanisms of External Control: Their Role in an Advocacy Coalition Model of Agency Policy-Making over Time." National Science Foundation Proposal, University of California at Davis, Institute of Ecology.

Sabatier, Paul, and Mazmanian, Daniel. "Relationships Between Governing Boards and Professional Staff: Role Orientations and Influence on the California Coastal Commissions." *Administration and Society,* 13 (August 1981), pp. 207–248.

Zald, Mayer N. "The Federal Impact on the Deinstitutionalization of Status Offenders: A Framework." Working paper commissioned by the Panel on Deinstitutionalization of Children and Youth, Assembly of Behavioral and Social Sciences, National Research Council, Washington D.C., June 1980.

· 7 ·

Organizational Change

Surely one of the most fundamental problems modern society faces is bureaucratization. "The two great German sociologists, Max Weber . . . and Robert Michels . . . were among the first to insist that the central political issue for all modern societies was no longer what type of economic structure prevailed—whether capitalist, socialist, or communist—but the increasing dominance of the public bureaucracy over the ostensible political leaders" (Scott 1981, p. 5; see also Burrell and Morgan 1979). Contemporary students of bureaucracy echo the same themes: "Although many critical problems face us today, most of the problems as well as proposals for their solutions are defined and shaped in bureaucratic organizations. . . . Our capacity to understand and modify bureaucracy in the present decade will greatly determine our capacity to solve our problems and thus shape the decades to come" (Littrell 1980, p. 263). "[O]ur public life is increasingly dominated by megastructures which take on a life of their own; they transcend human will, suppress individuality, initiative, and creativity in the interests of bureaucratic convenience. We experience alienation out of a sense of powerlessness" (Korten 1981, p. 610).

It is the dominance of bureaucracy that transcends all modern states, that assumes a life of its own, that works its way, toppling presidents, defying the commands from central party leaders, growing, adapting, demanding and extracting protection, asserting independence while posturing as the servant of the people. Bureaucracy provides order and stability in times of conflict and change; it frustrates and turns aside, swallows, and transforms demands and interests that conflict with its own. We now call on bureaucracy to solve virtually all of our social problems, and condemn it when it goes its own way.

Since Weber's time, bureaucracy has represented rationality, efficiency, predictability, orderliness, supervision, legality, and control—the prerequisites of the modern state. Bureaucracy, ideally, maximizes formality—the structure of rules and roles to govern behavior—and minimizes discretion and the role of personality. Bureaucracy represents the equal application of the law.

Although bureaucratization is characteristic of all modern states, our particular concern is with public bureaucracy in the liberal, social welfare state. Since the Depression, we have witnessed the dramatic growth of government at all levels. This growth reflects demands placed on the state and the attempt to rationalize the public role in all its myriad functions—regulating the economy, providing for an expansive system of social benefits, defense, transportation, and so forth. The conceptual framework, the ideology, the myth is Weberian—centralization, formalization, rationality, efficiency, control. The guiding principles of organizing the public sector are the definitions of policy goals by the political leaders and the neutral, objective, rational implementation of those goals through rules, structures, and accountability (March and Olsen 1979; J. W. Meyer 1980a; Gawthrop 1983).

The civil rights and legal rights revolution did not disturb this conceptual framework. Rather, it accepted the framework but insisted that existing laws be applied to minorities and the poor, or that new laws be enacted. It was a program of *rights*, to create rights-bearing citizens in their relations with government, and to insist that the bureaucrats obey the rules. A significant strategy of the civil rights and legal rights revolutions can be understood as an attempt to reduce bureaucratic discretion, to subject official decision making to rules that would be applied evenhandedly. The legal rights revolution accepted the ideology of the Weberian bureaucratic state, the demand for equal protection of the laws (DiMaggio and Powell 1983).

The purpose of this chapter is to present an alternative conception of bureaucracy. Part of the chapter is synthetic and descriptive. It looks at organizational theory and concludes that the Weberian model does not describe reality. Most students of organizations agree. Organizations are not hierarchical, formalized, rational, efficient collectivities; rather, they are loose collections of multiple centers of power, shifting coalitions, adapting and readapting to environmental influences. In current terminology, they are loosely coupled open systems. While there is lively disagreement as to whether *all* organizations can be so described, it seems clear that the organizations that we are considering—public agencies, in state and local settings, staffed by professionals, exercising discretion—fit this description (Gawthrop 1978; Smith 1983). In the first part of the chapter, I will describe briefly the competing theories of organizations and define the essential characteristics of the loosely coupled open system.

The second part of the chapter is normative. My thesis is that the loosely coupled open system is the *appropriate* form of organization to accomplish the goals of justice in the context of the discretionary decision. We have already traveled part-way along this route. The discretionary decision involves a relationship between the client and the agency that is not (or ought not to be) susceptible to solutions by rule. The goal is to strengthen the exercise of discretion but in ways that preserve and enhance liberal values in the client/agency interaction.

We have also seen that the legal rights approach has failed to fulfill its promise. Because of their powerlessness, clients have not been able to enforce rules where they exist, or to bargain successfully where rules do not govern. The bureaucracy has too many cards. Rules, centralization, and formalization are used as weapons against the client, not as protection (Lipsky 1980).

The theory of public action, and especially the role of social movement activities, in the formation and implementation of policy implies a decentralized, adaptive bureaucracy sensitive to contextual change. I argue that the way to use discretion creatively and at the same time create client empowerment is through the use of social movements, and that social movements ought to be considered an integral, essential part of the policy process. What this means, though, is that the public agency has to be responsive to the demands and activities of the social movement actors.

Discretion, decentralization, flexibility, and social movements openly introduce and acknowledge the element of contingency in public policy. Decentralization and discretion allow for the bad as well as the good; indeed, one of the animating ideas behind the normative side of Weberian bureaucracy and the legal rights revolution is to reduce the bad that flowed from decentralization and discretion—in Weberian terms, the bias and favoritism under traditional authority; in legal rights terms, the discrimination and lawlessness in, for example, old-style welfare as well as a great many other social welfare programs. Rationalization has its ethical content—equality and fairness in treatment; the appeal to formal, impersonal rules; the bourgeois demand for legal equality. Does the introduction of decentralization, discretion, flexibility, and social movements give up these goals? Does it open the way for the abuses of old-style welfare, of the South before *Brown* v. *Board of Education*? (Gilbert 1983).

There are other concerns as well. The attack from the right also speaks in terms of centralization versus decentralization, although it is usually phrased in terms of regulation versus deregulation. There are many threads to this argument, but one of them is to allow firms and organizations to operate free of many of the health, safety, environmental, consumer, and civil rights laws that have been so painfully constructed over the past two decades.

One answer to these concerns is that the promises of centralization and control are, to a great extent, illusory. We may believe that we have constructed rational, efficient, hierarchically controlled organizations that are pursuing agreed-upon goals, but this is not the truth (March and Olsen 1979; J. W. Meyer 1980a). It does not describe the behavior of organizations, public or private. Despite Weberian ideology, organizations are characterized by decentralization, discretion, bargaining, and adaptation. It is time to recognize the centrality of organization characteristics, to deal with these characteristics in a positive and creative attempt, to move discretion in desired directions rather than to deny or lament its existence. This is one of the important reasons for encouraging social movement activity. If a basic characteristic of an organization is its ability to adapt to environmental change, and if organizations bargain and negotiate rules rather than treat them as constraints, then the creation and enhancement of social movement groups will change the environment and the bargaining.

Nevertheless, the substantive outcome is still uncertain. All that I have said so far is that I want to change how organizational discretion is exercised, that there will be bargaining with social movement groups as well as clients. Outcomes are still open. The social movement organizations and the agencies may cooperate in ways that are contrary to public policy. There could be corruption, cooptation, discrimination, or other unacceptable views of public policy (Furniss 1974). Arguments in favor of decentralization and discretion speak of variation and flexibility as desirable, or at least as worth the cost of creative implementation along particular paths. But how high is that cost? In the social welfare programs that we consider, we are again talking about the most powerless in our society. If there is variation, corruption, discrimination, and other failures to achieve public goals, the burden, once again, will fall on the despised minorities, the poor, the deviant (Gilbert 1983).

I discussed this issue in arguing for the retention of the rule of law in consensual decision making. I endorsed Thompson's plea that however imperfect the rule of law was, it was too important in the history of liberalism to be jettisoned. This issue was discussed in terms of representation and access, and the argument was made that a system of rights had to be kept in reserve if social movement groups were not sufficiently responsive to members or outsiders. The same argument applies to the response of the bureaucracy. The object of the exercise is to have the bureaucracy respect and enhance the dignitary values of clients. It is reasonable and prudent to be prepared for failures here as well.

There can also be system or policy failures when, for example, groups and agencies together refuse to follow public values. A large part of the growth of the federal bureaucracy in social welfare was a response to the demands to correct and prevent systemwide failures on the part of states and localities. These were not only financial failures. One of the conditions of state participation in federal AFDC grants-in-aid was the requirement that the program be uniform throughout the state. In some states, there would otherwise be no program in counties that were heavily black or Indian. Under any system of decentralization and discretion, overriding national rights would have to be enforced.

It is important to determine the boundaries within which decentralization and discretion have to operate. The Weberian/legal rights approach contracts the boundaries, draws the circle tight, reduces the areas of discretion in the client/agency interaction. However, it is an illusion to push rules that far, and inappropriate as well. But where would the line be draw? One can obviously agree in terms of basic constitutional rights. There are many other boundary lines where there would be far less agreement. Substantive outcomes are uncertain. While this is viewed as a regrettable feature under the Weberian/ legal rights approach, it is openly acknowledged under the decentralized, discretionary approach. But where to draw the parameters of that discretion is not apparent; it depends on the substantive considerations of the specific program and the conditions of discretion.

I turn now to the descriptive section of the chapter: theories of organizations and the characteristics of the loosely coupled open system.

Organizations: Characteristics

Under what circumstances can an organization be induced to change along desired directions, and how can that course be maintained? In terms of the case example, how can a school district be induced to adopt and maintain a consensual form of decision making for special education? More generally, we ask the same questions for organizations where client/agency relationships are discretionary and continuous.

When we look at organizations for purposes of analysis, I start with two perspectives. One perspective looks at the internal structure. Under what circumstances are organizations flexible? How do they change? Is change purposeful? How is it maintained? The other perspective looks at the organizational environment. Since social movement activity is intended to be a crucial ingredient, we must inquire into the relationship between organizations and their environments. Under what circumstances are organizations adaptive to environmental influences?

The distinction that I have just made between an organization and its environment is a much debated point in the organizational literature. Many argue—and indeed, that is the position that will be adopted here—that the boundaries between organizations and their environments are permeable rather than fixed, blurred rather than distinct, and that organizations (at least the kind that we are concerned with) are constantly adapting or attempting to adapt to environmental conditions. Put more strongly, the very survivability of the organizations depends on its ability to adapt to changes in the environment. This view, of course, fits with the normative thesis, namely, that the essential role of social movement activity is to induce and maintain desired organizational behavior.

Organizations: Rational, Natural, and Open

Scott, in his recent text on organizations (1981), describes three basic views of organizations. The *rational* perspective views organizations as designed to achieve specific goals. The term "rational" is used in a technical sense: Is activity organized in such a way as to achieve the goals in the most efficient manner? The goals are given; rationality is concerned with implementation. According to Scott, the distinguishing feature of rational systems theorists is their emphasis on the specification of goals as desired ends and a formalized structure. Specific goals will determine the organizational structure; that is, they will specify the tasks to be done, the kind of personnel required, and the allocation of resources. Quite often an organization will have vague general goals but in its day-to-day operations will pursue fairly specific goals that allow choice among alternatives and determine organizational structure. The example Scott gives is education. There is little or no agreement on the fundamental goals of education but a lot of agreement on the disciplines to be represented, the number of units required for graduation, and the type of courses required.

Simon (1947) modified the rational system perspective by substituting the "administrative man" for the "economic man." The economic man is motivated by self-interest and has complete information about all possible alternatives. The administrative man may also be motivated by self-interest, but he does not always know what his interests are; he lacks complete information, he is aware of only a few of the possible alternatives, and he settles for an adequate solution instead of pursuing the optimal solution. He "satisfices" rather than optimizes. This is the concept of "bounded rationality." In Simon's view, organizations tend to simplify decisions and then to support the participants in the decisions that have to be made.

The importance of the rational Weberian theory is not so much whether it exists, or ever has (McNeil 1978; Smith 1983; March and Olsen 1979); rather, its importance lies in its ideology. The concept of the rational bureaucratic model is viewed as the norm, as the basic prerequisite of any modern, sophisticated society. It is the standard by which present organizations are judged. Disparities from the Weberian model are viewed as deficiencies, maladjustments (Gawthrop 1978). It is a conception of an orderly society that views implementation as the neutral, rational, efficient carrying out of policy (Edelman 1964).

The *natural* systems perspective developed out of a critique of the rational systems perspective. Whereas the latter viewed organizations as collectivities designed to achieve certain goals, the former views organizations primarily as collectivities only. Organizations are viewed more in terms of social systems, of self-maintaining systems, whose one overriding goal is survival as an end in itself rather than achieving agreed-upon goals. In order to survive, the organization must satisfy a stable set of internal needs and at the same time adapt to demands made in its environment.

The formal structure, while it exists, is supplemented, eroded, and transformed by informal structures. Natural systems theorists all emphasize that organizational participants bring to the job their whole personalities—their ideas, expectations, values, agendas, and abilities—and that these informal relationships are structured and orderly. Within organizations, there are informal norms and behavior patterns, systems, networks, working arrangements. Natural systems theorists argue that the rational system is often pathological, that attempts to program behavior are often misguided and inefficient and prevent an organization from using its talent creatively. Underlying the naturalist perspective is a structural-functional model of analysis. The organization has certain survival needs; specific structures are analyzed in terms of the needs that they meet.

Selznick (1949) agrees with the rationalists that organizations are designed to accomplish particular objectives, but he argues that these formal structures can never succeed in conquering the "nonrational" aspects of organizational behavior—individuals are "wholes" rather than organizational role players, and formal structure is only one aspect of the social structure that must adjust to various institutional pressures. Individuals in organizations bring commitments that restrict their capacity to act in rational ways; organizational procedures become ends in themselves; and the organization adapts to its environment as well as the characteristics and commitments of its participants in ways that compromise its objectives and limit its choices. The overriding need is self-defense, self-maintenance. In meeting these needs, one should look not only at formal structures but also at irregular methods such as informal structures, ideologies, and cooptation. One usually finds that organizations change their goals, not necessarily the stated goals but the operative goals, in the face of hostile environments (Scott 1981, p. 91).

The third perspective views organizations as *open systems* that are *loosely coupled*. Loosely coupled means that the parts of the organization are only slightly related to each other and are capable of fairly autonomous action (Weick 1976). This analytical framework is different from rational theory, where the parts of the organization are integrated through rules and hierarchical relationships, and from natural theory where the organization is viewed as an organic community. Theorists such as Cyert, March, Pfeffer, and Salancik view organizations as shifting coalitions of special interest groups, each pursuing its goals and objectives as it perceives them. This does not necessarily lead to chaos and self-destruction; on the contrary, these theorists maintain that loose coupling allows an organization to be highly adaptive to its environment (Scott 1981).

The distinguishing feature of the open-system perspective is the relationship of the organization to the environment (M. W. Meyer 1979). Because of the intimate connection between the organization and the environment, the difficulty comes in defining the boundary between the two. Individuals bring only part of themselves to the organization; their other activities relate to other subsystems, and all subsystems are parts of other systems. Open-system organizations spend a great deal of energy in both maintaining boundaries and spanning boundaries. The open systems theorists say that not only is there a close connection between the system and the environment, but the latter is also the source of diversity and variety in the system. As distinguished from the other views of organizations, the primary focus here is on the interdependence with the environment, the ultimate source for resources, information, and energy.

Within the open-system perspective are various theories. In view of the interdependence with the environment, it would follow that the effectiveness of the organization would depend on the nature of the environment. This is contingency theory. Organizations will do better to the extent that their internal structures match the demands imposed environmentally. Contexts characterized by uncertainty and rapid change will impose different kinds of demands on an organization than will a stable environment. Contingency theorists emphasize the importance of processing information. Structural arrangements, such as rules, hierarchies, and decentralization, are mechanisms for processing information. The more uncertainty, the greater the information processing needs, and structural arrangements have to be altered to meet these demands.

Other open-system theorists put more emphasis on the direct importance of the environment. This is a resource dependent model (Zald 1970). The environment is viewed as a source of resources and constraints that can act independent of an organization but also has the capacity to profoundly shape the activities of the organization. The organization, though, is not passive. It is actively engaged in dealing with the environment, in determining its own fate (Perrow 1979). Managers are actively engaged in trying to assert power over critical elements of the environment or at least in trying to reduce their dependency on these elements.

The analysis has been extended. According to Perrow, one needs to use a "network" analysis if one is truly to get a picture of organizational behavior. In network analysis, there is a wider definition of the organizational field. In the United States, for example, if one wanted to examine the behavior of a local public organization or a local private organization that had public monies, one would look not only at other public and private agencies at the same level but also at organizations at the state and federal levels. The same would be true for private firms. They too are affected by a host of federal and state laws. Organizations are "nestled" in hierarchies (M. W. Meyer 1979; Freeman 1980). Organizations at all three jurisdictional levels, both public and private, are the network.

It is the network, says Perrow, that is the unit of analysis. Within the network, organizations may be either tightly or loosely coupled. They may be aware of each other, but this does not mean that every change affects everything else. Parts of the network may be buffered from other parts; there may be strong or weak links between parts. Perrow would prefer to dissolve the boundaries between an organization and its environment; he would look at an organization in terms of the groups within and without the organization that are using the organization for their own purposes. He sees organizations as interactive processes, full of accidents and opportunities for short-run opportunities.

According to Scott (1981), the current view is to look at organizations as open natural systems; organizations worry primarily about survival rather than about achieving certain goals and, these theorists maintain, it is only rare that achieving goals and survival coincide. Because of the complexity and uncertainty of the environment, survival is a difficult game. In a highly structured environment, the organization will pay more attention to externally imposed rules than to achieving goals. In environments where goals and technologies are unclear, according to March and Olsen (1979), rational decision-making models have little applicability; there is little connection between individual preferences and behavior, between actions, choices, and environmental responses.

Organizational Change: Environments

How, then, do open systems change? First, we turn to environments; then, we will see how organization actors cope with environmental demands.

Scott (1981) reports that a widely employed approach is to view environments along two dimensions—as sources of information and resources. Information is related to the degree of uncertainty that organizations face; resources relate to problems of dependency. The issue then is what types of strategies organizations adopt to meet these two problematic situations.

Scott summarizes some of the factors that organization scholars point to as affecting these problem situations. Uncertainty is affected by the amount of heterogeneity in the environment, for example, the number of different kinds of clients a social agency has to serve; the amount of instability in the environment; the amount and type of other organizations that are linked together; the degree of organization in the environment. Factors affecting dependence are the degrees of scarcity, concentration, and organization. "The greater the scarcity of resources, the higher the degree of concentration, and the greater the degree of organization exhibited by entities within the environment, the greater the dependence of the organization" (Scott 1981, p. 169). Scott points out that the two dimensions do not necessarily co-vary; a high degree of concentration in the environment can reduce uncertainty but increase dependency.

Another way of looking at environments concerns levels; scholars talk of community, fields, networks, domains, or sets. The idea is to try to map the interconnections between the organization and the various entities that it deals with. Scott points out that all of these concepts are fraught with definitional and empirical difficulties. Of particular interest is the controversy over whether environmental characteristics are subjective (that is, dependent on the perceptions) or objective. Subjectivists argue that only perception is relevant since behavior can be based only on perception. Some go farther: organizational participants do not react to environmental stimuli; rather, they enact the stimuli. Structure and information-processing systems profoundly affect the information that is received by the organization. Individuals (in organizations) "see what they want to see and believe what they want to believe in" (March and Olsen 1979). Others argue that although environments have to be perceived if organizational behavior is to be affected, environments can still affect organizations whether perceived or not (Pfeffer 1981).

"The central insight emerging from the open system model is that all organizations are incomplete: all depend on exchanges with other systems. All are open to environmental influences as a condition of their survival" (Scott 1981, p. 179). On the one hand, an organization has to maintain its boundaries, its institutional integrity, to reduce uncertainty; on the other hand, because it is dependent on the environment for resources, it has to span boundaries. One set of strategies is called "buffering"—reducing uncertainty at the technical core of the organization—and the other is called "bridging"—increasing the security of the organization through links with environmental entities. The technical core refers to the central task of the organization, the mechanisms for doing the work—teaching in schools, laboratory work in research institutions, constructing products in factories.

Bridging strategies involve power and exchange relations. Power is not a generalized concept; it is specifically related to the particular needs and functions of the actors and varies from one actor to another. Power is specific to the context or relationship; a person is "powerful" in relation to another person or persons, not in the abstract. However, the power relationship is not necessarily related to a limited set of decisions (Pfeffer 1981). Power is not necessarily a zero-sum game, that is, when one gains, another loses. Rather, two actors can gain power by becoming interdependent.

Scott emphasizes the importance of the links between technology and the environment—in his view, "the major source of the work techniques and tools employed. Most organizations do not themselves invent their technologies but import them from the environment" (Scott 1981, p. 209).

While Scott emphasizes the influence of technology as well as other environmental forces—the market, the occupational system, the legal order—on organizational structure, other scholars look to different environmental influences. The political model would look to the importance of political groups both within and without the organization (Zald 1970; Perrow 1979; Pfeffer 1981). Pfeffer views organizations as political coalitions; when preferences conflict, the power of various social actors determines organizational choice. The power model differs from the rational model in that under the former there are no overarching organizational goals. Even if there are, decisions are made that are inconsistent with maximizing those goals, that is, they are made to further the political interests of the dominant coalition. In building coalitions, Pfeffer argues, organizations operate exactly in reverse of political institutions. In politics, the idea is the minimum coalition—getting just enough actors necessary to achieve the particular victory. Organizations, though, have to think in terms of long-term implementation. It makes no sense to reach a decision if there is a great deal of opposition and if implementation depends on the interdependence of hostile actors. In organizations, therefore, the strategy is to build a maximum coalition, and to continue to build the coalition after the decision is reached.

Depending on the situation, certain political strategies are useful. Many organizations build and use the support of outside constituencies. Agencies that deliver social services, money, or other benefits to various groups typically develop strong alliances with their beneficiaries, which can then be mobilized if the organization is threatened.

This is often an effective tactic, although there may be real costs to organizational autonomy. While the organization seeks to coopt others by bringing them into the decision-making structure, it introduces new sources of information, beliefs, and judgments. The new group may defer to the organizational group; or there may be mutual influences; or the organization may, over time, change as a result of the power and influence of the outside group. Lipsky (1980) argues that street-level bureaucrats are constrained by the need to keep their clients content. It is the political model that leads Perrow to conclude that the most useful way to view organizations is to dissolve as much as possible the boundaries between organizations and their environments, and to speak in terms of groups within and without the organization using it for their own purposes.

The common view is that there is a great deal of environmental uncertainty and that if organizations are to survive, they must be readily adaptable. DiMaggio and Powell (1983) challenge this view. Whereas others see change and seek to explain variation, they see great homogeneity and seek to explain stability. Their argument is as follows: Weber argued that bureaucratization resulted from three related causes—competition among firms; competition among states (thus, increasing the ruler's need to control his staff and subjects); and the demands of the bourgeoisie for equal protection by the laws. Weber considered the forces of the market most important. DiMaggio and Powell say that the causes of bureaucratization have now changed. The bureaucratization of the corporation and the state have largely been accomplished; hence, structural change today is driven less by competition. Today, the most important source of bureaucratization is what the authors call the structuration of the organizational field. The state and the professions have become the great rationalizers, and these highly structured fields lead, in aggregate, to homogeneity in structure, culture, and output.

Once an organization becomes structured into a field, powerful forces are set in motion which lead it to become similar to other similarly situated organizations. The metaphor is isomorphism, the constraining process that forces one unit in a population to resemble other units that face the same set of environmental conditions. Organizational isomorphism is of two types—competitive and institutional. Organizations compete not only for resources and customers but also for political power and institutional legitimacy.

DiMaggio and Powell identify three types of institutional isomorphic processes. There is *coercive* pressure. Sometimes organizations are forced to change as a direct result of a government mandate. Coercion can also be indirect—cultural expectations, persuasion, invitations to join. The existence of a common legal environment affects many aspects of an organization's behavior and structure. Organizations increasingly use rituals (for example, credentials) and ceremony to conform to their environment (J. W. Meyer and Rowan 1980), but these, in the opinion of the authors, are not without consequences; the actors become involved in advocating their functions, and may, in the long run, alter power relations within the organization (Scott 1981).

Less direct isomorphic change comes from *mimicry* and *normative* pressures. Uncertainty, argue the authors, encourages imitation. When technologies are poorly understood, or goals and environmental demands are conflicting or ambiguous, organizations will tend to model themselves after other organizations. Normative pressure stems primarily from professionalization. Formal education, professional networks, licensing, and credentialing all span organizations. The filtering of personnel makes people at the top virtually indistinguishable.

DiMaggio and Powell develop a number of propositions out of this analysis that are relevant to our concerns. For example, they argue that the more uncertain the relationship between means and ends, the greater the extent to which an organization will model itself after other organizations that it perceives to be successful. Thus, one would expect diffusion in areas characterized by discretionary decisions. Another proposition is that the greater the dependence of an organization on another, the more similar it will become in structure, climate, and behavior. Thus, the theory of public action, with its emphasis on social movement organizations, would predict organizational change.

Meyer and Rowan also use the isomorphism concept. They start with two related questions: What accounts for formal structure, and, more specifically, what accounts for loose coupling? That is, given the Weberian forces leading to bureaucratization, why would organizations become loosely coupled rather than tightly coupled? This, according to the authors, is because observers usually ignore another Weberian source of bureaucratization—the legitimacy of rationalized formal structures in the organizational domain.

We have powerful institutionalized rules in society which function as highly rationalized myths that are binding on particular organizations. Many of our ideologies define organizational functions—in business, sales, production, advertising, research; in universities, teaching, tenure; in hospitals, surgery, internal medicine. Classifications and specifications of function are prefabricated formulae available for organizations. Even technologies are institutionalized and become binding myths. Procedures for data processing, accounting, personnel management are taken for granted. Financial institutions have econometrics departments. Manufacturing plants have pollution and safety departments. Not only are these procedures taken for granted, they are considered appropriate, rational, and modern; their use displays responsibility and avoids claims of negligence (Meyer and Rowan 1977, pp. 343–345).

Meyer and Rowan claim that the impact of such institutionalized rules in society on organizations is enormous. Organizations incorporate these procedures to display their legitimacy. As rationalized, institutional rules arise, organizations may incorporate them as structural elements, or new organizations may arise. Many of these rules are based on legal mandates; thus, the stronger the rational legal order, the more institutionalized rules and procedures become organizational requirements.

Meyer and Rowan call the incorporation of institutionalized rules institutional isomorphism, and they argue that it promotes the success and survivability of organizations. By incorporating the externally legitimate formal structures, the organization increases the commitments of external constituents and internal participants. By conforming to institutional myths, the organization protects itself from being questioned.

The implications of these lines of analyses are that there is a great deal of organizational change. Three types of environmental factors are important: technology, interest group or social movement activity, and institutionalized myth and ceremony. All seem to be exceedingly active in contemporary America. The environment, according to Scott, is the primary source of new ideas and resources; given the state of the economy, the rapid development of certain kinds of industries, and the growth of scientific knowledge, it would seem that organizations susceptible to technological change are in a period of considerable uncertainty.

So too, we are still in a period of great social movement activity. If we view organizations as collections of shifting political coalitions engaged in forming and reforming alliances, then the rise and fall of citizen advocacy groups as well as the continued proliferation of special interest groups also contribute to an uncertain environment. Environmentalists, consumers, women's groups, and civil rights groups seek to influence organizations as much as suppliers, customers, competitors, and trade associations.

The growth of institutionalized domains continues without much sign of abatement. In some areas, there has been a slowing down of regulation, but this is probably only temporary, and it is limited. In other areas, for example, health, the drive seems to be to increase regulation. In addition, the legal liability system is expanding, thus inducing organizations to adopt even more ceremony and myth to preserve or enhance the appearance of accountability and responsibility. There does not seem to be a letup in professionalization, certification, and ceremonial evaluation.

But what kinds of changes will these environmental demands make in organizations? The common-sense view is that there will be an increase in organizational instability; some organizations will adapt, others will not. Yet, current thinking leans toward the opposite. Most seem to agree with DiMaggio, Powell, J. W. Meyer, and Rowan that the higher the uncertainty, the more organizations will come to resemble each other. Coercion, mimicry, normative pressures, the language of confidence and accountability will produce change. There will be widespread and rapid diffusion of institutionalized rules, but it will be isomorphic, homogeneous, and stabilizing rather than chaotic (Pfeffer; Perrow; J. W. Meyer; Lipsky). This is ironic, but the real problem, according to DiMaggio and Powell, is how to *maintain* and *encourage* organizational diversity in a pluralist society.

We turn now to the inside. Environments impose various demands on organizations. What determines organizational response?

"Inside" the Organization: Goals, Power, and Authority

How goals are determined, and what purposes they serve, depends on one's view of organizations. In a rational perspective, goals are determined and then used to direct and evaluate behavior. In a natural system, goals are used to attach participants and others in the environment to the organization as a social system. Goals can seek emotional, ideological, or motivational ends. Some researchers sharply challenge these views. Simon (1947) views organizational goals as constraints. If an actor can determine the constraints, he can in effect determine the decision. However, individuals in organizations have limited capacities to process information and limited research to look for the most rational alternatives. It was Simon who developed the idea of "bounded rationality," and coined the term "satisficing." March and Olsen (1979) view organizations as political coalitions. When preferences conflict, the power of various social actors determines the outcomes. They go farther; they argue that goals are rationalizations, justifications for actions already taken.

Organizational participants are problem solvers and decision makers. Organizational choice is always ambiguous because participants have limited attention and knowledge; they operate under constraints (and often are unaware of the constraints); and their choices may not be acted on. There are no overall organizational goals, and no powerful actors with defined preferences who possess sufficient resources to obtain those preferences. Rather, instead of preferences guiding choice, choice determines preferences. "In other words, one only knows what one likes after it has been experienced . . ." (Pfeffer 1981, p. 25). The action itself is the result of habit, custom, or the influence of other social actors in the environment.

Politics and the use of power will arise when there is scarcity and conflicts over goals and/or technology. One important source of goal and technology disagreement is differentiation, when there are dissimilarities in perspectives, goal orientations, and technological understanding. Different subunits have different tasks and receive different information. The more differentiated the work roles in the organization, the more heterogeneous beliefs and goals are likely to be.

Scarcity provides the incentive for political conflict, but scarcity is a relative concept. Resources that come to be defined as scarce are perceived as being more valuable. Slack resources reduce the amount of interdependence and the potential for conflict. One can also reduce conflict by avoidance, by labeling the decision as relatively unimportant. Political language is used to mask conflict. Choices are rationalized; issues are clouded; symbols are used to give the appearance of implementation (Pfeffer 1981; Edelman 1964). In organizations where ritual and ceremony are important, symbolic action maintains the legitimacy of the organization and quiets opposition. Symbolic political language is also important when participants have unclear preferences or when evaluation is problematic; key actors or constituents may then only want reassurance that their interests are being taken seriously. They may not want to know the actual results.

How, then, is power distributed in an organization? Subunits within organizations that are able to cope more effectively with environmental uncertainty are more likely to acquire power. These units can protect the other units from the disturbances caused by the uncertainty, but in so doing, they parlay environmental uncertainty into organizational power. If, over time, the uncertainty declines (or the work becomes routinized), power may decline.

When organizational tasks become divided, it is inevitable that some tasks will become more important than others, and those persons or units having the responsibility for performing the more important tasks will inevitably become more powerful. Although individual skills and strategies can certainly affect the amount and effectiveness of power, power is basically a structural phenomenon (Pfeffer 1981).

Power is also related to the substitutability and the centrality of the activities of the subunit. To the extent that the work of the subunit is important for other units in the organization, and to the extent that only that subunit can do the work, the subunit will be powerful in the organization.

Slack resources are important in the exercise of power. Slack resources are resources in excess of what has already been committed. Slack resources quickly become an integral part of regular operations. This absorption makes it possible to capture organizations with relatively small amounts of resources. Often great control can be exercised if there is discretionary control over even small amounts of resources. The difference is between the large, fixed portion of the budget and the small discretionary extra that will permit change, adaptation, new activities, and so forth. What was once slack and discretionary then quickly becomes necessity, and if the actors still have discretionary power over the funds, they become very powerful. The key factor is not the relative amount of the budget but the proportion of the discretionary funds.

Power is exercised through coalition building. Organizational politics may involve the formation of coalitions with others either inside or outside the formally designated organization boundaries. As previously discussed, coalition building continues after decisions are made; because decisions are continuous, there is a continous effort to build and maintain a consensus, to maintain commitments.

The political model suggests that organizations are characterized by uncertainty and conflict. How then do organizations control their subordinates? Scott's focus is on the structure of power and authority. Authority is defined as legitimate power. Legitimacy is the set of social norms that define situations as correct or appropriate. These norms guide the expectations of the participants; out of this stable role structure, leaders are expected to lead and subordinates are expected to obey. Personal power appears to be impersonal; authority structures become more stable and more effective control systems than power structures. Legitimacy also serves to restrain the exercise of power. Especially when subordinates are considered as a group, an area is defined in which power can be appropriately exercised. "[L]egitimate power is normatively regulated power" (Scott 1981, p. 281).

Beliefs and practices come to be accepted and bind together those within the setting. Activities that are accepted and expected within a context are legitimate within that context. The distribution of power within a social setting can become legitimated over time, so that those within a setting expect and value a certain pattern of influence. Power, then, becomes authority; the exercise of influence is transformed and becomes expected and desired in the social context. Once power is transformed through legitimacy into authority, it is not resisted and no longer depends on the resources or determinants that may have produced the power in the first place. In other words, authority is maintained not only by the resources and sanctions that produced the power but also by the social pressures and norms that define the power distribution as normal and acceptable. This adds stability and makes the exercise of power easier and more effective. But legitimation is also socially specific; thus, it is ultimately contingent and far from inevitable (Pfeffer 1981).

Given the power of lower-level subordinates (Mechanic 1962), the interesting question is why they do not exercise their power and resist instructions from managers. Employees do not behave this way. They do not compare their power with the power of managers and then decide whether to obey or not. "Rather, most of the time in most work settings the authority of the manager to direct the work activities is so legitimated and taken for granted, that issues of relative power and sanctions seldom become consciously considered" (Pfeffer 1981, p. 5). When power is transformed into authority, subordinates obey reasonable instructions because they expect to. Thus, control can be exercised regardless of the balance of power possessed by the respective groups.

In the end, power is stable in most organizations most of the time. Administrators usually persist in their commitments. Beliefs and practices become institutionalized, become unquestioned and taken as objective reality, mainly because of presumptions of rationality, stability, and authority. Those who possess power usually have the means of increasing it (Pfeffer 1981).

Thus, looking at organizations from the inside out or the outside in, one comes to the same conclusion: the dominant patterns are those of stability, routinization, and homogeneity. This, of course, follows the definition of loosely coupled open systems with its great emphasis on the importance of the environment. The amount of uncertainty or stability, of change or institutionalization that one sees in the environment depends on the eye of the beholder. What seems to be less problematic, though, is the response of the organization. Loose coupling allows for change and adaptation. There seems to be a great deal of diffusion throughout similarly situated organizations. Through isomorphic processes, beliefs and practices become so widespread that they are accepted without question. These changes can be either symbolic or real. In certain organizations (for example, education), the symbols of ceremony and myth are the very essence of survival. In other organizations, according to Starbuck (1983), changes in symbols only are a sure road to death.

Schools as Organizations

It should come as no surprise that schools are generally considered loosely coupled open systems. Indeed, Weick (1976) first used the term in describing schools; much of the empirical work of March and his colleagues concerns universities, and the basic articles of J. W. Meyer, Rowan, and Sproull concern public schools.

Meyer and Rowan have done the most systematic analysis of public schools. The view that they present is one of both tight and loose coupling. Schools are tightly coupled in such matters as hiring and credentialing of teachers, assigning students, scheduling. On the other hand, there is very little supervision or evaluation of what goes on in the classroom. Schools have elaborate tests to evaluate pupils, but the data are rarely used to evaluate teachers, schools, or school systems. There is relatively little concern with teaching technology or detailed instructional programs. Educational administrators have little control over what goes on in the classroom. The result is that there are elaborate rules specifying when education occurs, but not as to what the categories of education actually mean.

Schools are remarkably successful organizations. Despite occasional ups and downs, schools enjoy widespread public confidence and support. They are stable, they have the ability to command large amounts of public resources, and they have grown rapidly. How do they manage to do this?

Meyer and Rowan's interpretation is that schools produce education for *society*, not for individuals and families. They are the central agency defining personnel. In order to do this for a market economy, there has to be a standardized product, readily identifiable—in their words, a trustworthy currency. In education, this is accomplished by the "schooling rule": education means a certified teacher teaching a standardized curricular topic to a registered student in an accredited school. The legitimacy (and success) of the school depends crucially on close adherence to the rituals and forms that comprise the shared social understanding of what constitutes a school—accreditation, credentials, "innovative" programs, prestigious faculty, and the like.

But the close adherence to societally determined rules presents problems. The rules may be inconsistent; they may be burdensome or difficult to implement in a particular school or classroom; they may be inappropriate. How, then, does the school maintain adherence to institutionalized rules but still carry out its work? It does so by loose coupling. The formal structure (the institutionalized rules) is decoupled from the technical activities (the teaching). Evaluation and inspection are avoided, thus reducing uncertainty. Decoupling allows for flexibility in the classroom; it reduces the costs and stress of coordination; it allows the school to adopt inconsistent or conflicting policies. At the same time, public adherence to the institutional rules is maintained by the logic of confidence. The avoidance of inspection is accompanied by elaborate displays of confidence and trust, which also serve to increase the commitment of the participants. Teachers assume responsibility for upholding the rituals. But in order to pull this off, the "sacred rituals must be carried out by all with the utmost good faith" (Meyer and Rowan 1980, p. 101). The parties bring to each other the good-faith assumption that each is doing his or her job. No one looks behind the credentials, the rituals, the ceremonies; avoidance and the myth of professionalism are applied universally.

Public schools as organizations are the empirical base for the Meyer and Rowan theory of the institutionalized organization. The formal structure is in large part myth. Schools reflect environmental demands by incorporating the wider institutional structures as their own, thereby gaining internal and external legitimacy. The structure presents the appearance of rationality, that what needs to be done is in fact being done. Decoupling is used to accommodate appearances with reality, to separate institutionalized demands from activity (Miles 1980; Purkey and Smith 1982).

This is not to say that schools are impervious to change. Quite the opposite. One of the advantages (and characteristics) of a loosely coupled open system is its adaptiveness. Decoupling allows for environmental response and, at the same time, avoids internal uncertainty. With schools, the response to environmental demands and the ready incorporation of institutionalized rules and roles are highly adaptive. Organizations that can do this, such as schools, derive legitimacy, power, resources, and authority from the environment. Dependency on the environment, then, is a source of strength, not weakness. Thus, their ultimate effectiveness (survivability) is a matter of political agreement and social definition negotiated with the environment (J. W. Meyer 1980b).

Not only are schools responsive to larger, more general institutional demands, they are also highly responsive to local environmental conditions. Schools are attentive to their reputations; they seek out ways to satisfy their local constituencies. There is considerable innovation in the classroom, but it is not centrally directed. Classrooms are relatively autonomous. While this allows the adoption of fashion by individual teachers, such innovations are unlikely to become institutionalized without organizational support.

In short, schools operate within highly pluralistic, multilayered environments. At the macro-level, one sees homogeneity, the institutionalization of societal expectations, the ritual and ceremony. But local environments also make demands on schools. Schools accommodate by decoupling, by avoiding close inspection and evaluation by ritual and ceremony. This strategy is not without consequences for the organization. To maintain their legitimacy, schools must demonstrate that they are obeying the institutionalized rules. The line between technology and institutionalized environments is not clear. In time, technology itself becomes institutionalized. The units within the organization created or redefined to satisfy institutional demands may, in time, become important political actors within the organization.

Loosely coupled open systems can adapt to small changes; large-scale change is more difficult but is usually not necessary to meet environmental demands (Weick 1982).

Change in a loosely coupled organization requires leadership techniques that are different from those in tightly coupled organizations. Leadership in the former requires the management of those symbols that tie the organization together, that is, the articulation of general directions and values. According to Weick, similar socialization is one reason that loosely coupled systems remain systems; socialization is the glue, the source of cohesion. Effective leaders centralize the system on key values. It is their voice and vision that teachers have in common. "People need some shared sense of direction for their efforts which must be built and reaffirmed in loosely coupled systems. . . . People need to be part of sensible projects. Their action becomes richer, more confident, and more satisfying when it is linked with important underlying themes, values, and movements" (Weick 1982, p. 675).

Implications

Where does one emerge from this foray into organizational theory? The initial impression is nowhere, that the theory is in chaos. Some theorists see organizations as rational problem solvers, the collective efforts of people, ideas, and resources. Others see organizations as collections of groups and actors in a continual, dynamic struggle for their own survival.

All seem to agree on the importance of the environment, but how important is it, and for what purpose? Some emphasize the ability of organizations to deflect environmental pressures through the use of myth and ceremony. Others stress isomorphism, the various ways organizations mimic the environment. Still others view boundaries between organizations and environments with skepticism and see organizations as fields of activity for political groups both within and without the organization, using the organization for their own ends. Some go farther, seeking to obliterate the lines between organizations and their "fields" or "networks."

Despite the apparent chaos in organization theory, certain ideas and principles are useful to this essay. The concern here is with organizational change, specifically to restructure school districts to enhance their capacity to utilize consensual forms of decision making. More generally, the goal is to restructure other bureaucracies where client/agency relationships are characterized by discretionary decisions. In light of these tasks, certain statements can be made on the basis of organization theory and research.

The first statement is that organizations do change and are subject to change. This may seem obvious, but it is not. The commonplace view is the opposite. The scholarly literature, especially recently, contributes to this perception.

This view, we know, is not based on reality. Organizations are adaptable, are susceptible to change, and do change. They are sensitive to the environment. The issue, then, is: Under what circumstances do they change, in what directions, and with what results? In keeping with the analysis of this chapter, but for the purposes of analysis only, I will again discuss environmental considerations first, and then turn to the internal dynamics of the organization. At the conclusion of the section, interconnections will be made.

In discussing schools, scholars point to two levels of environmental influence. One is the general, societal, macro-level—the legal, cultural, social, political, professional, and organizational systems and networks; relations with governmental units at the various levels; the broader national influences. The other environmental influence is at the local level—the community, the school board, local government, parents, and citizens. Schools are highly responsive to environmental influences on both levels. For schools, perhaps as distinguished from other organizations, the environment is a source of strength. Schools are successful organizations.

The normative prescription of this book is to change environmental influences, at both levels, through social movement activity. Under the theory of public action, social movement groups are to be active throughout the policy formulation and implementation processes. They bargain for the creation and definition of values, for the structure and content of the legal and administrative framework, for program funds, and they have the responsibility for creating patterns of communicative conflict for all points in the system, especially for parent/teacher interactions, through the creation and support of parent groups, the conducting of workshops and other sources of information, supplying trained parent advocates, the collectivization of grievances and experiences, and the mobilization of resources for change.

In Chapter 8, I will discuss the extent to which this role is likely, but for the purposes of this chapter, I will assume that social movement groups can perform these tasks. What, then, are the likely consequences for school districts? First, I will discuss the optimistic or affirmative side of the case; then, I consider the problems.

To the extent that the social movement groups are successful, there will be uncertainty in the environment. The school districts will react through myth and ceremony; they will respond to the demands of the social movement groups by incorporating institutionalized rules, structures, and procedures and perform enough activity to demonstrate adherence to the rules of the game. We saw this happen with the procedures of the Education for All Handicapped Children Act (P.L. 94–142). There was a rapid diffusion of the procedural structures and rules. The National Academy of Sciences found a high degree of formal compliance with the law. Moreover, this was not just law on the books. The procedures were implemented, after a fashion. There was a large increase in special education enrollments, there were multidisciplinary evaluations and conferences, informed consent forms were signed, there were placements, hearings, and evaluations. In Meyer and Rowan's terms, the schools went to great lengths to demonstrate that the law was being applied.

The facts showed that there was loose coupling, that is, the myth and ceremonial compliance with P.L. 94–142 were decoupled from the teaching tasks, and the law was not working as intended. There was contact with the parents but no communication. Conferences and evaluations tended to be pro forma; once placements were made they tended to stick. Instead of flexibility, experimentation, professional judgments, and reevaluations, deep patterns of routine were established quickly.

The social movement groups, in the jargon of the organizational literature, are supposed to span ceremonial compliance with the work at the classroom level, to change the organization from a loosely coupled to a tightly coupled one in that the work is to be responsive to environmental demands. In the language of those who view organizations in terms of power and politics, the social movement groups form alliances and coalitions with organizational participants and use the schools for their own purposes (Perrow 1979).

The consensus seems to be that at the local level, schools are highly responsive to environmental demands, that a great deal of innovation occurs, but that the innovation needs organizational support if it is to endure. The task, then, is to have the social movement groups create the environmental demands for change and also work for institutional and organizational support. This is done by encouraging communicative conflict at all levels. It is important not to view this relationship in adversarial terms. Rather, it is expected that most often the relationship will be closer to those seen in political alliances. Those who emphasize isomorphism, myth, and ceremony note that these adaptations have organizational consequences. The organization has to demonstrate to its constituents that it is complying; this means the creation of organizational subunits which, over time, may acquire power and influence. Those within an organization who are successful in dealing with environmental uncertainty tend to gain power in the organization. Within school districts, units created to respond to social movement activity will become more powerful to the extent that they can form cooperative relationships (political alliances) with the demanding social movement groups.

Although I am citing social movement groups for their ability to create responsiveness, they represent only one small part of the system. Weick and others note it is relatively easy for a loosely coupled system to accommodate demands for small change; it is much harder to accomplish widespread change. Pfeffer (1981) makes the same point—it is relatively easy to effect organizational change with small amounts of money. This is the perspective to keep in mind. Although I am talking about a large change, it is within the context of a small unit of the organization that can easily be segregated from the other parts of the organization if the school districts so desire. In other words, there is no reason to assume that consensual decision making has to be adopted for other decisions.

Social movement groups, while essential, cannot accomplish these objectives alone. This is a major point of this book. There have to be changes in the leadership and staff of the school districts as well.

The staff has to be committed. Ultimately, the test of the program rests on the quality of the interaction between the teacher, the parent, and the pupil. Here, ideology can be important. Ways of looking at people and problems make a difference. It will be recalled that the Madison School District adopted several crucial conceptual positions—that parents are part of the solution rather than the problem, and, because special education decisions have to be tentative, flexible, and experimental, that decisions are to be continuous and not in terms of winners and losers. Changes in attitudes precede changes in structure. Perrow argues that technology is not objectively determined; rather, ideology—the varying ways in which organizations view mental patients, students, welfare recipients, the handicapped—determines technology. It was the change in ideology on the part of the leadership and the staff that makes consensual decision making work in the Madison School District. The fundamental concepts reduce adversarial conflict and allow for the growth of communicative conflict. Conflict can now be handled within the overarching frame of flexibility, autonomy, and consensus.

In addition to preserving and enhancing dignitary values in the discretionary decision, there are two other features of this model that have distinct benefits. The model results in diversity of application. Social movement activity, decentralization, individualized treatment, flexibility, and continuous processes are messy. There will be a variety of forms, various styles of application, and the full range of successes and failures. This type of implementation does not comport with the Weberian ideal for a sophisticated modern government. It does not comport with conceptions of bureaucratic government arising out of the New Deal. the modern, efficient, centralized, uniform welfare state. Rather, the model welcomes and encourages discretion at the local level. As argued in Chapter 6, to impose uniformity of application is impossible. There are many reasons in support of this assertion, but the principal one is that we lack the administrative and political capacity to control local government, especially in areas such as education with such strong local traditions. But, it is the position here that in view of the values and interests involved and the substantive nature of the work, it is inappropriate to even strive for uniformity of application. Both the work—the education of handicapped

children—and the dignitary values of individualism require flexibility, experimentation, and discretion, which have to be supported by
social movement activity. Social movement activity, in turn, means
diversity. Movements will vary in terms of character, strength, values,
and success, which in turn will produce various effects on the organization. In sum, there is virtually no chance of fulfilling substantive
and liberal values in a hierarchical, legalistic, uniform system; but
there is, I think, a good chance if the theory of public action is
adopted, carrying with it diversity at the local level.

The second beneficial feature of this model is the larger value of
myth and ceremony. Granted, Meyer and Rowan argue, myth and
ceremony in a loosely coupled system may not be efficient in the
specific, day-to-day operations, but in the long run it may be better for
society if organizations adopt the larger societal values. To some extent we do this now—with the mythical and ceremonial adoption of
the rule of law and the procedural due process values of P.L. 94–142,
although it is far from obvious that this is a social benefit. Indeed, the
myth and ceremony of P.L. 94–142 look more like the symbolic reassurance that serves to mask the underlying realities of bureaucratic
domination and control (Edelman 1964). The consensual form of
decision making will, I hope, encourage a richer variation on the
values of autonomy and individualism in client/agency interactions.
By deemphasizing the means/ends distinctions and the adversarial
process, there will be a more complete concept of the individual to the
modern welfare state.

I believe that these benefits are possible, but only after major problems are addressed. In my model, the actors are committed, they
believe in themselves and what they are doing; they are professionals
who are trained in their tasks. Nevertheless, organizational participants work with limited resources. Inevitably, there will be problems
of routinization, cooptation, and the development of new myths and
ceremonies. Under the best of circumstances, routinization will be a
great danger. Conflict produces stress. Even under the model presented here, there will be stress and great demands on energy. It is
impossible for decision makers to avoid the temptation to classify
today's problem in terms of yesterday's categories and solutions. We
noticed that the dedicated and supportive teachers in the Madison
School District worried a great deal about routinization.

In addition, there is the specter of cooptation. Ironically, the very success of the system increases the risk. A proud belief in the values and successes of achievement infects the participants and constituents.

It seems to me that the problems of routinization and cooptation are every bit as serious as the problems of creating a properly functioning consensual model. The burden of continuous implementation cannot be handled by the leadership and staff alone. A heavy burden is also placed on the social movement groups. I am relying on them to challenge the process of routinization, cooptation, and the negative consequences of myth and ceremony. But social movement groups are also organizations—they too are subject to the processes of routinization and cooptation. There are two sides to this issue. One is concerned with the relationship between the social movement groups and the agency. To what extent will the social movement groups become partners with the school districts, resulting in corporatism, or, to use Lowi's (1969) phrase, institutionalized pluralism? The other question is the relationship between the social movement group and the parents. To what extent will it coopt or exclude efforts at change from below? These two questions are the subject of the next chapter.

REFERENCES

Bardach, Eugene, and Kagan, Robert A. *Going by the Book: The Problem of Regulatory Unreasonableness.* Philadelphia: Temple University Press, 1982.

Benson, J. Kenneth. "Innovation and Crisis in Organizational Analysis." *Sociological Quarterly,* 18 (Winter 1977), pp. 3–16.

Benson, J. Kenneth. "Organizations: A Dialectical View." *Administrative Science Quarterly,* 22 (March 1977). pp. 1–21.

Burrell, Gibson, and Morgan, Gareth. *Sociological Paradigms and Organizational Analysis.* London: Heineman, 1979.

Christensen, Soren. "Decision-Making and Socialization." In J. G. March and J. P. Olsen (eds.), *Ambiguity and Choice in Organizations.* Bergen, Norway: Universitetsforlaget, 1979.

Clune, William H., and Van Pelt, Mark. "A Political Method of Evaluating 94–142 and the Several Gaps of Gap Analysis." *Law and Contemporary Problems,* December 1984.

Cohen, Michael D.; March, James G.; and Olsen, Johan P. "People, Problems, Solutions and the Ambiguity of Relevance." In J. G. March and J. P.

Olsen (eds.), *Ambiguity and Choice in Organizations.* Bergen, Norway: Universitetsforlaget, 1979.

DiMaggio, Paul J., and Powell, Walter W. "The Iron Cage Revisited: Institutional Isomorphism and Collective Rationality in Organizational Fields." *American Sociological Review*, 48, 2 (April 1983), pp. 147–160.

Edelman, Murray. *The Symbolic Uses of Politics.* Urbana: University of Illinois Press, 1964.

Fesler, James W. "Centralization and Decentralization." In D. L. Sills (ed.), *International Encyclopedia of the Social Sciences*, Vol. 2, pp. 370–379. New York: Macmillan and Free Press, 1968.

Freeman, John H. "The Unit Analysis in Organizational Research." In M. Meyer (ed.), *Environments and Organizations.* San Francisco: Jossey-Bass, 1980.

Furniss, Norman. "The Practical Significance of Decentralization." *The Journal of Politics*, 36, 4 (November 1974), pp. 958–982.

Gawthrop, Louis C. "Organizing for Change." *The Annals*, 466 (March 1983), pp. 119–134.

Gawthrop, Louis C. "The Political System and Public Service Education." *American Behavioral Scientist*, 21, 6 (July/August 1978), pp. 917–936.

Gilbert, Charles E. "Preface." *The Annals* 466 (March 1983), pp. 9–21.

Gormley, William; Hoadley, John; and Williams, Charles. "Political Responsiveness in the Bureaucracy: Views of Public Utility Regulation." *The American Political Science Review*, 77 (1983), pp. 704–717.

Hannan, Michael T., and Freeman, John H. "Internal Politics of Growth and Decline." In M. W. Meyer (ed.), *Environments and Organizations*, San Francisco: Jossey-Bass, 1980.

Holland, Thomas P., and Cook, Martha A. "Organizations and Values in Human Services." *Social Science Review*, 57 (1983), pp. 59–77.

Kasarda, John D. "The Structural Implications of Social System Size: A Three-Level Analysis." *American Sociological Review*, 39, 1 (February 1974), pp. 19–28.

Kochen, Manfred, and Deutsch, Karl W. *Decentralization: Sketches Toward a Rational Theory.* Cambridge, Mass.: Oelgeschlager, Gunn & Hain, 1980.

Korten, David C. "The Management of Social Transformation." *Public Administration Review*, 41 (November/December 1981), pp. 609–618.

Kreiner, Kristian. "Ideology and Management in a Garbage Can Situation." In J. G. March and J. P. Olsen (eds.), *Ambiguity and Choice in Organizations.* Bergen, Norway: Universitetsforlaget, 1979.

Lawrence, Paul, R., and Lorsch, Jay W. *Organization and Environment: Managing Differentiation and Integration.* Homewood, Ill.: Richard D. Irwin, Inc., 1969.

Lipsky, Michael. *Street-Level Bureaucracy: Dilemmas of the Individual in Public Services.* New York: Russell Sage Foundation, 1980.

Littrell, W. Boyd. "Bureaucracy in the Eighties: Introduction." *Journal of Applied Behavioral Science*, 16, 3 (July–September 1980), pp. 263–277.

Lowi, Theodore I. *The End of Liberalism.* New York: W. W. Norton & Co., 1969.

Macaulay, Stewart. *Law and the Balance of Power: The Automobile Manufacturers and Their Dealers.* New York: Russell Sage Foundation, 1966.

March, James G., and Olsen, Johan P. *Ambiguity and Choice in Organizations.* Bergen, Norway: Universitetsforlaget, 1979.

March, James G., and Simon, Herbert A. *Organizations.* New York: John Wiley & Sons, Inc., 1965.

Mashaw, Jerry L. *Bureaucratic Justice.* New Haven, Conn. Yale University Press, 1983.

Mazmanian, Daniel A., and Nienaber, Jeanne. *Can Organizations Change?* Washington, D.C.: Brookings Institution, 1979.

McNeil, Kenneth J. "Understanding Organizational Power: Building on the Weberian Legacy." *Administrative Science Quarterly,* 23 (March 1978), pp. 65–90.

Mechanic, David. "Sources of Power of Lower Participants in Complex Organizations." *Administrative Science Quarterly,* 7(1962), pp. 349–364.

Meyer, John W. "Organizational Factors Affecting Legalization in Education." Paper prepared for the IFG Seminar on Law and Governance in Education, October, 1980a.

Meyer, John W. "Strategies for Further Research: Varieties of Environmental Variation." in M. W. Meyer (ed.), *Environments and Organizations.* San Francisco: Jossey-Bass, 1980b.

Meyer, John W., and Rowan, Brian. "Institutional Organizations: Formal Structure as Myth and Ceremony." *American Journal of Sociology,* 83, 2 (September 1977), pp. 340–363.

Meyer, John W., and Rowan, Brian. "The Structure of Educational Organizations." in M. W. Meyer (ed.), *Environments and Organizations.* San Francisco: Jossey-Bass, 1980.

Meyer, John W.; Scott, W. Richard; Cole, Sally; and Intili, Jo-Ann. "Instructional Dissensus and Institutional Consensus in Schools." In M. W. Meyer (ed.), *Environments and Organizations.* San Francisco: Jossey-Bass, 1980.

Meyer, John W.; Scott, W. Richard; and Deal, Terrence E. "Institutional and Technical Sources of Organizational Structure Explaining the Structure of Educational Organizations." In H. D. Stein (ed.), *Organization and the Human Services: Cross-Disciplinary Reflection.* Philadelphia: Temple University Press, 1981.

Meyer, Marshall W. *Change in Public Bureaucracies.* Cambridge: University Press, 1979.

Meyer, Marshall W. *Environments and Organizations.* San Francisco: Jossey-Bass, 1980.

Meyer, Marshall W., and Brown, M. Craig. "The Process of Bureaucratization." In M. W. Meyer (ed.), *Environments and Organizations.* San Francisco: Jossey-Bass, 1980.

Miles, Matthew B. "Common Properties of Schools in Context: The Backdrop for Knowledge Utilization and 'School Improvement.' " Paper prepared for Program on Research and Educational Practice, National Institute of Education, Center for Policy Research, New York, April 1980.

Olsen, Johan P. "Choice in an Organized Anarchy." In J. G. March and J. P. Olsen (eds.), *Ambiguity and Choice in Organizations.* Bergen, Norway: Universitetsforlaget, 1979.

Olsen, Johan P. "University Governance: Non-Participation as Exclusive Choice." In J. G. March and J. P. Olsen (eds.), *Ambiguity and Choice in Organizations.* Bergen, Norway: Universitetsforlaget, 1979.

Perrow, Charles. *Complex Organizations: A Critical Essay,* 2nd ed. Glenview, Ill.: Scott, Foresman, 1979.

Pfeffer, Jeffrey. *Power in Organizations.* Boston: Pitman, 1981.

Pfeffer, Jeffrey, and Salancik, Gerald R. *The External Control of Organizations.* New York: Harper & Row, 1978.

Purkey, Stewart C., and Smith, Marshall S. "Effective Schools: A Review." Paper published by the Wisconsin Center for Educational Research, School of Education, University of Wisconsin-Madison, September 1982. (To be published in an upcoming edition of the *Elementary School Journal.*)

Rai, Gauri S. "Reducing Bureaucratic Inflexibility." *Social Service Review,* 57 (March 1983), pp. 44–58.

Ritti, R. R., and Goldner, Fred H. "Professional Pluralism in an Industrial Organization." *Management Science,* 16, 4 (December 1969), pp. 233–246.

Scott, W. Richard. *Organizations: Rational, Neutral, and Open Systems.* Englewood Cliffs, N.J.: Prentice-Hall, 1981.

Selznick, Philip. *The T.V.A. and the Grass Roots: A Study in the Sociology of Formal Organization.* Berkeley: University of California Press, 1949.

Simon, Herbert A. *Administrative Behavior.* New York: Macmillan, 1947.

Smith, Bruce L. R. "Changing Public-Private Sector Relations: A Look at the United States." *The Annals,* 466 (March 1983), pp. 149–164.

Sproull, Lee S. "Managing Education Programs: A Micro-Behavioral Analysis." *Human Organizations,* 40, 2 (Summer 1981), pp. 113–122.

Sproull, Lee S. "Responding to Regulation: School Superintendents and the Federal Government." In Samuel Bachrach (ed.), *Organizational Analysis of Schools and School Districts,* forthcoming.

Sproull, Lee S. "Response to Regulation: An Organizational Process Framework." *Administration and Society,* 12, 4 (February 1981), pp. 447–470.

Starbuck, William H. "Organizations as Action Generators." *American Sociological Review,* 48, 1 (February 1983), pp. 91–102.

Weatherley, Richard, and Lipsky, Michael. "Street-Level Bureaucrats and Institutional Innovation: Implementing Special Education Reform." *Harvard Educational Review,* 47, 2 (May 1977), pp. 171–197.

Weick, Karl E. "Administering Education in Loosely-Coupled Schools." *Phi Delta Kappa,* 63 (June 1982), pp. 673–676.

Weick, Karl E. "Educational Organizations as Loosely-Coupled Systems." *Administrative Science Quarterly,* 21 (March 1976), pp. 1–19.

Weiss, Carol H., and Barton, Allen H. (eds.). *Making Bureaucracies Work.* Beverly Hills, Calif.: Sage Publications, 1979.

Wright, Erik Olin. "To Control or To Smash Bureaucracy: Weber and Lenin on Politics, the State, and Bureaucracy." *Berkeley Journal of Sociology,* 19 (1974–1975), pp. 69–108.

Zald, Mayer. *The Political Economy of the YMCA.* Chicago: University of Chicago Press, 1970.

Zey-Ferrell, Mary, and Aiken, Michael. *Complex Organizations: Critical Perspectives.* Glenview, Ill.: Scott, Foresman, 1981.

· 8 ·

Social Movement Groups

Under the theory of public action, organizations of parents of handicapped children have two critical functions. One function is classic interest-group lobbying. Parent organizations would lobby, negotiate, supply information, and build coalitions. These functions would be performed throughout the entire policy-formation and implementation process—from the state and federal levels down to the school room. What is different, though, is the theoretical position of the parent groups. Under classic democratic theory, interest groups are only grudgingly tolerated; at best, they are a regrettable necessity, attempting to mitigate deficiencies in the representation processes. Traditionally, there has been a deep distrust of intermediate groups claiming the right to represent citizens (Anderson 1979; Moe 1981). Our liberal political tradition was a reaction to the corporatism of medieval Europe. In an ideological regime of individualism, unless an organization does in fact represent its members, it lacks the legitimacy to bargain; and in America, it is difficult for a group to creditably maintain that it is truly representative. There remains the profound conviction that organized interest groups are not fully legitimate participants in public processes (Salisbury 1979).

The second function of the parent organization is to address the distribution question in the client/agency interaction. The groups would provide a number of services for the parents at the grass roots level—social activities; workshops; training sessions; meetings with teachers, administrators, special education professionals, advocates, officials; and service (assisting parents in their negotiations with the school). The groups would supply lay advocates and other forms of representation; they would also have the capacity to collectivize the individual grievances and to press for systematic reform. Thus, the work at the grass roots level would be linked to the work at the political and administrative level (Reifner 1982).

To the extent that the groups can perform these tasks at the grass roots level, parents will have the needed information, will obtain additional skills, and have access to advocacy resources. They will have a sense of community. As noted, quite often parents of handicapped children experience feelings of shame and guilt; they are alienated. An important function of the group is to help overcome these feelings, to show the parents that they are not alone, that others share their burdens. Acquiring skills and a sense of community will change perceptions of efficacy. Parents will see that valuable things can be done for their children and that they can play a role in this process. Through the group activities—at both the grass roots level and in the political process—the parents will be in a better position to negotiate.

Thus, the theoretical role of the social movement groups confronts and transcends the three major problems of liberalism in the modern welfare state. The first of these issues arose at the very inception of liberalism—the antimony of the individual and the community, the conflict between the person as an individual and as a social being, the reality of the social bond and its threat to individualism. Atomic individualism leaves the parents in a hopeless, dependent position. By the development of shared ends through common experiences, "men come to understand and respect what beyond the boundaries of their shared purposes makes each person unique" (Unger 1975, p. 152). The imparting of skills and the development of efficacy contribute to the uniqueness of the individual; the building of community is the development of shared ends. Thus, there are both the shared values and the recognition of concrete individuality. There are boundaries between the individual and the group—some matters are "properly beyond politics"—but they are not inherently fixed (Unger 1975, pp. 152, 183, 274). The relationship between the individual and the group will be discussed in this chapter.

The second and third issues of liberalism, while not unique to the modern welfare state, have become more salient with the growth and penetration of government. These are the public/private distinction and substantive inequality. The distinguishing feature of liberalism as political theory is its insistence on specifying determinate limits on public authority (Levine 1981). In the critique of equating adversarial advocacy to liberalism (see Chapter 5), I challenged this distinction as no longer apt in the broad range of decisions characterized by discretionary, continuing relationships. The continuing relationship between the individual and the agency has necessitated a redefinition of the public and the private; there has to be a sharing of interests, a recognition that individual and public ends are to be realized in cooperation, not in separateness, and that procedural forms should facilitate community, not atomic individualism. In the discretionary relationship, politics cannot be wholly separate from social life. Nevertheless, as with the individual and the group, there still remain boundaries between the individual and the state; they may shift, but they must continue to exist.

The third issue addresses the monumental failure of liberalism to deal with substantive justice. By failing to come to grips with inequality, liberalism to a great degree forfeits its ethical claim. It grants access in form, but denies the fruits of society to all but the rich and powerful. It opens its doors to all, but only a few can pass. Its system of justice, its crowning achievement—the rule of law—is rationed by social reality. We praise the defense of property and liberty; we glory in the dramatic defense of the underdog, the heroic victim of oppression, but the masses are untouched. For them, just as the economic and social rewards of society are beyond their grasp, the system of justice is beyond their imagination. Formal justice perpetuates substantive injustice.

Social movement groups (in the theory of public action) seek to redress the balance. It starts with a group of individuals facing a common set of problems. By building a community at the grass roots level and by engaging the state—even at the lowest level—a concrete political act is performed; it starts the process of fulfilling the promise of liberalism (Unger 1975). It is a small beginning, but it contains the seeds of possibility.

In order to fulfill this promise, three conditions have to be met. The first concerns the formation of groups. What leads people to join organizations? What ties people to these groups? Unless individuals join the groups, most will not obtain the benefits. Unless groups are sufficiently strong, they will not be able to perform their tasks. Yet, under many circumstances, particularly for people who suffer most from the maldistribution of wealth and power, it is difficult to form and maintain strong, cohesive groups (Handler 1978; Olson 1965).

The second issue concerns the relationship of the organization to the state. If the group is weak, it is ineffectual. It may be ignored by the state or it may be easily coopted if the state feels the need for symbolic legitimacy. The relationship of the group to the state also raises the issue of corporatism (Schmitter & Lehmbruch; Lowi; Salisbury).

The third issue concerns the relationship of the individual to the group. For a group to enter into a successful relationship with the state, it must be able to guarantee control over its membership. In corporatism, the state aids this process by strengthening the position of the group leaders. The state is a valuable source of information and resources which allows the leaders to strengthen their position vis-à-vis the rank-and-file and any potential challengers (Lowi 1969). This raises the specter of domination and hierarchy within the group; the group suppresses rather than enhances individualism.

The boundary between the individual and the group parallels the ultimate issue of this book—the boundary between the individual and the state. The ultimate issue for liberalism is autonomy, but not autonomy in the classic sense of atomic individualism. The social bond cannot be denied. The issue is not whether there is interdependence, but whether the appropriate *conditions* of interdependence are present (Luhmann 1983). Autonomy as it relates to group membership will be discussed in this chapter. Autonomy as it relates to the state will be the subject of the next chapter.

What Are Social Movement Groups?

As with so many terms in social theory, "social movement group" has been used in a variety of conflicting and diverse meanings. In describing the deinstitutionalization of juvenile status offenders in the theory of public action, I used the term to include voluntary organizations, individual activists, judges, citizen groups, and officials in government agencies; in short, "social movement group" was synonymous with "social movement activity." It is also used interchangeably with "collective action." The three terms describe an enormous range of phenomena—crowds; riots; broad changes in culture; spontaneous, unconnected challenges to authority (for example, the hippie movement); organized campaigns (civil rights, the environment); and classic special-interest groups, whether economic (unions, trade associations) or noneconomic (religious, charitable). The forms of the organizations also vary tremendously, from spontaneous and ephemeral to staff-led professional with little or no contact with members.

For Marwell and Oliver (1985) social movements are about *goals*. They also argue that social movements ought to be distinguished from collective action. Collective-action theorists include any activity aimed at providing a collective good—contributions to charity, volunteer fire departments, as well as the civil rights movement. They argue that social movements should be understood in terms of *aggregates* of acts or events—meetings, rallies, riots, petitions, conversations. These activities are performed by different kinds of people in varying organizational forms. Although social movements are fluid and complex, the emphasis is on the *activities* of people. Other scholars emphasize ideas. Marwell and Oliver think that ideas are important, but largely for their effect on what people *do*.

In order to clarify the concept, I turn to a real-life example described by Wahrhaftig (1982). It concerns a neighborhood mediation organization, the Community Association for Mediation (CAM) in Pittsburgh, Pennsylvania. The advantage in considering this organization lies in its minimal qualities; yet, it seems to perform many of the kinds of personal and community functions that the parents' groups would perform at the grass roots level.

CAM is in a black neighborhood. Gloria Patterson, the originator, was an active worker in the area; she had participated in most of the volunteer organizations and had a wide range of contacts. CAM started without any financial support. Patterson began by identifying people in the community that she knew were problem solvers—agency paraprofessionals, block leaders, involved parents, and social workers. They met informally and discussed community mediation, which many were already doing, although they did not identify it as such. They designed a continuing education program for additional training and contacted other community leaders to advise them of their project.

The project consists of a network of people who have completed the training. They mediate disputes that come to them through their jobs and other social networks, and they meet together bi-weekly to discuss their experiences. They have expanded their contacts by meeting with a group of housing development residents to find out what kinds of problems these people have and who should be involved as problem solvers.

This is a very informal organization. No records are kept. "Members mediate in homes, bars, on the telephone—anywhere and any time." Wahrhaftig evaluates CAM as follows:

> The unresolved disputes that fester in the gap between informal dispute resolution resources and formal agencies are handled, and the skills of indigenous mediators are enhanced. Community growth is fostered at the biweekly meetings of mediators, which discuss not only the effectiveness of mediation techniques but also the substantive problems encountered. Mediators are linked with most of the agencies in the target area, so that the information can be channeled to an appropriate body when intervention is necessary. They are part of nonagency community networks that can be mobilized. Thus, in a case that initially involved a confrontation between a neighbor and a young single mother who had left her eighteen-month-old child at home unattended, CAM members were able to integrate the mother with others on her block who could watch her child while she ran down to the grocery store. . . . CAM thus quietly operates to build a community [Wahrhaftig 1982, p. 94].

CAM provides a useful analogy. It mediates disputes between both residents and agencies. In addition, it attempts to collectivize its experience in its bi-weekly meetings and seeks systematic reform. It is a minimal organization in that it uses volunteer time, does not require outside funding, and has virtually no overhead. It survives, apparently, because it performs a service; yet, this service is more than individual- or client-oriented; it also builds a sense of community.

CAM does not seem to be unique. There are tens of thousands of neighborhood groups or associations throughout the country. Most grew out of the experiences of the 1960s and 1970s. They exist in both white and minority communities; they are in both poor and middle class neighborhoods. Their principal concern is with community control over local land use and services. They engage in a variety of tactics: campaigning and block voting; lobbying and petitioning; self-help projects; and participation in government projects. There is also an extensive amount of coordination and coalition building with other neighborhood associations; there are almost a dozen national organizations (Oliver 1983; Boyte 1980; Perlman 1976).

Some thought should be given to what we expect social movement organizations to do. Marwell and Oliver (1985) point out that outcomes are often subtle, complicated, and mixed. Gusfield (1981) takes an even more encompassing view. He draws a contrast between a "linear" perspective and a "fluid" perspective. Characteristically, social movements are viewed in terms of activity directed toward particular ends. The focus is on the public arena—the underdog challenging authority—and the measure of success or failure is whether there have been changes in legislation or policies. Gusfield argues that there are more social movements than public policy controversies. He reminds us that a great deal of day-to-day interactions are only dimly affected by public policies. The women's movement, gay rights, and other broadly based movements are also reflected in everyday social relations. Attention to political goals, he argues, overstates the public as an arena and underemphasizes these broader effects.

> Effects of movements on change arise not only from their direct impact, but on those who perceive that a change is taking place, who reflect on the fact of the movement's occurrence. The recognition that something that has been taken for granted has now become an issue. These perceptions affect ordinary discontents—the housewife now has a new label for her discontents; the secretary no longer wants to serve coffee; husbands are warier about past habits. The awareness of the movement itself becomes a crucial and significant phenomenon [Gusfield 1981, p. 126].

Gusfield draws attention to the old idea that "politics" does not necessarily have to result in state policy. Politics as civil discourse can result in changed attitudes and practices, with law only in the background. Most modern social movements understand this; they are as concerned with consciousness-raising as with influencing government action. These are important considerations. The idea of the parent groups is to increase the capacity of the individual parent to negotiate with the school district. This is the political outcome. But in order to reach that outcome, two other processes have to happen. There has to be a sense of community, a sense of belonging to the group, a sharing of experiences, and a willingness to contribute. There also has to be a sense of personal efficacy; not only must the parent feel discontent but the parent must also believe that he or she can do something about it. These perceptions are not only important for the immediate tasks—negotiation and community building among similarly situated parents—but also for broader societal effects.

Incentives: Formation and Maintenance of Groups

What leads people to join organizations? What leads them to contribute, to stay, to work for the success of the group? Currently, there are three theories that seek to answer these questions—pluralism, the work of Mancur Olson, and critiques and revisions of Olson. The pluralists stress the motivational role of the common interests (Moe 1981). When people find they have common interests that can be advanced by collective action, they will join together to pursue them. The members will stay in the group and contribute only insofar as the group continues to reflect their interests. The central task of the group leaders is to sustain cohesion around group goals. Group goals have to be consistent with the wishes of the membership; otherwise, dissatisfied members will leave. Internal politics and leadership decisions are thus constrained by the goals of the members. The pluralism of these groups should reflect the pluralism of the society; at any one point in time, the spectrum of the groups should be a pretty fair indicator of the spectrum of interests in society. Under pluralist theory, social movement groups are a means of political expression alternative to electoral politics.

Mancur Olson, an economist, has sharply challenged the pluralist perspective. He argues that it is nonrational (in economic terms) for an individual to contribute to the collective good. The definition of a collective good is a good whose consumption is nonexclusive, that is, an individual cannot be denied consumption even though that individual has not contributed to the cost of providing that good. An example is an appeal to support public radio. Any one individual's contribution is not going to have any effect on whether public radio will be supplied or not; and that individual can listen to the Saturday afternoon opera without sending in a dime. In these circumstances, it is economically irrational for the individual to make a contribution.

Olson says that there are a number of exceptions to this general proposition, but they are still consistent with it. If the group is dominated by a few large members, the benefits of receiving the collective good might outweigh their costs in providing the good, and if they do not contribute, the good will not be provided. Another exception is coercion. People may have no choice about whether they contribute or not. This, of course, is the situation in organized society; we have to pay our taxes for the provision of public safety, national defense, and parks. This is also the theory behind the closed or union shop; unless workers are forced to contribute to the union, they will take a free ride.

In Olson's view, people will join small groups for noneconomic reasons and these may overcome the free rider, but for large groups, there have to be side payments. The survival of the large group depends on its ability to meet the demands for the side payments. Individuals join these groups, then, whether or not they agree with the goals. The leaders are not constrained by the goals of the members, and there is no reason to think that these large groups do, in fact, represent the membership interests. Small groups are different. Contributions are based on cooperation; leaders do have to respond to the preference of members, and these groups do tend to be representative (Moe 1981).

Olson's theory calls into question the major assumptions of the pluralists. At least with large groups pursuing collective goods, formation and maintenance are problematic; it is not at all certain that individuals with common interests will join together to pursue those interests. The existence of these groups does not necessarily reflect the interests of the members nor are they necessarily an accurate reflection of the varying interests in society. It cannot be claimed with any degree of assurance that they represent an alternative, reliable means of political expression (Moe 1981).

Nevertheless, if Olson is correct, why then do we see so many organizations pursuing collective goods? Most observers agree that there has been a fantastic proliferation of organizations in America (Walker 1983; Boyte 1980). Many, of course, are economic organizations dominated by large members or with coercive powers. But the overwhelming majority cannot be explained by these characteristics.

A great deal of the explanation lies in an interesting variation of the large member. Olson uses the example of the trade association, but a similar phenomenon occurs with purposive and administrative or political incentives. With large members, the benefits of supplying the collective good outweigh their costs. A great many social movement groups are funded by "external sources" (Walker 1983). External sources are contributors who are not necessarily members of the group in that they do not expect to consume the collective good—at least directly. For example, most contributors to organizations to abolish the death penalty would derive only vicarious pleasure if the goals of the organization were accomplished. McCarthy and Zald (1978) distinguish between *beneficiaries* and *adherents;* the former directly consume the collective good, the latter only vicariously.

Adherents are analogous to Olson's large members of economic organizations. The benefit of achieving the collective good overcomes the free riders, and the organizations are maintained. The adherents of these noneconomic, purposive organizations are foundations, churches, elites, corporations, or individuals. Government is also a great source of external support. This has given rise, according to McCarthy and Zald, to the "funded social movement" organization. These are organizations led by professional, salaried staff whose main function is to package grievances and manipulate the media to stimulate contributions from elites. The connection with the members is tenuous; in fact, many may be paper organizations. Organizations founded and maintained by external sources are extremely widespread. Walker (1983), in a large survey of interest groups, found that the overwhelming majority do not rely on the provision of selective incentives. Instead, they rely on funds outside of the immediate membership.

Government also plays a large role in the formation and maintenance of groups. The government role takes a variety of forms, but the basic idea is that various government agencies find it useful to have citizen organizations help in the political process. This could be the formation of allies in lobbying efforts, or to lend legitimacy to programs, or to help in the implementation and provision of services.

One noteworthy development has been the rise in government-mandated citizen groups. Although citizen advisory groups have been around for a long time, the real impetus came with the War on Poverty's mandate for "maximum feasible participation." This resulted in a significant amount of conflict between citizen groups and local political leaders. In 1966, Congress passed the Model Cities Act—local governments would have control over programs and there would be "widespread" citizen participation. Other programs followed this pattern. For example, under the Housing and Community Development Act, there was to be "adequate opportunity for citizen participation." The idea has spread widely, and today there are a great many mandated citizen organizations. In fact, since 1964, practically all of the major federal legislation aimed at sharing resources with state and local governments has included some form of participation mandate (Kweit and Kweit 1981). A number of questions have been raised about the mandated organization, but they do account for a large number of citizen groups. Again, this is not inconsistent with Olson; the government is acting as a large member.

Walker (1983) observed another interesting characteristic of external sources of support. His research concentrated on the federal level. As noted, he found that the bulk of the groups were supported by external sources. Many of the groups came about at the urging of federal officials who had to have regular contact with state and local agencies; thus, the organizations were sources of information. Both the government and foundations are important patrons of interest groups, especially in programs that depend heavily on federal funds—health care, education, welfare, mass transportation, and scientific research. Moreover, he found that most of these groups came into being at the bidding of the patrons themselves and were formed *after* the passage of the dramatic new legislation that established the policies in their area. In other words, contrary to the pluralist theory, these organizations were formed from the top down; they were the *consequence* of the legislation, not the *cause*. Thus, rather than representing an alternative means of political expression for the members, the organizations represent the efforts of political entrepreneurs, both in and out of government, who are using the organizations to further their particular interests.

In one respect, the funded social movement is not inconsistent with Olson. Large members are willing to provide the collective good; this

overcomes the free rider. However, the collective good is not restricted to economic incentives. This accounts for the existence of
large numbers of organizations that have purposive goals. The implication of these organizations will be discussed in the next section
dealing with corporatism.

Most of the criticism of Olson deals with the formation and maintenance of small groups. The basic theme in this research is that Olson
has too narrow a definition of rationality, that people have a variety of
incentives that make it rational, in their eyes, to contribute to collective goods (Marwell 1982; Moe 1981; Oliver 1980a, b). Moe argues,
first, that whether or not an individual's contribution has any
significance for the provision of the collective good in an objective
sense may not be important; rather, what may be more important is
whether the individual *thinks* that the contribution makes a difference. In other words, a perception of efficacy may be determinative.
Second, many incentives are noneconomic; they are purposive or
solidary. The smaller the group, the greater the interaction, the
greater the importance of solidary incentives. Purposive incentives,
which come from religious, ideological, or moral bases, shape an individual's evaluation of collective goods.

Marwell and Oliver make the same point. Marwell and Ames (1979,
1980, 1981) conducted a number of controlled experiments in which
they found that contrary to Olson's hypothesis, collective goods were
in fact provided in significant amounts even though it was economically nonrational for the participants to do so. The explanation that
Marwell offers is altruism. Altruism is usually contrasted with self-
interest. This is not necessarily so. People receive rewards not only
directly, but also indirectly through the pleasure of others. These
indirect rewards are very common. We gain pleasure from the pleasure of our children, our friends, and, Marwell notes, even from
fictional characters. "The fact is that humans have an enormous capacity to identify with the pains and pleasures of others" (Marwell
1982, p. 212). These indirect rewards are side payments (selective
incentives) and they lower the cost of providing the collective good.

The economic view, argues Marwell, is to view the group as a collection of individuals who have some interest in the provision of the
collective good; this is similar to the concept of the interest group in
political science. Social psychologists view human interaction in more
than strictly individualistic terms. Humans develop individualism and

separateness, but they learn dependence as well. Wanting others to be happy is both normative and functional in growing up. "It's a basic lesson—when others in the environment are happy, it usually helps us as well."

Altruism has not been analyzed that closely, but Marwell offers the following points. There is a connection between altruism and noticeability. Rewards tend to reverberate within the group, multiplying and incrementally increasing in value at each step. Within an interdependent system, contributions by any one individual have the possibility of increasing the contributions by others. People see that they can gain indirect rewards, which are also stimulated by norms of reciprocity. To the extent that the indirect rewards multiply and grow, they further reduce the cost of supplying the collective good. Small groups of people not only share in the collective good, but they also receive the side payments. There are both solidary and purposive incentives. This leads to the formation and maintenance of groups. In the real world, people belong to groups and social networks and have caring relations.

While Marwell concentrates mostly on small groups, Moe thinks that large groups are not so disadvantaged as Olson would have it. To the extent that people do feel efficacious and do share in the values of the organization, they will be attracted. If the incidence of efficacy and purposive values is high, the leaders can concentrate on maintaining the political goals of the organization. They can also manipulate information to maintain the sense of efficacy. Empirically, purposive incentives are important; there are in existence many more such organizations than Olson's model would predict. Motivational incentives are important. The problem with the pluralists is that they focus almost exclusively on the political; the problem with Olson is that he focuses almost exclusively on the nonpolitical (Moe 1981).

In the small groups that we are considering, there would seem to be a full range of both selective and collective goods. In fact, at the grass roots level, it would seem that the incentives are primarily selective. In the Community Association for Mediation (CAM) the good was the mediation services and other kinds of access and negotiation with agencies. This is a selective good. A person cannot consume that good without paying for the cost. The cost, though, is minimal; the person "joins" the group by coming to it and asking for its service. This benefits the group; they have a new member, even if only for this one particular event; they gain more information about community problems; they gain more in the eyes of the community because people are coming to them for service. They also gain the indirect rewards that Marwell is talking about: they are helping people, which lowers their cost of providing the service. The theory is that the new member will remain with the association after the particular service is completed. There are other selective incentives. To the extent that the organization is successful in a particular mediation or bargain, both the new member and the organization will have an increased sense of efficacy, and this should produce more of a willingness to contribute.

It would seem that the same analysis should apply to grass roots groups of parents of handicapped children. Certain kinds of benefits can be consumed without any participation in any group activities. For example, if the school and the parents' group offers a special event, it would seem that parents could not be excluded because they were not members of the group. Again, the hope would be that the more contact there is between similarly situated parents, the more networking and caring begins to develop.

Parents can acquire information and skills without making any contribution to the organization. Thus, at least to some extent, there will be a free rider problem. But, there are a great number of selective incentives. Many parents have difficulty in acquiring the necessary information, many lack confidence, feel bewildered and alone. Overcoming these problems is a selective good.

If all of these good things happen, then the obvious question is: Why don't more of these groups exist? One answer is that they do— the thousands of neighborhood organizations that Oliver, Perlman, Boyte, and others write about. With special education (as well as other areas), there may not have been enough organization, or there may be special problems in organization. I will return to this question at the conclusion of this chapter, but would like to point out that once the importance of these organizations is recognized by the school system—if it wants to accomplish its goal of parental participation—then more active support should be given to the formation and maintenance of the groups. This would be external support. External support has many problems, which will be examined in the next section, but again it is useful to note that it is a fairly common phenomenon. Most neighborhood organizations receive some form of external support, primarily for paid activists. But paid activists do not have divided loyalties; in fact, as Oliver (1983) found, they have deeper commitments to the organization.

External Support: Advocacy, Cooperation, Cooptation

Organizations attempt to obtain outside resources and not rely on membership contributions. Needless to say, external sources of support can create problems for the organizations. At the very least, seeking outside support implies a certain level of bureaucratization and formality. There are other dangers. There is the fear of a loss of independence, of the piper no longer calling the tune. Oliver (1983) reports that paid activists of neighborhood and block organizations are more dedicated to the group than the average volunteer. Boyte (1980), on the other hand, says that citizen, populist, neighborhood, and community groups, so widespread in this country, seek to avoid governmental or external support. They rely on membership dues and, quite extensively, on door-to-door solicitation. Gittell et al. (1980) draws sharp distinctions between advocacy organizations and government-mandated organizations, arguing that the rise of the latter has signaled the decline of the former.

The most prominent recent example of organizations relying on external support were the CAP agencies of the War on Poverty. These were organizations of local citizens funded by grants from the federal government. The idea was community empowerment; local groups would form to help themselves. In doing so, they would address "structural" problems that were considered to be barriers to the social mobility of the poor. The problem was that many of the major difficulties of the poor had to do with local public agencies, and quite quickly, local CAP agencies were pitted against the local political power structure. Needless to say, local and state politicians found it amazing that public money was being used to finance local political opposition. President Johnson also found it amazing, and in a very short time, the federal government pulled the string. Subsequent legislation modified "maximum feasible participation" to "widespread participation" or "adequate opportunity for citizen participation," but whatever the language, it was clear that local governments had final authority over these programs (Matusow 1984).

The aftermath of the CAP agencies was the rise of the mandated citizen group. Practically all major federal legislation that shares resources with state and local governments has included some form of participation mandate. The state or local agency administering the program is to organize the population that is to be served. Representatives are chosen in a variety of ways, and perform many different functions. They may or may not be representative of the client groups. Sometimes they only advise, while in other situations they are responsible for the actual delivery of the services. They act as intermediaries between citizens and officials. They can be viewed as democratizing the public process or as a clever way of avoiding conflict on the part of the government by bringing potential troublemakers into the system (Kweit and Kweit 1981). Gittell et al. (1980) report that local public agencies come to depend on the mandated group as the sole, legitimate representative of the clients.

The importance of the style of the group depends on what the group is supposed to do. Parent organizations are expected to perform the full spectrum of tasks. Some of their activities would be highly visible, for example, lobbying to prevent budget cuts. Other lobbying activities would combine two types of tasks, for example, lobbying for the creation of certain programs, and monitoring their implementation. There would also be combinations at the grass roots level. The basic thrust of the entire effort is to improve the relationship between the parents and the teachers, not only for the formation of the special education plan, but also for the interaction during the school life of the child. This is continuous, low-visibility activity. The role of the organization is to provide information, social support, and advocacy services if needed.

The grass roots organizations will also collect grievances and press for systematic reform. This will be a combination of functions in that the groups will be engaged in a visible act of reform, but will have to monitor implementation.

When the full range of tasks is considered, the distinction drawn between advocacy and service (see Gittell et al. 1980) collapses. At the grass roots level, bargaining with the school district looks like advocacy, but the continued contact with the teachers and the willingness to experiment and renegotiate look more like service. If the contact is suspicious and distrustful, it would look like advocacy; if the contact is cooperative and the exchange of information ongoing, it looks like service.

The argument made in this book is that the confrontational, adversarial style cannot work, at least in the long run. The bulk of the activities of the parent group require continuous, day-to-day contact with the bureaucracy. This is self-evident with parent-teacher interaction at the grass roots level, but it is also true when one considers the implementation monitoring that is required at the systemic reform phase. A social movement group cannot maintain the pressure for these long-term relations. The group simply lacks the resources and staying power. The bureaucracy holds too many cards, and the day-to-day operations can wear the members down (Handler 1979). This is not to say that adversarial, confrontational tactics might not be useful. They may be necessary for the early stages of the relationship. They also may be necessary to establish, from time to time, some of the conditions of cooperative bargaining. In special education, I discussed the importance of retaining due process procedures and alternative points of access for parents who felt that they were not being treated adequately by the cooperative system. Confrontational tactics may be necessary to counter cooptation, an issue which will be discussed shortly.

In Chapter 6, I described social movement groups in the deinstitutionalization of juvenile status offenders. One of the important lessons of that experience is that there is no one formula for the support of social movement groups. They take a variety of forms and nurturing; they have to maintain contact and be part of the local social configuration. In some areas, they "take," in others they do not. If one is serious about the importance of sharing power in the exercise of discretion, one has to accept variety. There will be successes and failures. In some school districts, autonomous groups will function, in others they will not. The first step is to clearly establish what functions the social movement groups are to perform. Then comes the task of how to support the formation and maintenance of the groups.

Avoiding the obvious dangers of the adversarial, confrontational style is easy enough to conceptualize, but there are also important problems with organizations that receive external support, but fall in between the two polar types. The danger of public funds is not so much the direct confrontation, the dramatic assertion of public will over the organization; rather, it is the danger of cooptation and corporatism. Organizations that secure and grow used to public funding tend to form stable alliances with the granting agencies. A regular supply of funds frees the leadership from dependence on members. The agency helps the leadership in other ways; it provides information and access and gives the leadership the symbols of importance and efficacy. The organization, in turn, helps the agency by legitimating the process, by providing political support for the program, and by avoiding negative publicity for the agency and the relevant political leaders. For this partnership to work, there must be stable leadership that can deliver the organization (Lowi 1969).

Here, we need to say something about corporatism. Corporatism, a term that received notoriety with twentieth-century fascism, is actually a common form of social organization in western Europe. There it is referred to as liberal corporatism, implying the voluntary nature of the relationships. Liberal corporatism is commonly found when the state is trying to implement an income policy. Organized labor, along with organizations representing major businesses, form a tripartite relationship with the government to reach agreement on wages, prices, and other monetary issues. In theory, the difference between liberal corporatism and interest group pluralism is that under the former, the organizations are formally designated as partners with the state for the development and implementation of public policy. With interest group pluralism, labor and business influence policy but the arrangements are episodic and ad hoc; they do not have the legitimacy one finds in liberal corporatism (Schmitter 1979).

The distinction between liberal corporatism and interest group pluralism may not be real, or at least may not amount to very much in a practical sense. The claimed advantage of liberal corporatism is stability; yet, the wage bargains become unstuck and the rank-and-file members force the unions to withdraw from the alliances (Schmitter Lehmbruch 1979; Panitch 1979). Liberal corporatism is stable only to the extent that the leadership can guarantee control of its members. Conversely, Lowi (1969) finds a great amount of stability in certain important sectors of American policy; agricultural producers, for example, are closely tied to the relevant subcommittees in Congress and the U.S. Department of Agriculture.

The distinction between formal and informal recognition of organized interests becomes even thinner when one considers organization theory as discussed in the previous chapter. Both the state (education bureaucracies in this instance) and the social movement groups are organizations. Under the open systems analysis, these organizations are responsive to their environments, that is, to each other. The environments are sources of information, alliance and coalition building, and political support. The organizations themselves are collections of shifting political groups and individuals. To the extent that the social movement group is strong and active, it is creating environmental uncertainty for the state. Those actors within the state bureaucracy who can manage this uncertainty will gain power and influence. And those social movement leaders who have access to agency leaders will be able to deliver for their groups and maintain their leadership position. Open systems theorists, it will be recalled, deemphasize the distinction between an organization and its environment. Perrow (1979), in fact, says that there is no distinction at all and that organizations can be considered only in terms of their fields.

The concept of liberal corporatism draws attention to the issue of cooptation. Cooptation is the important issue in the relationship between social movement groups and the state. Corporatism highlights the strong incentives that the state and the social movement groups have in forming alliances. Open systems theory challenges the concept of cooptation, at least in terms of analytic distinctions. If boundaries between organizations and their environments are shifting and indistinct, what is the difference between cooptation and mutual influence? Cooptation is said to occur when the outsiders lose their independence of judgment and assume the goals of the insiders. But the outsiders bring a different perspective, different sources of information, and the ability to help manage environmental uncertainty. Over time, this may have influence on the perceptions and behavior of the insiders.

The line between the state and the social movement group fades; yet, under the theory of public action, we expect the social movement group to stand apart from the state, to be a source of information and control, to keep the bureaucracy honest. How can there be a concept of state when according to the open systems theorists there is little or no distinction between the organization and its environment?

Empirically, we see the full range of possibilities. We see social movement groups in conflictual, adversarial postures or in virtual partnerships. The answer to the conceptual paradox is to shifting reality rather than conceptual compartments. The safest prediction is that in whatever position a social movement group finds itself in relation to the bureaucracy at a given point in time, that position is likely to change over the course of time. Even assuming an ideal position, according to the prescription of the theory of public action, in time either of two things will happen—the organization will grow weak and lapse into irrelevance or it will develop a stable alliance with the bureaucracy and assume corporatist characteristics. A third alternative is a possibility—through the introduction of new blood, the leadership will remain responsive to the original mission. This is a difficult alternative, and the history of social movement groups is not promising in this regard. What this means, then, is that alternative structures and avenues of redress have to remain open. We are dealing with a dynamic, fluid relationship. Not only will change come, but it must be anticipated.

What conclusions, then, can one draw concerning the problem of cooptation? The groups of parents will need a variety of external sources of support. In order to accomplish the social networking, the exchange of information, and perceptions of personal efficacy, incentives will have to be provided, especially for those least likely to want to participate. We have already seen some valuable forms of external support—for example, state-supported workshops and training sessions with stipends to cover child care and dinners. There was also support for picnics, outings, and other kinds of social events. The idea is to get parents of handicapped children to develop personal ties with similarly situated parents, to feel comfortable with them, to want to share feelings and concerns and information. Moreover, this form of support will have to be more or less continuous since there is a natural turnover with "new classes" of parents. There also could be support for paid organizers. As noted, this is quite common in many grass roots organizations.

External support carries real problems for support groups. If the bureaucracy does not come to believe in the importance of parental cooperation and the need for social movement groups to help foster that cooperation, then three possibilities are likely to happen, none of which is desirable. The relationship will be confrontational, in which event the bureaucracy will terminate its support and the group will die. If the bureaucracy wants parental cooperation but does not understand the functions of the social movement group, it will become overzealous and create a mandated organization. Or, the group will become coopted; the leaders will be devoting their energies to maintain a stable alliance with the bureaucracy. With both the mandated and the coopted group, there will be no incentives to engage in the grass roots activity, and, of course, that is the whole point.

In sum, if cooptation is to be avoided, it is crucial that the bureaucracy fully understand the importance of social movement activity to its goal of parental participation. The principal danger is the misconception about service. The common assumption is that providing service accomplishes the mission. This is important, but it is not enough. The Madison School District provided service—the teachers were more than ready to consult with parents—but parental participation lagged. The same would be true if the mandated or coopted organization provided service. More has to be done to educate and stimulate the parents. The bureaucracy has to come to understand that a variety of activities is necessary.

Attitudes toward the social movement group have to parallel attitudes toward parental participation. The key concept here, it will be recalled, was the use of conflict by the Madison School District. Conflict was encouraged to increase communication. The same approach must be taken toward the organization of parents. Again, I am not talking about adversarial, confrontational conflict; rather, the idea is *communicative conflict*. The bureaucracy must view its relationship with the parent organization as a window, a source of information, another trouble-shooting mechanism. Within a lowered conflictual relationship, where there is a habit of listening and learning and an effort to compromise, it is possible to avoid being defensive. The Madison School District has done this with parents, advocates, and outside specialists. The same is called for in relationship with parent groups.

While external support is important, it must foster grass roots development. In some neighborhoods, there might be strong organizations already in existence and parents of handicapped children could be a part of existing groups. These groups may or may not be connected with education. There is no reason why a community development group, for example, could not also sponsor and encourage a parent group.

Just as there will be a variety of grass roots possibilities, there ought to be a variety of sources of external support. We noted that in the Madison School District the State Department of Public Instruction was an important source of support. It would seem that other public agencies would have an interest in lending a hand to the parent groups. This, of course, would lessen the dangers of cooptation, although it might increase the administrative demands on the leadership, thus leading to increased bureaucratization.

Social Movement Organizations and Their Members

The core of liberalism is the individual, the basic unit of society. Liberal theory views the individual as an atom. Like atoms, individuals come into contact with each other but only as a matter of instrumental necessity; the union is not constitutive of human nature. Associations, especially institutional, are always instrumental. Persons interact in terms of ends and means, subjects and objects. Thus, group life is suspect; it threatens the individual. The problem of the individual in the group is fundamental. The tension between people as individuals and people as social beings is perhaps the greatest dialectic in modern political thought (Nisbet 1978; Lustig 1982).

In the theory of parent groups proposed here, the end of the group is the individual. The purpose of the group is to enhance the power of the parents in their bargaining with the school district. At the grass roots level, the groups are minimal rather than inclusive. Parents participate not as whole beings but for their discrete interests in the education of their handicapped children. They may use the groups for other purposes, such as social networking, recreation, or other community and political activities, but these would be by-products. Diversity of interests among parents would, of necessity, have to be recognized if the groups are to flourish. The emphasis is on conflict and pluralism at both the individual and the group level. Differences between members of the group are not considered contradictions; rather, they are expected. The purpose of providing information, a sense of *personal* efficacy, and the concept of the parent advocate is to create autonomy, not effect the incorporation of the individual into the general will (Wolff 1968).

Nevertheless, group members are dependent people. Strong, aggressive, knowledgeable parents do not need social movement organizations. They do not need them even in traditional bureaucratic relations; and they certainly can find their way with a cooperative bureaucracy such as the Madison School District. The problems lie with the parents who are most in need of the collective strength offered by the group. For these parents, despite the theory behind social movement groups, there is great risk of losing autonomy and individualism in the practical working out of relations. These problems have to be confronted if there is to be a coherent concept of the individual in the group.

We return to the question of incentives. Why would parents participate in the social movement group? If the parents are knowledgeable, they will deal with the school system on their own. They will understand what the school system is proposing, evaluate the proposition, weigh the costs and benefits, and make their decision. The parents that I am concerned with are different. They have to be persuaded to participate in the activities of the group, to bring themselves up to the position of the informed, active parents. They will do so only if they have the requisite information and the incentives; and this will happen only if the social movement group can deliver on its promises.

Two basic tasks are asked of the social movement group, and they are potentially contradictory. The organization is asked to participate in the formation of policy and the implementation process, to become, over time, an institutional bargainer, with the real potential of forming a regular alliance with the bureaucracy. At the same time, the group is being asked to represent individual parents in their relations with the schools. There is a potential conflict. It is analogous to the problem of the "institutional litigant" or "repeat player" verses the "one-time player" identified by Galanter (1974). Examples of repeat players are plaintiff's lawyers in tort cases and defense lawyers in criminal cases. Over time, these lawyers develop continuing relationships with their counterparts—insurance adjusters in tort law and prosecutors in criminal law. In bargaining over individual cases, the two sides become sensitive to their long-term interests. The plaintiff's lawyer will yield a little on this case to help out the adjuster who can then be expected to help out the plaintiff's lawyer on the next case. This happens in the plea bargain. The defense attorney makes adjustments to the needs of the prosecutor to preserve the long-term relationship (Galanter 1974).

This sounds like the sacrifice of an individual's interest (a one-time player) for the sake of the institutional litigants, but this is by no means clear. It may be that the individual is better off in the negotiated settlement than he or she would be as the result of a full adversary confrontation. The plaintiff's lawyer and the defense lawyer fill important needs for their adversaries; they come not as supplicants but as valuable allies whose needs have to be met, and this may rebound to the betterment of the individual client. Furthermore, the standard by which the negotiated settlement is questioned is an ideal standard—what would have happened if there had been a full adversarial confrontation? This standard is hardly ever met, and this is important to keep in mind. What has to be compared is the negotiated settlement with what is likely to be the relative position of the parties in real life.

The same issue is present in the dual roles envisaged by the parent groups. To what extent will the group (the institutional litigant) represent particular parents? The long-term interests and relationships of the group may be jeopardized by obstreperous parents. Over time, the group comes to perceive the school officials and teachers as reasonable, responsible people, especially when they have made the cooperative, conceptual moves. The school people can appeal to the leaders of the organization. The viability of the alliance between the group and the bureaucracy depends on the ability of the group to control its members. Will the repeat player compromise the interests of the one-time player for the sake of the long-term relationship?

There are other potential difficulties for parents. We speak of incentives to participate, and this implicitly assumes voluntariness, but how realistic is this assumption? Corporatist theorists point out that when an organization in effect becomes licensed by the state as the official representative of the members, membership is no longer voluntary (Anderson 1979). To the extent that the social movement group forms a continuing, stable alliance with the education bureaucracy, it may in effect become licensed by the state. The most severe situation the parents might face would be if the school considered the group the exclusive bargainer or representative of the parents in their dealings with the school. This would be similar to the mandated organization. Then the parents would be stuck. But even if there is no monopoly relationship, particular parents may still be disadvantaged. What is the school to think of them when reasonable, responsible leaders of the group disavow them? The outsider is the deviant.

The parents face similar difficulties in the larger community. Here, we run into the issue of systemwide cooptation. The people in the community view the program with satisfaction. They have seen the results of the changed attitudes on the part of the school system, the cooperative relationships with the social movement group, the reduction in conflict, and the general rise in satisfaction. Along come some parents who claim a grievance. They will be viewed suspiciously. Why can't they get along with the system when everyone else can? Are they the problem rather than the school?

Finally, there are those who question the value of informalism in protecting legal rights. This issue was discussed in Chapter 5. It is argued that the procedural formalism under current attack is actually one of the few weapons that the powerless have at their command. Procedural due process equalizes the poor with the rich before the law. If these protections are removed, then one more restraint on the dominating class will have been removed. As Lazerson (1982) has pointed out in his study of the New York City Housing Court, informalism, by curtailing the procedural rights of the weak, actually increased the power of the landlords. The answer to that argument is that the comparison is being made between an informal system and an idealized version of adversarial advocacy. It has been amply demonstrated that the defenseless are, in the overwhelming majority of situations, not made any less defenseless under procedural formalism. I also concede that an informal system, alone, would hardly improve the position of the weak. What I am arguing for is an informal system set in the context of social movement activity *and* the changed position of the bureaucracy.

The group and the school have it within their power to suppress the individual, but if they choose to go this route, they will have forfeited their goal of parental participation. The dangers to autonomy are just that—the resolution can go either way; it is not inevitable that individualism cannot survive and flourish within a group, but the first step is for the group and the bureaucracy to recognize the primacy of autonomy.

It is not self-evident that the social movement group will compromise the interests of individual parents in order to preserve its relationship with the bureaucracy. The group has to deliver for its members. Recruitment depends on the supply of selective incentives, which in this case means adequate representation of the interests of the parents. To the extent that the group fails in this regard, the parents will either seek help elsewhere or simply lose interest. Either event can be a serious blow to recruitment. Further, the group may not be able to hide its lack of effort. Ordinarily, lack of information or passiveness can be a problem, but here, by hypothesis, the parents are causing trouble. Not to serve them is dangerous for this group. If the bureaucracy asks the leadership to control the parents, the existence of the group and its own objective of encouraging parental participation is threatened.

The organization of the parent groups is such as to foster individualism. At the grass roots level, the group will consist of volunteers. The lay advocates are knowledgeable parents. Parents will also be the ones who organize and lead the informal social gatherings in their homes. These people contribute their time and energy for nonmaterial reasons. They know the system and are perfectly capable of bargaining for themselves and others with or without the authority of the group. The weakness of the incentive system within the organization is also its strength; it lacks the ability to control the rank-and-file and thus compromise their interests for the sake of the top-level alliance. Since the group cannot guarantee its membership, its alliance with the bureaucracy is unstable. This is a benefit—instability reduces corporatist tendencies and increases democratic ones.

The characteristics of the membership should also encourage instability and autonomy. The membership will be naturally fluid and diverse. New parents are continually eligible; parents with older children will "graduate." In addition, the interests of parents change as their children progress through the school system. Parents of entry-level children are very concerned about the initial diagnosis and treatment plan; parents of older children tend to be more concerned with vocational education and what will happen to their children after they leave the school system. What this diversity means is that the organization is inherently unstable. There is constant recruiting merely to stay alive. Parents come and go, interests change, the leadership is more likely to rotate. This should serve to reduce corporatist tendencies and increase the incentives to serve the individual members.

Finally, one should not automatically assume that because there is a negotiated settlement the particular parents are worse off. As with the institutional litigant, the bureaucracy and the group need the services of each other. The group does not come to the bureaucracy as a supplicant. Because the bureaucracy needs the active participation of the group, the group can extract a better deal for the parents. The group and the bureaucracy are in an *exchange* relationship. We saw such a situation in the Madison School District. There, the school yielded to a parental request to get a child into a certain program. Once in the program, the teachers felt that adjustments could be worked out in the course of time. The important point is that the parents in this particular case had something to offer (their child's participation) that the school system wanted. The parents were not in a dependent, powerless position. Similarly, the school system wants a functioning group; the group can fulfill the school's needs but not from a coopted position.

In discussing the problems of autonomy, it is easy to slip out of context. In the liberal tradition, individualism and autonomy are considered against the backdrop of the rule of law. It is traditional and natural to compare the interests of an individual in a group with the interests of the individual in the liberal, due process system. When we think of parents and their relationship to the bureaucracy, and the effects of group membership on that relationship, we implicitly think of rights, the individual versus the state. It is the liberal, legal, adversarial cast of mind.

Here, the context is changed. Merely by conceiving of parents as part of the solution rather than the problem, and by viewing all decisions as experimental and flexible rather than in terms of winners and losers, one immediately reduces the level of conflict. The term lay advocate becomes a misnomer; it is probably more accurate to talk of skilled interpreters or communicators. Etiquette barriers are probably a more accurate description than legal barriers. Conflict is to produce communication and consensus, not the articulation of rights and duties. Procedural forms are to uncover shared ends, not adversarial positions.

With the development of shared ends, the role of law is reduced. There is less of a need to arbitrate disputes according to rules; the parties fashion their own solutions in terms of common goals. Formal contract law recedes in importance as long as there are shared ends. Yet, autonomy is not diminished. People can live both as individuals and as social beings. The negotiators are simultaneously ends and means.

Legal rights become less important, but they are not unimportant. While procedural due process declines in importance in a consensual system, it would be foolhardy to jettison one of the crowning, hard-won achievements of liberal society (Mills 1970). There has to be an avenue of redress. Procedural reform is never enduring. The relationships that I am arguing for here are dynamic, fluid, and unstable. Groups will grow weak or strong and client interests will suffer. The bureaucracy may become disenchanted and revert to old ways, or bureaucratic pathologies may dominate. Budget cuts alone may seriously compromise, if not defeat altogether, the system that I envisage. Not only procedural due process but also other community resources must be held in reserve.

The theory of social movement groups offered here, therefore, differs from conventional group theory. Here, the individual is not incorporated into the general will. The individual does not find fulfillment only within the shared purposes of the group. Rather, the purpose of the group is to enhance the individual. But others have also said this. The difference here lies with the behavioral end. The end is not group behavior. Rather, it is individual behavior. It is the behavior of the parents in their negotiations with the school district. And the key to this relationship is that it is one of *exchange*, not of dependency. If the bureaucracy is to fulfill its organizational task, it has to have knowledgeable, understanding parents. The purpose of the group is to bring the parents to that level.

When all is said, autonomy in social groups will remain problematic. A number of factors in the Madison example *may* preserve individuality—the voluntariness of the group, the posture of the bureaucracy, the lack of inclusiveness of the group, the differing and changing interests of parents—but if we generalize to other social groups in other contexts, these factors may or may not be present. Voluntariness with dependent people should always give one pause. To the extent that the group is effective and the individual needs the services, we move on the continuum toward domination. The existence of alternatives in the environment should make a difference. If the individual rejects (or is rejected by) the group, are there other sources of aid? To what extent is there systemwide cooptation? A key element in the Madison example was the exchange between the bureaucracy and the parent. What if there is no exchange in the substantive relationship? What if the relationship is more episodic than continuous? The answers and implications to these questions are not known. The problem of the individual in the group is subtle and difficult.

Intermediate Groups, Liberalism, and the Administrative State

Intermediate groups, *together* with the changed position of the bureaucracy, have the capacity to overcome the three major problems of liberalism in the modern administrative state. The three problems that I have addressed are the relation of the individual to the group, the public/private distinction, and the relationship between formal and substantive justice, or equality. These are all old problems; they take on new urgency with the growth and penetration of the state, the increasing dependency of the citizen on the state, and persistent, widespread inequality.

The legal rights revolution recognized the erosion of the public/private distinction and the growing threat to the citizen in the administrative state (Reich 1964). It sought to protect the citizen by erecting additional defenses. In addition to its conceptual weaknesses, adversarial advocacy failed because it could not deal adequately with the distribution question. The bureaucracy was to be changed through force—in the 1960s in the street, in the 1970s in the courts. But the citizen lacked the necessary power. Here, too, the reconceptualization of the public/private distinction will fail unless the third major problem of liberalism is addressed—the distribution question. It is the failure to deal with inequality that has so compromised the promise of liberalism, and especially the rule of law.

Hence, the importance of the intermediate group. The properly functioning social movement group addresses the distribution question by supplying resources and information to the parent, by its ability to collectivize grievances and press for systematic reform, and by its political activist program. There can be no illusions that the social movement group can adequately perform these functions on its own, in the face of an implacable or hostile bureaucracy. The state must come to realize the importance of social movement activity for the definition and implementation of policy (the theory of public action) and the grass roots work that is necessary for client/agency interactions. The change in approach must come from within the organization; it will not come through demonstrations and lawsuits.

The theory of the role of social movement groups not only addresses the distribution question, it also addresses the two other issues of liberalism. It recognizes the mutual dependence of the citizen and the state; it seeks to build continuity and cooperation; and it addresses the role of the individual in the group.

Although the social movement group holds the promise of addressing the problems of liberalism, it also raises problems of its own. I have identified three such problems: corporatism and democratic values; the contingency of public policy; and the preservation of individualism in the group.

The issue of corporatism has been discussed. It is a danger that can be expected to emerge from time to time. Social conditions, incentives, and attitudes will change. There are, however, countervailing tendencies within social movement groups—the rotating membership, the constantly changing interests of the members, and the pressure to deliver services. An important consideration is the position of the coopting agent—the bureaucracy. If the bureaucracy engages in cooptation, it will gain peace, but it will lose parental participation. The latter depends on grass roots activity, which will decline to the extent that cooptation takes hold. The bureaucracy has to view parental challenge as an opportunity for communication, not as a threat to its prerogatives. This is possible within a relationship of overall reduced conflict. The Madison School District has done this. They welcome outside specialists and parent advocates.

Interest group representation, let alone corporatism, is suspect in democratic theory because groups represent special interests rather than the general interest. Anderson (1979) argues that interest group representation can be made compatible with democratic theory if the criteria of interest representation themselves are embedded in the substantive standards of policy. In this example, the social movement group is not a general group of consumers or like-minded citizens. It is a specific group dealing with the education of handicapped children. Would this satisfy Anderson's criterion of political accountability? The criteria of special education are vague and discretionary; they do not narrowly prescribe the scope and activities of the group. Yet, this public policy configuration has been arrived at by democratic means. It was the legislature that decided to enact the vague statute. The enabling legislation is thus a broad delegation to administering units—in this case, the states and the local school districts. This is very common; there are vast delegations of power to administrative agencies. It has always been difficult to "fit" broad delegations of power with constitutional theory, but there is little doubt that it is a firmly accepted practice. The participation of the social movement group, then, rests on the same theoretical footing as does the administrative agency. The agency, of course, is public. It is a creature of public law; it is supported by public funds; and its personnel are public employees. But in real life, the distinction is not very sharp. There are many private associations that perform public functions and receive public funds. Quite often, there is no clear line between public and private organization in the administration of public programs. Anderson recognizes these close connections. He is saying that compatibility is achieved to the extent that the private group is operating within the same substantive standards that govern the agency. It is the democratically arrived at charter, and not the internal structure and membership, that counts. As long as social movement groups are specific to the public purposes of the program, they are no more and no less consistent with democratic theory than the rest of the administrative state.

The requirement of consistency with substantive standards meets the objection of contingency. This is not to say that contingency will be overcome. Quite the opposite is true. As long as discretion has been delegated to lower units of administration, policy outcomes will be contingent on local conditions. In many programs, such as special education, contingency is both inevitable and desirable. On the other hand, an attempt is made to contain discretion within certain parameters. There are constitutional standards and other uniform statutory and administrative requirements. Again, conceptually, the introduction of social movement groups is no different than delegation to lower administrative units. The local units are supposed to operate within the parameters; so too should the social movement groups that participate in the process.

What is different, though, is the concept of discretion. The fact of discretion is recognized. The theory of public action views discretion as a positive good, a method of introducing creativity in administration and enhancing liberal values. But this positive view of discretion, by itself, does not alter the issue of contingency. Contingency arises from discretion, however discretion is exercised.

The ultimate test is the relationship of the individual to the group. The interest group not only must pursue the public interest (that is, operate within the substantive policy criteria) but also must be so constituted as to supplement rather than supplant popular representation. If parent groups are considered necessary and desirable for the development and implementation of special education, then some attention has to be paid to the people that the group represents; efforts have to be made to reach those parents who would not normally join. Anderson (1979) argues that intermediate associations act as buffers between the individual and the state; they give the individual supplemental and differentiated access to decision makers. They enhance democracy by protecting against mass movements. Whether they do so in fact, is, of course, the issue. They may suppress dissent; they may coopt rather than represent. Here, the role of the group is different. Although the ends are shared, *the* end is autonomy, not cooperation. Although collective action is called for in lobbying and systemic reform, the basic goal is to enhance the individual bargaining position of the parents. This is the goal of the bureaucracy; it wants individual parental participation, and the group is encouraged to that end. There are valuable by-products of the social movement group— networking, social events, information, participation, community— all of which will contribute to the richness of social life and a sense of personal efficacy. The organizing principle, the principle that legitimizes the group in terms of democratic theory, is its commitment to liberalism. The end is not collective behavior. The end is the individual.

REFERENCES

Abel, Richard L. (ed.). *The Politics of Informed Justice, Volume I, The American Experience; Volume 2, Comparative Studies.* New York: Academic Press, 1982.

Alfano, Geraldine, and Marwell, Gerald. "Experiments on the Provision of Public Goods by Groups. III. Nondivisibility and Free Riding in 'Real' Groups." *Social Psychology Quarterly,* 43, 3 (September 1980), pp. 300– 309.

Alford, Robert R. "Paradigms of Relations Between State and Society." In Leon N. Lindberg, Robert Alford, Colin Crouch, Claus Offe (eds.), *Stress and Contradiction in Modern Capitalism.* Lexington, Mass.: D. C. Heath 1975.

Anderson, Charles W. "Political Design and the Representation of Interests." In Philippe C. Schmitter and Gerhard Lehmbruch (eds.), *Trends Toward Corporatist Intermediation.* Beverly Hills: Sage Publications, 1979.

Berger, Peter L., and Neuhaus, Richard John. *To Empower People: The Role of Mediating Structures in Public Policy.* Washington, D.C.: American Enterprise for Public Policy Research, 1977.

Boyte, Harry C. *The Backyard Revolution: Understanding the New Citizen Movement.* Philadelphia: Temple University Press, 1980.

Cole, Richard L. *Citizen Participation and the Urban Policy Process.* Lexington, Mass.: D. C. Heath, 1974.

Follett, Mary Parker. *The New State.* New York: Longmans, Green, 1918.

Galanter, Marc. "Why 'Haves' Come Out Ahead: Speculations on the Limits of Legal Change." *Law and Society Review,* 9 (1974), pp. 95–160.

Garlock, Jonathan. "The Knights of Labor Courts: A Case Study of Popular Justice." In Richard L. Abel (ed.), *The Politics of Informal Justice, Volume 1, The American Experience.* New York: Academic Press, 1982.

Gittell, Marilyn, with Bruce Hoffacker, Eleanor Rollins, Samuel Fosler and Mark Hoffacker. *Limits to Citizen Participation: The Decline of Community Organizations.* Beverly Hills, Calif.: Sage Publications, 1980.

Goodwyn, Lawrence. *Democratic Promise: The Populist Moment in America.* New York: Oxford University Press, 1976.

Gordon, Robert. "New Developments in Legal Theory." In David Kairys (ed.), *The Politics of Law: A Progressive Critique.* New York: Pantheon, 1982.

Granovetter, Mark. "Threshold Models of Collective Behavior." *American Journal of Sociology,* 83, 6 (1978) pp. 1420–1443.

Gusfield, Joseph R. "Social Movements and Social Change: Perspectives of Linearity and Fluidity." In Louis Kriesberg (ed.), *Research in Social Movements, Conflict and Change,* Vol. 4. Greenwich, Conn.: JAI Press, 1981.

Handler, Joel F. *Protecting the Social Service Client: Legal and Structural Controls of Official Discretion.* New York: Academic Press, 1979.

Handler, Joel F. *Social Movements and the Legal System: A Theory of Law Reform and Social Change.* New York: Academic Press, 1978.

Hardin, Russell. *Collective Action.* Baltimore: Johns Hopkins University Press, 1982.

Harrington, Christine B. "Delegalization of Reform Movements: A Historical Analysis." In Richard L. Abel (ed.), *The Politics of Informed Justice, Volume 1, The American Experience.* New York: Academic Press, 1982.

Hofrichter, Richard. "Neighborhood Justice and the Social Control Problems of American Capitalism: A Perspective." In Richard L. Abel (ed.), *The Politics of Informal Justice, Volume 1, The American Experience.* New York: Academic Press, 1982.

Jessup, Bob. "Corporatism, Parlimentarism and Social Democracy." In Philippe C. Schmitter and Gerhard Lehmbruch (eds.), *Trends Toward Corporatist Intermediation.* Beverly Hills, Calif.: Sage Publications, 1979.

Kaufman, Herbert. "Administrative Decentralization and Political Power." *Public Administration Review,* 29 (January 1969), pp. 3–15.

Korten, David C. "The Management of Social Transformation." *Public Administration Review,* 41 (November/December 1981), pp. 609–618.

Kweit, Mary G., and Kweit, Robert W. *Implementing Citizen Participation in a Bureaucratic Society.* New York: Praeger, 1981.

Lazerson, Mark H. "In the Halls of Justice, the Only Justice Is in the Halls." In Richard L. Abel (ed.), *The Politics of Informal Justice, Volume 1, The American Experience.* New York: Academic Press, 1982.

Lehmbruch, Gerhard. "Consociational Democracy, Class Conflict and the New Corporatism." In Philippe C. Schmitter and Gerhard Lehmbruch (eds.), *Trends Toward Corporatist Intermediation.* Beverly Hills, Calif.: Sage Publications, 1979.

Lehmbruch, Gerhard. "Liberal Corporatism and Party Government." In Philippe C. Schmitter and Gerhard Lehmbruch (eds.), *Trends Toward Corporatist Intermediation.* Beverly Hills, Calif.: Sage Publications, 1979.

Levine, Andrew. *Liberal Democracy: A Critique of Its Theory.* New York: Columbia University Press, 1981.

Lowi, Theodore J. *The End of Liberalism: Ideology, Policy, and the Crisis of Public Authority.* New York: W.W. Norton, 1969.

Luhmann, Nicholas. Presentation at the Reflexive Law Conference, Wisconsin Law School, Madison, Wisconsin, July 1983.

Lustig, R. Jeffrey. *Corporate Liberalism: The Origins of Modern American Political Theory, 1890–1920.* Berkeley: University of California Press, 1982.

Marwell, Gerald. "Altruism and the Problem of Collective Action." In Valerian J. Derlega and Janisz Grzelak (eds.), *Cooperation and Helping Behavior: Theories and Research.* New York: Academic Press, 1982.

Marwell, Gerald, and Ames, Ruth E. "Economists Free Ride, Does Anyone Else?" *Journal of Public Economics,* 15 (1981), pp. 295–310.

Marwell, Gerald, and Ames, Ruth E. "Experiments in the Provision of Public Goods. I. Resources, Interest, Group Size, and the Free-Rider Problem." *American Journal of Sociology,* 84, 6 (1979), pp. 1335–1360.

Marwell, Gerald and Ames, Ruth E. "Experiments on the Provision of Public Goods. II. Provision Points, Stakes, Experience, and the Free-Rider Problem," *American Journal of Sociology,* Vol. 85, No. 4 (1980), pp. 926–937.

Marwell, Gerald, and Oliver, Pamela. "Collective Action Theory and Social Movements Research." In Louis Kriesberg (ed.), *Research in Social Movements, Conflicts and Change,* Vol. 7. Greenwich, Conn.: JAI Press, 1981.

Matusow, Allen J. *The Unraveling of America: A History of Liberalism in the 1960's.* New York: Harper & Row, 1984.

McCarthy, John D., and Zald, Mayer N. "Resource Mobilization and Social Movements: A Partial Theory." *American Journal of Sociology,* 82 (1978), pp. 1212–1241.

Mills, C. Wright. "The Social Scientist's Task." In Henry S. Kariel (ed.), *Frontiers of Democratic Theory.* New York: Random House, 1970.

Moe, Terry M. "Toward a Broader View of Interest Groups." *The Journal of Politics,* 43 (1981), pp. 531–543.

Nedelmann, Brigitta, and Meier, Kurt G. "Theories of Contemporary Corporatism: Static or Dynamic?" In Philippe C. Schmitter and Gerhard Lehmbruch (eds.), *Trends Toward Corporatist Intermediation*. Beverly Hills, Calif.: Sage Publications, 1979.

Nisbet, Robert. "Conservatism." In T. Bottomore and R. Nisbet (eds.), *A History of Sociological Analysis*. New York: Basic Books, 1978.

Oberschall, Anthony. "Loosely Structured Collective Conflict: A Theory and an Application." In Louis Kriesberg (ed.), *Research in Social Movements, Conflicts and Change*, Vol. 3. Greenwich, Conn.: JAI Press, 1980.

Oberschall, Anthony. "Protracted Conflict." In Mayer N. Zald and John D. McCarthy (eds.), *The Dynamics of Social Movements*. Cambridge, Mass.: Winthrop Publishers, 1979.

Oliver, Pamela. "The Mobilization of Paid and Volunteer Activists in the Neighborhood Movement." In Louis Kriesberg (Ed.), *Research in Social Movements, Conflicts and Change*, Vol. 5. Greenwich, Conn.: JAI Press, 1983.

Oliver, Pamela. "Rewards and Punishments as Selective Incentives for Collective Action: Theoretical Investigations." *American Journal of Sociology*, 85, 6 (1980), pp. 1356–1375.

Oliver, Pamela. "Selective Incentives in an Apex Game." *Journal of Conflict Resolution*, 24, 1 (March 1980), pp. 113–141.

Olson, Mancur, Jr. *The Logic of Collective Action*. Cambridge, Mass.: Harvard University Press, 1965.

Panitch, Leo. "The Development of Corporatism in Liberal Democracies." In Philippe C. Schmitter and Gerhard Lehmbruch (eds.), *Trends Toward Corporatist Intermediation*. Beverly Hills: Sage Publications, 1979.

Pateman, Carole. *Participation and Democratic Theory*. Cambridge: At the University Press, 1970.

Perlman, Janice. "Grassrooting the System." *Social Policy*, 7, 2 (September/October 1976), pp. 4–20.

Perrow, Charles. *Complex Organizations: A Critical Essay*, 2nd ed. Glenview, Ill.: Scott, Foresman, 1979.

Piven, Frances Fox, and Cloward, Richard A. *Poor People's Movements: Why They Succeed, How They Fail*. New York: Pantheon, 1977.

Poulantzas, Nicos. *State, Power, Socialism*. London: Verso, 1980.

Preston, Larry M. "Freedom and Authority: Beyond the Precepts of Liberalism." *The American Political Science Review*, 77 (1983), pp. 666–674.

Reich, Charles. "The New Property." *Yale Law Journal*, 73, 5 (April 1964), pp. 733–787.

Reifner, Udo. "Individualistic and Collective Legal Action: The Theory and Practice of Legal Advice for Workers in Prefascist Germany." In Richard L. Abel (ed.), *The Politics of Informal Justice*, Volume 2, *Comparative Studies*. New York: Academic Press, 1982.

Salisbury, Robert H. "Why No Corporatism in America?" In Philippe C. Schmitter and Gerhard Lehmbruch (eds.), *Trends Toward Corporatist Intermediation*. Beverly Hills, Calif.: Sage Publications, 1979.

Schmitter, Philippe C., and Lehmbruch Gerhard (eds.), *Trends Toward Corporatist Intermediation* Beverly Hills, Calif.: Sage Publications, 1979.

Spitzer, Steven. "The Dialectics of Formal and Informal Control." In Richard L. Abel (ed.), *The Politics of Informal Justice, Volume 1, The American Experience.* New York: Academic Press, 1982.

Thomas, John L. *Alternative America: Henry George, Edward Bellamy, Henry Demarest Lloyd and the Adversary Tradition.* Cambridge, Mass.: Harvard University Press, 1983.

Turner, Ralph H. "Collective Behavior and Resource Mobilization as Approaches to Social Movements: Issues and Continuities." In Louis Kriesberg (ed.), *Research in Social Movements, Conflicts and Change,* Vol. 4. Greenwich, Conn.: JAI Press, 1981.

Unger, Roberto M. *Knowledge and Politics.* New York: Free Press, 1975.

Useem, Bert, and Zald, Mayer N. "From Pressure Group to Social Movement: Organizational Dilemmas of the Effort to Promote Nuclear Power." *Social Problems,* 30, 2 (December 1982), pp. 144–156.

Wahrhaftig, Paul. "An Overview of Community-Oriented Citizen Dispute Resolution Programs in the United States." In Richard L. Abel (ed.), *The Politics of Informal Justice, Volume 1, The American Experience.* New York: Academic Press, 1982.

Walker, Jack L. "The Origins and Maintenance of Interest Groups in America." *American Political Science Review,* 77 (1983), pp. 390–406.

Weisner, Stan. "Fighting Back: A Critical Analysis of Coalition Building in the Human Services." *Social Science Review,* 57, 2 (June 1983), pp. 291–306.

Wolff, Robert Paul. *The Poverty of Liberalism.* Boston: Beacon Press, 1968.

· 9 ·

Social Autonomy

The purpose of a theory of public action is to enhance the capacity of individuals for self-determination in the modern social welfare state. Our major concern has been with individuals. One of the great failures of the liberal state—and its contemporary manifestation, the legal rights revolution—has been its inability to halt the increasing powerlessness of the ordinary person. The state has expanded; more and more we are dependent on it; yet, less and less do we have meaningful control over the shape of our lives. The legal rights revolution promised redress. By establishing rights and procedural due process, citizens could protect themselves from the power of the state, but this has not happened.

The question is whether liberalism can exist in the modern state. Liberalism has many meanings—political freedom, the market, the free exercise of religion. I take the core definition of individualism, or autonomy. Autonomy tracks the initial definition of administrative justice. Administrative justice, in my conception, is the sharing of power in the discretionary decision. Autonomy, variously defined, usually comes down to self-determination. Autonomy, say Beauchamp and Childress (1983), is "where the individual determines his or her own course of action in accordance with a plan chosen by himself or herself. The most general idea of autonomy is that of being one's own person, without constraints either by another's action or by a psychological or physical limitation. Both internal and external constraints on action can limit autonomy." Kant and John Stuart Mill approached the idea of autonomy from different perspectives, but, at least for our purposes, did not really differ that much. For Kant, autonomy was a matter of will, of governing oneself in accordance with moral principles that are personally derived but that are universal, that is, valid for everyone. For Kant, respect for autonomy is founded on the conception of each person having unconditional worth; each person is an end, never a means. "To treat a person merely as a means always involves a violation of autonomy for Kant, because the person is then being treated in accordance with a rule not of his own choosing" (Beauchamp and Childress 1983, p. 58). The principle of respect for persons is based not on utilitarian concepts but on the idea that each person is a person and rightfully a determiner of his or her own destiny.

Mill was concerned with autonomy of action.

> There is a non-contingent argument which runs through *On Liberty*. When Mill states that "there is a part of life of every person who has come to years of discretion, within which the individuality of that person ought to reign uncontrolled either by any other person or by the public collectively," he is saying something about what it means to be a person, an autonomous agent. It is because coercing a person for his own good denies this status as an independent entity, that Mill objects to it so strongly and in such absolute terms. To be able to choose is a good that is independent of the wisdom of what is chosen [Dworkin 1976, p. 188].

These are the classic concepts of individualism. For our purposes, they are incomplete. One reason is the historical context in which individualism has been considered in classic liberal political philosophy. There, autonomy (as individualism) has been used in a number of senses that must be distinguished here. One important sense has been the connection between individualism and free enterprise (Macpherson 1962; Wolff 1968). It has been argued that historically and conceptually, individualism cannot be separated from the idea of private property and the market. Liberalism, in its classic sense, is atomic individualism. Each person pursues his or her self-interest, as free as possible from the constraints or considerations of others. The possession and acquisition of property are indispensable to individualism. Government, social groups, indeed society, are instrumental only (Levine 1981).

Here, I am not concerned with the connection between private property, or the market, and the individual. The concern here is with people and their relations to the state. While this relationship has been characterized as the "new property" (Reich 1964), that is the language of legal rights, and, as I have indicated, not productive of autonomy in the modern welfare state.

The other point of difference with classic liberalism is the concept of atomic individualism. Both Kant and Mill emphasize the liberty of the individual to choose, free from the restraints of others. Classical liberalism is concerned with conditions of independence. I am starting not with the solitary independence of the client but with the relationship of the client to the agency. I begin not with the independent, free-standing person, but rather with a person in a social relationship. The concern is not with the conditions of independence but, with the conditions of *interdependence*. Hence, the title of this chapter—"Social Autonomy"—to draw attention to the distinction between classical liberal autonomy and autonomy in the social relations.

A further distinction has to be made, the one discussed in Chapter 8. The conception offered here also differs from the classic alternative to classic liberalism—the individual finding identity within the social group. Among traditional group theorists, there is no distinction between the interests of the individual and the interests of the social group. As explained in Chapter 8, that is not the conception here. The function of the group is to help mitigate the effects of the maldistributions of wealth and power, to enhance the power of the individual, to increase autonomy *in the bargaining relationship;* in other words, to change the conditions of interdependence rather than to create the conditions of independence or to lose identity in the social bond.

The distinction that I am trying to make has been articulated most fully in the field of medical ethics. There, the social nexus is central; indeed, there is no point in talking about informed consent other than in the context of the physician/patient relationship. To the extent that the ideal is approached, the patient is autonomous, but the concept and its characteristics are embedded in the social relationship. We consider the patient autonomous not in the abstract but in relation to the health care decision. I am exploring a similar idea here—the autonomy of the client (or the parent) not in the abstract but in the context of the discretionary decision.

Informed Consent in Medical Ethics

The Theory

The theory of informed consent in medical ethics can be stated fairly simply. It follows the definition of autonomy but is placed in the physician/patient relationship. The President's Commission for the Study of Ethical Problems in Medicine and Biomedical and Behavioral Research defines informed consent as a process of shared decision making based upon mutual respect. It is based on two ethical values—personal well-being and self-determination. It is a mutual relationship. The President's Commission says that although it is fundamental that individuals (adults) are entitled to accept or reject care on the basis of their own values, patient choice is not absolute. The patient is not entitled to insist on care that violates accepted practice or a professional's own deeply held values. That is, professionals are also autonomous and entitled to mutual respect (President's Commission 1983).

Katz (1984) introduces the concept of "psychological autonomy" by which he draws the distinction between the right to make a choice and the psychological capacities that underlie that right, that is, the ability to reflect about contemplated choice. Psychological autonomy is just as essential to self-determination as the act of choosing. Psychological autonomy is the capacity of persons to reflect, choose, and act with an awareness of internal and external influences. Self-determination is an ideal; as such, it is unattainable in ordinary human affairs. We are never wholly free of the influence of others. The issue is the point on the continuum between self-determination at the one end and physician paternalism at the other.

What are the conditions or elements of informed consent? Again, there are various formulations among the ethical philosophers. Beauchamp and Childress (1983) say that informed consent must be solicited whenever a procedure is intrusive, whenever significant risks might be involved, and whenever the purposes of the procedure might be questionable. The components of informed consent are information, which in turn requires disclosure and comprehension; and consent, which requires voluntariness and competence. Neither of the components is simple. How much information must be disclosed? What would a reasonable person want to know? What would this particular patient want to know? According to Beauchamp and Childress, the emerging standard is that the patient should be provided with information that a reasonable person in the patient's circumstances would find relevant and could reasonably be expected to assimilate. They and others (for example, Katz) criticize this standard as being removed from the needs of the particular patient, the *individual,* not some hypothetical, abstract, uniform, "reasonable" person. They would add that the physician has to go further and ask whether this *particular* patient desires any more information. Katz argues eloquently that the process of mutual conversation has to occur patiently, over time, and with great skill in order for both the physician and the patient to know what and why they are deciding.

Adequate comprehension is a necessary condition for valid informed consent. Beauchamp and Childress say that the requirement of "full" disclosure is a red herring. "The fact that we are never *fully* voluntary, fully informed, or fully autonomous persons, does not follow that we are never *adequately* informed, free, and autonomous" (Beauchamp and Childress 1983; p. 26).

A difficult problem, on which the informed consent theorists divide, concerns waivers. Empirical evidence shows that many (some say over 60 percent) patients want virtually no information about the procedures and the risks. Some argue that it would be paternalistic to force the information onto the patient and that autonomy demands that the patient's wishes be respected. Others argue that there can be no such thing as informed consent if the patient is not informed. Beauchamp and Childress conclude that there is no clear theoretical resolution of this problem—either alternative is risky. Katz would insist on more conversation, more exploration of why the patient does not want more information. He concedes the paternalism point but argues that the goals and benefits of more informed decisions by patients are worth the risks to autonomy. In answer to the argument that patients want to trust their physicians, he says; "Trust, based on blind faith—on passive surrender of oneself to another—must be distinguished from trust that is earned after having first acknowledged to oneself and then shared with the other what one knows and does not know about the decision to be made" (Katz 1984; p. xv).

Is the patient competent to understand the information and make a decision? What are the standards for judging competency? Beauchamp and Childress say that "a person is competent if and only if that person can make a decision based on rational reasons" (1983, p. 69). The "rational" requirement, as they admit, is troublesome. It, as well as the conclusion "competence," can easily be used to hide a value judgment about what a rational person *ought* to consent to. Competence is thus cast in the form of an empirical question, which is seldom true. A person can be considered incompetent because he or she does not agree on the treatment that the physician recommends.

Katz also draws attention to the problem of rationality. As a psychoanalyst, he is concerned with the role of the unconscious and the irrational that influence both physicians and patients. The assumption (with which Katz agrees) that the unconscious and the irrational are inferior to the conscious and the rational for purposes of reaching decisions is often manipulated by physicians. Physicians will make the decisions for the patients' "best interests," that is, the decisions that the patients would have made if their rational selves had been in control. Katz believes that the impact of the unconscious and the irrational can be reduced through conversation and self-reflection. "Individual freedom should be equated neither with simply permitting patients to do what they initially desire nor with requiring them simply to make complete sense to their physicians. True freedom requires constant struggle" (Katz 1984, p. 114).

Then, there is the issue of voluntariness. Having received the necessary information and reached an understanding of the facts, is the patient free to choose among the alternatives? Again, we are on a continuum. Decisions are always made in the context of influences and pressures, of competing needs and wants, family concerns, obligations, persuasive arguments made by others. Beauchamp and Childress say that we must distinguish between "mere influence or pressure" and coercion or undue influence. Coercion is when "one person intentionally uses an actual threat of harm or forceful manipulation to influence another. . . . Undue influence is whenever someone uses an excessive reward or irrationally persuasive techniques to induce a person to a decision the person might otherwise not reach" (1983, p. 80).

In the abstract, informed consent is a simple idea and one on which there is virtually universal agreement. At least in Western society, it reflects our most fundamental conceptions of human dignity. There is hesitation and disagreement only when people begin to consider specific patients and specific illnesses. Once these problems are raised, the complications that the philosophers have noted—how much information? what is competence? what is voluntariness?—have to be addressed. But the point now is to recognize the fundamental basis of the idea of informed consent—liberty and self-determination. Why, then, is it such a difficult and troublesome problem?

The Tradition of the Medical Profession

Given the fundamental nature of the idea of informed consent, it may come as a surprise to learn that it has been unalterably opposed by the medical profession ever since its recorded history began, 2,000 years ago. In briefly reviewing the medical profession's position, I want to make two distinctions. First, I will review their theoretical or professional reasons for opposing informed consent. Then, I will discuss the more "mundane" reasons—self-interest, psychological factors, attitudes toward patients, training, the need to maintain the image of authority, problems of uncertainty, and so forth. In real life, of course, all of these factors operate on us. A theoretical or professional reason may be no more than a rationalization for the need to perform an operation that week to make a car payment. Certainly our mundane needs influence in varying degrees our principles. Nevertheless, to discuss only the reasons involving self-interest misses an important part of the equation. Throughout the history of medicine, as well as other professions, thoughtful people have consistently and sincerely opposed informed consent as not being in the best interests of the client. The idea of informed consent calls for a redefinition of the idea of professionalism. Although this is a central problem for medicine, it clearly applies to the area that I am discussing. Educational professionals as well as nonprofessional bureaucrats have more or less similar attitudes and conceptions of the client relationship. The theoretical position of traditional medicine will expose the elements of this position.

Just as self-interest can determine principles, principles can serve as masks for self-interest. It is important therefore, to examine as thoroughly as possible the principled reasons for the opposition to informed consent to uncover underlying reasons not based on principle. Katz and others argue that before physicians will embrace informed consent, they not only have to come to a theoretical understanding but they also must come to grips with a variety of underlying, nonprincipled reasons. The methodology of this book is similar. In order for informed consent to work in the context of the discretionary decision, the bureaucrats, too, have to come to both sets of understandings.

The final reason for understanding the theoretical arguments against informed consent is to determine where informed consent may not be valid. Although a fundamental value in the abstract, informed consent is controversial in the real world. There may be good reasons why, in certain circumstances, liberty and self-determination need to be limited. This is true in medicine (incompetence; small children) and may also be true in other areas of bureaucratic and professional relations (for example, child abuse and neglect). A careful understanding of theory can shed light on these cases.

Katz says: "Contemporary and historical evidence shows that patients' participation in decision making is an idea alien to the ethos of medicine. The humane care that physicians have extended to patients . . . is based on the humaneness of services silently rendered" (1984, p. xvi). Historically, good patients follow doctors' orders. Consent only applied to recalcitrant or "bad" patients. Disclosure meant getting patients to "consent" to what the doctor recommended.

This tradition can be traced back to the Hippocratic oath where the only explicit reference to disclosure is to advise against it:

> [p]erform [these duties] calmly and adroitly, concealing most things from the patient while you are attending to him. Give necessary orders with cheerfulness and serenity, turning his attention away from what is being done to him; sometimes reprove sharply and emphatically, and sometimes comfort with solicitude and attention, revealing nothing of the patient's future or present condition [Katz 1984, p. 4].

According to Katz, the physicians of ancient Greece would have been puzzled by the idea of shared decision making. "They viewed the doctor and the patient as having an identity of interests, united in friendship, which makes conversation unnecessary. Cooperation led to trust, obedience, and then to cure" (p. 5). And so it was with the medical profession. For the next 2,000 years liberty was never even considered part of the caring relationship. There was no mention of informed consent, in any form, in the codes of the organized profession, until 1957. Then, in response to current developments in malpractice law and to comply with congressional legislation for the conduct of research, the American Medical Association (AMA) required disclosure in three specific instances—in surgery ("all facts relevant to the need and performance of the operation"), for experimenters of new drugs and procedures, and for investigators in clinical-treatment programs. It was not until 1981 that the AMA addressed the question of informed consent, concluding that a patient has the right of self-determination and, in order to exercise that right, has to have "enough information" to make an intelligent choice. It is not justification for the physician to withhold the information simply because the patient might be prompted to forego needed therapy. There are limitations on the duty to disclose: in addition to incompetence, in cases when the failure to treat will result in harm.

Why has it taken organized medicine so long to come to even this limited position? In part, it was the pressure of the law, which will be discussed in the next section. But the main reason is that physicians do not believe in the validity of informed consent in the doctor/patient relationship. The task of the physician is to provide the best, most humane care for the patient. Physicians believe that this task will be compromised if they try to engage in shared decision making. There are multiple reasons for this position. There is a great deal of uncertainty in medicine, even about what may appear to be a most routine procedure. Medical knowledge is both esoteric and uncertain. Furthermore, the condition of the patient is never static; as it evolves, different considerations become relevant. Physicians feel that it is both impossible and harmful to convey this uncertainty. Physicians themselves have great difficulty in sorting out what they know and do not know. How, then, can they convey this information to patients in a sensible fashion?

Even if the physicians wanted to convey this information in an honest and forthright manner, do the patients have the capacity to comprehend? Many physicians think not. They view patients as child-like, and there is some degree of truth in this perception. Because of the helplessness, anxiety, and dependence that illness engenders, patients do appear more like children than like adults (Katz 1984). They want to believe in their doctors, to trust in their professional judgment; they want reassurance, not conversations about uncertainties, problems, and alternatives. As Stone has said: "One does not have to be a psychiatrist to know that the vulnerability and helplessness of sick people manifest in their relation to their doctors will not often be resolved by information" (1979, p. 323). Doctors insist that a certain amount of trust is essential to the caring function. To raise these issues with patients who are unprepared and unwilling to hear about them may cause more harm than good. In the end, the patient will insist that doctors do what they think "best"; in the meantime, a great deal of anxiety will have been created, and, in the process, a lack of confidence may have developed.

Patients may be incompetent and disclosure may be therapeutically harmful, but how can physicians justify making the decisions themselves? They have knowledge and experience, but why should they be trusted to make decisions in the patients' best interests and not their own self-interest? The answer is their devotion to service and altruism. Physicians have a commitment not only to give the best available technical care but also to put the patients' best interests first.

The Law of Informed Consent

From the beginning of recorded medicine, then, the doctor/patient relationship consisted of a doctor who would decide and then provide the patient with a recommendation; the patient's ordinary role was to acquiesce (Lidz and Meisel 1982). There was not complete silence; under the law of battery, the patient had a right to know what a surgeon proposed to do and the surgeon had to have the patient's consent. The patient's right was narrow; it was only a right to refuse treatment. If the patient submitted, the doctor had obtained consent.

According to Katz, as late as the 1950s, allegations as to the *adequacy* of the physician's disclosure—the seriousness of the operation, the risks, and the alternatives, including no treatment—were virtually unheard of. The first use of the term "informed consent" appeared in a 1957 case where the plaintiff, a young man, suffered paralysis of his lower extremities after an aortography. He claimed that the physicians negligently failed to warn him of the risks inherent in the procedure. The decision was reversed on a number of errors but in the concluding paragraph, the court quoted from the *amicus curiae* brief of the American College of Surgeons: "A physician violates his duty to his patient and subjects himself to liability if he withholds any facts which are necessary to form the basis of an intelligent consent by the patient to the proposed treatment." How much should the physician disclose? The court continued: "In discussing the element of risk, a certain amount of discretion must be employed consistent with the full disclosure of facts necessary to an informed consent." The American College of Surgeons was concerned because a new and risky procedure was being used and there was a feeling that patients should be told something.

In subsequent cases, the courts attempted to define more precisely the duties of the physicians. Liability for failure to obtain informed consent was firmly placed in the law of negligence instead of in the law of battery. No mere technicality, the law of negligence clearly favored the doctors. Physicians would be liable only if they failed to disclose what a reasonable physician would have revealed under the circumstances. Furthermore, there is a therapeutic privilege—the physician can withhold information that would seriously jeopardize the well-being of the patient.

Under negligence law, the patients have to prove that they would have refused the proposed treatment had they been fully informed *and* that by submitting to the treatment, they suffered harm. Negligence law generally does not redress injuries to dignitary values in the absence of physical injuries. Yet, it would seem that the core idea of informed consent is an injury to self-determination. A subsequent court restricted patients' interests even further. In deciding whether the patient would have rejected the treatment if fully informed, the jury would consider what a reasonably prudent patient would have decided, not what this particular patient would have done. Again, this objective standard conflicts with the idea of self-determination, which is supposed to protect individual choice, even if idiosyncratic. The court was concerned that a subjective standard would put too great a burden on doctors—they would have to find out what their particular patients wanted to know.

According to Katz, courts, juries, and legislatures have deferred to standard medical practice. The law, as developed, protected the physicians and limited disclosure to the bare minimum. The courts invented the duty of informed consent, but when confronted with the more difficult questions of how much information and under what circumstances, they were reluctant to interfere with the doctor/patient relationship. They deferred to standard medical practice. And what is that standard? Physicians continue to think that "patients are too ignorant to understand the information, that disclosure will increase fears and anxieties and reinforce 'foolish' decisions, and that informing them about uncertainties can undermine the faith so essential to the success of therapy. Therefore, the doctor must be the ultimate decision maker" (Katz 1984, p. 64).

Informed Consent in Operation

The law's vision is that medical decisions should be made jointly by both the physician and the patient. The physician brings to the decision medical expertise. The patient brings personal values. The law then imposes on the doctor the duty to give the patient information, thus equalizing the relationship and enabling the patient to instruct the doctor as to how to proceed. Procedurally, there is a single occasion on which the doctor talks to the patient about the condition, the diagnosis, the alternative procedures, the risks and the benefits. Then, the patient makes the decision by signing the informed consent form (Lidz and Meisel 1982).

In actual practice, there is a disclosure of risks rather than a dialogue with the patient. The purpose of the disclosure is defensive—to avoid malpractice liability. The end is to get the patient to accept the recommendation. The major finding of research prepared by the President's Commission for the Study of Ethical Problems in Medicine and Biomedical and Behavior Research is that "the manner in which decisions are made about which treatments patients will get bears little resemblance to the decision making process contemplated

by the informed consent doctrine" (Lidz and Meisel 1982, p. 390). As
the study put it:

> [A]n entirely different vocabulary must be employed if reality is
> to be more accurately portrayed:
> (1) "Disclosure" does not typically occur. Rather patients learn
> various bits of information, some relevant to decision making,
> some not, from doctors' and nurses' efforts to obtain compliance
> and from "situational etiquette."
> (2) "Decisions" are not made by patients. "Recommendations"
> are made by doctors to patients.
> (3) "Consent" does not exist. Instead what we find is "acquies-
> cence," the absence of "objection," or occasionally a "veto" [Lidz
> and Meisel 1982, p. 401].

Katz reached the same conclusion. Although physicians have become more aware of their new obligations, "by and large, disclosures
are limited to risks and benefits of proposed treatment, not about
alternatives, and not about the certainties or uncertainties inherent in
most treatment options. Most importantly, conversations with patients are not conducted in the spirit of inviting patients to share with
their physicians the burdens of decision. Without such a commitment,
dialogue is reduced to monologue" (Katz 1984, p. 22). "Thus, what
passes today for disclosure and consent in physician/patient interactions is largely an unwitting attempt by physicians to shape the disclosure process so that patients will comply with their recommendations"
(p. 26).

To be sure, there is variation. Some doctors give what amounts to
orders; others will present neutral statements. Some patients know
more than others, or will be more aggressive. Sometimes the presence
of family helps the patient decide. The practice of informed consent
also varies by the setting, the procedures, and the type of illness.

The amount of information that physicians give patients seems to
vary with the discreteness of the diagnosis (surgical in-patients receive
more information than cardiology in-patients) or the uncertainty of
the disorder. Nevertheless, despite the uncertainty about the nature
and the etiology of the problem, medical personnel go to great
lengths to convey a sense of certainty.

The President's Commission study found a difference between the acute and the chronically ill. With the latter, the physician/patient role came closest to the idea of informed consent. These patients were given more information than acute-care patients, they had a better understanding of the information, and both physicians and patients understood the patients to have a greater role in deciding on their treatment. The conversations between the physicians and the chronic patients extended over a period of time and, with the passage of time, understanding grew. The study noted, however, that the information given to the chronically ill patients was not necessarily for the purposes of shared decision making. Rather, it was to assist them in learning to cope with a new way of life and to comply with the treatment. Moreover, when the chronic patients suffered an acute illness, the physician/patient role reverted. The patients were then given only enough information to help them agree to the recommendation and to lessen surprise in the event of untoward results (Lidz and Meisel 1982).

Perhaps the harshest criticism of the study centered on the role of informed consent forms in the decision-making process. It was here that the reality was at sharp variance with the law's vision. Neither the physicians, the nurses, nor the patients viewed the form as part of the decision-making process. Rather, it was a bureaucratic formality imposed upon them by hospital administrators, lawyers, and the legal system. In most cases, it was a preprinted form with a minimal amount of information. In effect, the patients were asked to sign the forms after the decisions were made. The surgery form was presented the night before the scheduled operation. The nurses were responsible for obtaining the signatures; they did not view their role as being responsible for providing information.

Why the Failure of Informed Consent in Medicine?

There are three clusters of reasons why informed consent does not work in medicine: the attitudes of the physicians, the attitudes of the patients, and the nature of the *medical* decision-making process. All interact and reinforce each other. The attitudes and perceptions of the physicians have already been discussed. It is a mistake to think of this attitude as merely self-serving in a narrow, parochial, or greedy sense. As Stone says, "Many good physicians find personal satisfaction and fulfillment in the parental role. What is more, most doctors believe that it is a therapeutically useful and efficient role. Resistance to transforming the doctor/patient relationship is deep-seated because in its current format, it both serves the psychological needs of the doctor and is thought to be useful" (1979, p. 322).

The attitudes of the patients reinforce the predispositions of the doctors. According to Katz, adults regress under the stress of illness; they become childlike and dependent and look to the physician as the all-powerful, omniscient parent who will help them in their distress. The conclusion of the President's Commission study was that, fundamentally, patients do not feel equal to making these decisions. Even when provided with the information, they remain passive and still act as if the doctor should make the final decision. For the most part, the patients were not even interested in the information. It was the opinion of the authors of the Report of the President's Commission that the doctors know this about the patients and therefore do not take the time and effort to pursue informed consent.

The uncertainty in medicine combined with what the physician brings to the case produces a medical decision-making process that is sharply at odds with the law's vision. The diagnosis of the physician usually involves the rapid formulation, quite often on a preconscious level, of a series of conclusions including preferable treatments. Diagnosis and treatment decisions are a temporal process rather than a discrete decision. In the course of the process, however, the physician rarely sees alternative possibilities. For each problem there exists a medically preferred alternative rather than a series of alternatives. Thus, according to the President's Commission study, to the doctor, the issue is not a decision-making process but a problem in persuading the patient to accept proper treatment. By the time the physician is conversing with the patient, "The decision has been made—by the doctor. It is now, in the medical view, time to make a recommendation to the patient" (Lidz and Meisel 1982, p. 400).

The conclusions reached by most observers is that informed consent in medicine is largely a failure; it really does not exist in most situations. This is both unfortunate and serious. It is unfortunate if one believes in self-determination, as a value in and of itself. It is serious because the controversy and failure of informed consent in medicine has spilled over into other areas of life. Looking at the medical experience, one often concludes that shared decision making is "hopeless," "it doesn't work," or it is "utopian."

Actually, medicine is probably the most difficult setting for informed consent. All of the characteristics of the physician/patient relationship work against it. The information is truly difficult. It is highly technical and esoteric; but making the problem of understanding far more difficult is the uncertainty of diagnosis and prognosis. That is, not only must the physician be able to transmit in understandable form the benefits and costs of alternatives, but added in are statistical probabilities (if they even exist) of the alternatives. This kind of information is not easy to understand for the purposes of making a choice about treatment. What does it mean to say that there is a 1 percent chance of total paralysis of the lower extremities? For a great many medical procedures, the 1 percent is not a real figure, something that has been verified by scientifically controlled experiments. More often, it is a hunch, based on clinical experience.

In addition, consider what the patient is being asked to decide. The patient, in most situations, has not had any experience with the problem. The condition is new and the future is unknown. How can the patient know what choice to make without any basis for experience?

Some argue that informed consent will lead to better medical decisions. If physicians can be persuaded to believe this, then there are incentives for them to pursue informed consent. This, apparently, is the situation with the chronically ill. There, it is in the professional interests of doctors to ensure that patients understand the nature of their illness and agree with proposed alternatives. This is in the physicians' interests, because only with this understanding will the patients learn to live with their new conditions *and* follow the prescribed treatment. In other words, cooperation and understanding are necessary for both the physician and the patient, and the research indicates that chronically ill patients learn a great deal about their conditions and have a lot to say to doctors about alternative treatments (Lidz and Meisel 1982).

But suppose it is not clear that informed consent will lead to better medical decisions, or that physicians are not persuaded that such is the case? What, then, will induce them to engage in this process? A belief in the dignity of people? Perhaps, for a few doctors. But a belief in the dignitary value of informed consent was not the motivating factor with the chronically ill; rather, informed consent was a by-product of the process of pursuing the professional or medical goals of the physicians. There were strong incentives to gain understanding and cooperation.

Then, there is the issue of trust. As noted, many physicians believe that trust is essential for therapy (Relman 1984). Some argue that a situation where patients ask many questions is fundamentally anti-thetical to trust. The latent message from the patient is "I do not trust what you are telling me, and I want to be sure," and from the doctor, "See how open and honest I am?" Where there is trust—for example, with a long-standing physician/patient relationship—there will be less substantive communication and more obedience (Lidz and Meisel 1982). Katz (1984) criticizes this view; he calls it "blind" trust, and argues that with meaningful communication, trust can develop based on understanding and confidence. The paradox may be that physicians who explain more create a more trusting atmosphere, which does not produce more autonomy but rather less of a need for more disclosures.

It is in this subtle, exceedingly complex setting that the law intervenes and produces the wrong results. The ethical idea of the law is correct; as argued throughout this book, the bedrock foundation is the belief in the autonomy of the individual, the primacy of self-determination in important decisions that affect one's life and well-being. But the law is trapped by its liberal legal tradition. It views the physician/patient relationship as antagonistic. The law of informed consent grew out of the law of battery—an intentional tort—and the idea of battery still makes far more sense than negligence. How can one give consent to something that one is ignorant of? The use of negligence is a fiction, a device to make things easier on the medical profession. The law views the transaction cross-sectionally: there is disclosure and there is agreement; a contract establishes rights and liabilities rather than an on-going organic process. The primary purpose of the informed consent as administered is defensive—to avoid malpractice liability. The President's Commission study views the informed consent form as fruitless at best; it probably impedes patient participation in the decision-making process (Lidz and Meisel 1982). In short, adversarial advocacy truncates the relationship. By defining the relationship in terms of rights and liabilities, it pulls the parties apart. Physicians are concerned with lawsuits, not communication.

And, at least in the physician/patient relationship as presently constituted, if physicians do not take the responsibility for sharing decision making, it is not going to happen (Katz 1984).

The Comparison with Special Education

The reasons for the failure of informed consent in medicine point to the possibilities for its success in special education (and hopefully, in other discretionary decisions). We start again with organizational incentives. In medicine, there were no positive incentives to engage in meaningful conversation; and there were strong incentives not to. The one exception—which is important for our purposes—was with the chronically ill. And here, it is important to note that informed consent was a by-product; it grew out of the professional incentives to heal. Informed consent worked because there was an *exchange* between the chronically ill and their physicians. In order for the physicians to succeed, they had to get something that only the patients could give—understanding, agreement, and cooperation. Further, all three were necessary. If there were no understanding and agreement, there would not be cooperation. We found the same to be true in the Madison School District. When the District decided that they could succeed in their mission only if the parents were part of the solution, the relationship became one of exchange. The parents had to understand and agree if they were to cooperate in the school's program. Autonomy, self-determination, participation—from the school's perspective—were by-products of organizational incentives. Attitudes and beliefs become harmonious with professional tasks (Weimann 1982). Teacher and parent become both ends and means. There is a conjunction, not a conflict, between ethics and work.

The technical and uncertain nature of medical knowledge is considered by physicians to be an impediment to informed consent. With special education, knowledge is also technical and uncertain, but the Madison School District uses this state of the art to foster communication rather than silence and acquiescence. By recognizing the uncertain state of the art, the District is able to adopt a flexible, experimental approach. This is not a tactical ploy. They honestly believe that the surest way to proceed with handicapped students is by trial and error.

The effect of this approach is to reduce the level of potential conflict and to increase the opportunities for discussion. Parents and teachers do not have to think of themselves as winners and losers. They can be flexible and experimental. The parents can listen to the school's point of view, knowing that there will be reconsideration. If parents are particularly worried about a placement, the school can defer and see how the child progresses in an alternative setting.

Both the medical decision-making process and special education take place over a period of time. The difference is that the formal informed consent part of medicine takes place at only one point in time. In the Madison School system, the dialogue (at least ideally) takes place over the school-life of the child. The process is not only more realistic but also allows for the building of trust and experience. Physicians ask their patients to speculate, to project how they would feel about certain things that are completely unknown to them. With a continuous dialogue, parents can make decisions on the basis of past experience.

Physicians feel that authority and trust are important to therapy, and for these reasons informed consent is not a good idea. The Madison School people also believe in themselves; they are well-trained, highly motivated, and experienced. But they are not defensive. They welcome outside professional opinion and different points of view. To them, uncertainty is not a threat; time will tell which approach is better. There is also trust in the Madison School District, but the staff view trust as more problematic than the physicians do. The problem, in Madison, is blind trust, the trust that leads to passiveness and acquiescence. Their goal is the trust that Katz argues for—trust based on mutual understanding. What seems to happen in Madison, though, is that as the child ages, the parents, for a variety of reasons, begin to lose interest in maintaining the levels of communication and participation that the teachers would like. This is similar to the problem that the President's Commission study noted—the more conversation and understanding, the more trust, which paradoxically leads the physician to dispense with disclosure. In Madison, it is the teachers who want to maintain the communication—they still have the organizational incentives. It is the parents who no longer feel the need to communicate.

There are differences in the technical nature of the information and the stakes involved, but how important are these for the purposes of informed consent? In the abstract, the differences are very great. From the point of view of the parents the idea that their child may be retarded is extremely anxiety-producing. They too have difficulty coping with the technical information, the test scores, the evaluations, the jargon. While the nature of the information and the stakes involved may make informed consent more difficult in medicine, the situation with handicapped children is by no means easy.

The implementation of the law also has differential consequences. As to some of the formalities, the law operates the same in both medicine and special education. In special education, the parents have to agree in writing to the major decisions of selection and placement. In most jurisdictions, the informed consent procedures are viewed defensively, bureaucratically, as obstacles to overcome—much as we find in medicine. In special education, the law requires that the parents be present at the multidisciplinary conferences, but this, too, is often only a formality. Most decisions are made beforehand by the school staff; the parents have little understanding as to what is going on; there is no effort to communicate with them in language that they can understand; there is no effort to find out what they think and want. Most observers agree that the informed consent process in special education is form only (see Chapter 3).

In both medicine and special education, the law is intrusive and dysfunctional in its requirements. It separates the parties instead of building cooperation. It creates adversaries when there should be friends. It creates winners and losers when there should be community. It creates bureaucratic requirements when there are already enough barriers.

The law also applies to Madison. The Madison system of cooperative decision making still has to deal with the Education for All Handicapped Children Act, the state statutes, and the administrative regulations. Informed consent forms still have to be signed; parents can still get two administrative hearings and judicial review if necessary. But the law recedes in importance. It is there to protect those who still feel aggrieved, and, on a few occasions, it has been used. But it does not dominate. The participants in Madison do not think in terms of legal rights, of hearings, of lawsuits. Their focus is on shared decision making, on communication, on reaching understandings at a reduced level of conflict.

Conclusions

Informed consent in medicine is a hard case. It is not working, and, given the obstacles, it may never work. But it does not follow from the experience in medicine that informed consent is an impossible dream in other settings.

In special education, informed consent is not working for similar reasons. In most districts, there is bureaucratic domination. The law intervenes crudely, inappropriately, and exacerbates conflict rather than fostering community. The parents are seen as part of the problem. They lack self-determination in important matters that affect their children.

Yet, we have seen that in the Madison School District informed consent seems to work. By "work" I mean that the school people have thought through in a coherent manner what conditions are necessary for the autonomous functioning of parents and school people. They work hard at trying to implement the idea, and, based on limited interviews with a range of participants and knowledgeable observers, there seems to be some degree of success. The system is by no means perfect, as those who are involved readily admit, but the weaknesses seem to be amenable to moderation. One does not get a sense of near hopeless intractability as seen in medicine.

In the preceding chapters, I have discussed in detail the conditions of shared decision making. Initially, the key moves have to come from the bureaucracy. In Madison, this consisted of reconceptualizing the organizational task so that parents become part of the solution rather than the problem. It is important to repeat that this change in position on the part of the bureaucracy is not necessarily based on sentiment, ethics, goodwill, or the like (although these worthy traits are not excluded either); rather, it is based on organizational incentives—the schools can do a better job of educating handicapped children with parental participation.

The Critique of Liberalism

This book presents a form of decision making that is at variance with current ideology and practice. I use the term "variance" to emphasize both change and continuity; significant elements of what I am proposing have been drawn from history and contemporaneous practice. Indeed, my principal empirical example—the Madison School District's special education program—is a real-world case. And many of the ideas are as old as political philosophy itself. What I have tried to do is to bring together various strands and elements of ideas and practices into a different way of conceptualizing, designing, and implementing public programs to better accomplish justice in the discretionary decision. The idea is to preserve the old liberal values of autonomy, responsibility, and progress in the social context of the modern welfare state. An economical way to illustrate the similarities and differences between what I am proposing and the current theory and practice is to examine the recent criticisms of the liberal state. It is out of the critique of the current practice that the new form emerges.

As I have described, there are four principal conditions of discretion. The first condition is a decentralized system. In a sense decentralization is obvious when there is discretion; the two are inseparable. The difference in my proposed theory is that decentralization is viewed as an opportunity rather than a regrettable necessity. The aim of policy is to encourage the creative use of discretion. Accepting the fact that there will be variation, policy will necessarily be contingent. Discretion is desirable if the other three conditions are fulfilled.

The second condition is the changed role of the bureaucracy. Great emphasis is placed on the importance of incentives and structures at the agency level. In a word, the bureaucracy has to be part of the community, otherwise the program fails.

The third condition is the role of social movement groups, particularly, but not exclusively, at the grass roots level. The groups address the distribution question. They provide the resources to enable parents to take advantage of the opportunity to participate. They key here is *communicative* conflict, not *adversarial* conflict. The bureaucracy, as part of its organizational task, has to want parental participation.

The fourth condition is cooperative decision making between the parent and the school. Borrowing an analogy, we might call this informed consent (in its ideal form) in the administrative state. This is the ideal of informed consent, as eloquently stated by Katz and others, rather than the current practice in medicine. It contemplates "a process in which two or more parties influence each other in making plans, policies, or decisions. . . . It excludes merely taking part in group activity, merely getting information on a decision before execution, and mere presence but no influence" (Pateman 1970, p. 68).

All of the conditions are necessary; none can be avoided. Cooperative decision making necessarily implies contingency. If parents are to participate, then social movement groups have to be autonomous. Participation and autonomy can succeed only if there is community with the bureaucracy, and this can come about only if there is decentralization and discretion.

How, then, do the conditions of discretion differ from liberalism? As will be brought out at the conclusion, the conditions reaffirm what I believe are the essential values of liberalism. Moreover, they are rooted in traditions and theory as old as the liberal state. Nevertheless, they are strongly opposed to the current theory and practice of the liberal state. In order to demonstrate this, I will first discuss the critique of liberalism and then compare the conditions of discretion.

First, a disclaimer. Needless to say, there is a vast and ever-growing literature on what liberalism is. I cannot hope to thoroughly explore these very complex issues, the very issues that have been at the core of political philosophy in Western civilization. What I will try to do is describe in brief fashion what I believe are some of the basic criticisms of liberalism and where the argument of this book meets and transcends these criticisms.

The criticisms of liberalism come from all directions, including from many who consider themselves liberals. One strand, from the left, has been labeled democratic radicalism (Shiffrin 1983) and is in the tradition of radical communitarian politics. This strand, also very old, has never really taken hold; two objections have been utopianism and the threat to individualism. In addressing the critique of liberalism, I will also discuss the two objections to democratic radicalism.

At the risk of oversimplification, the critique of liberalism can initially be grouped into two broad categories—political and epistemological. The objections under the first grouping are excessive egoism and the public/private distinction. Under the second, the objections are to positivism or scientism, the separation of facts from values and subjects from objects, relativism, and neutrality. The epistemology and political theories inform each other; the result, it is charged, is at best conservatism and the perpetuation of inequalities and the status quo, and at worst, technocracy, authoritarianism, domination, and even fascism. Under either result, there is a loss of liberal values (Spragens 1981; Shiffrin 1983).

The distinguishing feature of liberal political theory is the radical separation of public life from private life and its insistence on clear, determinate limits to public or political authority. It is in society (private) where individual ends are realized. Freedom, for liberals, is concerned with the relation between individuals and each other and the state (or other groups). The state is necessary only insofar as it guarantees or promotes the freedom of individuals—the familiar "nightwatchman." The public is separated from the private, politics from economics, and the state from the market (Spitzer 1982; Nedelsky 1982). It is in the market that freedom flourishes; political life is conceived of in terms taken from the market. The acquisitive market man is the basic unit of society; contract is the "paradigmatic social relationship" (Lustig). The radical separation of politics from society, and the conception that society is the principal arena for the development of human activity creates a powerful presumption for contracting politics and expanding society (Levine 1981).

Liberal theory is most commonly linked with the development of the market. Not accidentally, the development of the political theory coincided with the rise of modern science, the Age of Enlightenment, utilitarianism, all of which contributed, in the most profound sense, to the conception of the autonomous individual. Scientific methodology would allow for the dissemination of knowledge; one could understand and consider nature without the risk of blasphemy. The truth value of knowledge depended on what one could verify through one's senses. Utilitarianism—the greatest good for the largest number— was the sum of individual interests, not an organic group interest. These theories of politics, morals, and epistemology rested on an optimistic view of human nature. Free of medieval restraints, free from state interference with thoughts, feelings, and private conscience, limited only to the minimum amount necessary to prevent harm to others, individuals, as rational and free agents, would flourish, and happiness would be maximized (Spragens 1981; Wolff 1968).

This was the classical position. Although the world has changed drastically since the formative period of liberal theory, a great deal of the ideological heritage lives on, which, in turn, has prompted a large volume of criticism. Utilitarianism and the emphasis on the market reduces people to unbridled pleasure seekers and leads people to treat each other as means to ends. Under the individualism of utilitarianism, all is instrumental—the people one deals with, social groups, the state. There is no concept of people as social beings, as belonging to groups or other social units except for individual instrumental purposes. There are no group or social values other than the sum of the individual values. Groups, indeed all social bonds, are unstable since the ends of the individuals are unstable. Social life, in classical liberal theory, is atomic individualism. Each person is an independent entity; social intercourse, a series of collisions.

Not only does this individualistic, pleasure-seeking conception impoverish the human but it is false to the nature of humanity. As an immediate reaction to the earliest expressions of liberalism, conservative thought argued that individuals cannot be thought of in isolation; people are what they are only as defined socially; they can survive, let alone flourish, only as part of the group (Nisbet 1978). The older traditionalists harked back to the church, the family, the guild, the clan. But communitarians were also progressive. They believed that the individualism of the market and utilitarianism were basically destructive of the person, and that humanity could flourish only when individualism was merged into the community.

Thus, throughout the history of liberal theory there has been the countertheory. People are individuals; yet people live in society, they are social beings (Mensch 1982; Levine 1976). How can the individual personality survive in the group? Liberal theory has never been able to resolve the contradiction or to develop a theory of social autonomy (Sandel 1982). As Unger puts it:

> Alone, a man is deprived of the supports of individuality. Without the social productions of culture, he cannot develop his characteristic human capacities. Without the recognition of his personality by others, he cannot arrive at a definition of his own identity. But in the company of others, he must conform to their expectations in order to be understood and to be recognized. This submission undermines his uniqueness. Thus, men are in the position of Schopenhauer's porcupines, who huddle together to protect themselves from the cold, but who, when they come together, wound one another with their spines [Unger 1975, p. 156].

The public/private distinction similarly serves to obscure underlying social relations. Liberal political theory holds that the state is minimal and that individuals achieve their ends primarily by their own acts in the private (social) arena. Yet, from the earliest times, the state has been deeply implicated in the market. As Kennedy states:

> The private owner's "freedom" to exclude others from his possessions has as its corollary his "power" to control the lives of those who cannot live without access to the means of production. Admission to the use of property is the carrot, exclusion the stick that orders our lives. It is a familiar notion that, through the definition and enforcement of legal rights in things, the state is deeply implicated in the particular order that emerges from the inter-action of private individuals [Kennedy 1979; p. 264].

Kennedy goes on to discuss the implication of maintaining the myth of the public/private distinction: by masking the role of the state, particular outcomes are considered to be outside collective control. Instead, they are the "natural" functioning of the market.

Rather than the classic liberal state, we now have the welfare-corporate state. More and more, the government has assumed responsibility for the workings of the market and the distribution of social and economic benefits. At the same time, intermediate associations (unions, corporations, associations) have penetrated into the inner workings of government and have assumed a larger role in the definition of public policy (Unger 1975). In the modern welfare state, the government has become privatized, while private groups have been clothed with public power. We have developed a system described as "institutional pluralism" (Lowi 1969). Institutional pluralism, in many respects, differs little from liberal corporatism (Lustig 1982), where government and the relevant special interest groups are in stable alliances pursuing common ends. The range of government activity has grown so large and so extensive that it is difficult to think of significant areas that are not in some manner or other affected by public policy. At the same time, economic and social life is also dominated by large-scale enterprises working closely with the public sphere. The classical liberal conception of the separation of public and private and the dominant importance of the latter for the realization of human ends is now widely at variance with the modern state. Because of the failure of liberalism to deal with the question of equality, we lack democratic participation (Levine 1981); because of the lack of theory to reconcile the individual with the group, we lack a theory of associational participation. (Lustig 1982). We either rely on the myths of an earlier age that there is a sharp distinction between the public and private spheres; that individuals are free, autonomous, and equal participants in public life; or we believe that groups form to express their interests before a neutral government (pluralism) and that the state of public policy at any given time represents the sum of the represented interests.

The legal system, whether viewed as a mirror of the dominant interests of society (Friedman 1973) or as a more or less autonomous source of mediation (Kairys 1982), basically reflects the older, liberal tradition. The net result is the same. Either the public/private-individualism myth serves to support the "natural" order or the pluralism myth serves to mask the role of the state in reproducing the interests of the dominating coalitions (Alford 1981). The status quo is perpetuated.

At first blush, this assertion seems palpably untrue. As government has grown over the last decades, so have legal institutions. Law, in the classical liberal state, was used primarily to defend the property rights of individuals. Today, we see regulatory agencies, the substantive allocation of rights by states, and discretion rather than rights (Nonet and Selznick 1978; Teubner 1983). Yet, at base, we still rely on adversarial advocacy for the protection of rights. We continue to view relations between individuals and associations and government in terms of entitlements, rights, and procedural due process. Although the social reality is cooperation and discretion, the legal ideology and structure are in terms of adversarial relations, the assertion of rights either in courts or in trial-type hearings before administrative agencies (Michelman 1977). The adversary system, which in ideology and practice is the dominant form of conflict resolution by far, posits a conflictual relationship of winners and losers, of means and ends (Simon 1978). The parties are instrumental to each other. Under its mask of neutrality and formal equality, it, too, perpetuates the competitive egoism of the individual and the existing order by adding to the "natural" state of the market the mythology and sanctity of the law (Frug 1980; Spitzer 1982; Gordon 1982).

Underlying the various strands of the critique of liberalism— utilitarianism, atomic individualism, the liberal state, the legal system—is the epistemological base of positivism. Here, too, the argument is complicated, subtle, and controversial. Instead of liberating humanity by the dissemination of knowledge, understanding, and the progressive development of liberal qualities, positivism has led to conservatism, manipulation, hierarchy, and domination. How has this happened? How have the great, promising scientific breakthroughs of the seventeenth century served to enslave rather than liberate? Positivism made the radical separation of fact from value and asserted that knowledge was based only upon what could be observed—the hard, simple data that come from our sensory perceptions. Concepts such as morality, justice, fairness, beauty, and love—if not reduced to the "facts" of utilitarianism—were consigned to the irrational. Moral sentiments were either dismissed or converted into what people found agreeable and useful (Spragens 1981; Unger 1975).

The liberating concept of positivism in its earliest days was that nature was subject to objective, observable, rational, and scientific laws. This was liberating in at least two senses. It freed society from theocracy and offered hope that progress could be made through the understanding and manipulation of the laws of nature. The problem was that humanity was also considered part of nature, and if the world of plants and animals, tides and stars, was subject to observable, scientific, objective laws, so too were the activities of people. This view, in turn, led to two consequences. First, there was the conservative bias, which tended to view with favor the "natural" order of things; the parts of nature that are "functional." The unwillingness to rely on any knowledge claims that do not rest on hard, observable, simple facts leads to skepticism and to reliance on careful, trial-and-error experimentation as the only correct approach. One cautiously tinkers to make adjustments in the complex ordering of life. There is no basis for transcending the existing order (Spragens 1981).

Second, and somewhat contradictorily, positivism leads to the manipulation of people through the "authority of science" (Spragens 1981; p. 150). If nature (including humanity) is subject to scientific laws, then who better than the scientists to know what is good for those who do not understand science? Rather than democratizing knowledge, replacing the medieval clerics with the educated citizen, positivism has now substituted the scientist, the expert, the official. They are the interpreters of the scientific laws that determine the course of human events and guide people toward maximizing their happiness.

Spragens, in his book, *The Irony of Liberal Reason,* reminds us of Bentham's Panopticon. This was his model prison, a circular structure where the keeper, at the center, could observe the interior of every cell but the inmates could not observe the keeper, thus providing an effective method of control and domination. The Panopticon was not a lighthearted idea tossed off by the father of utilitarianism. Rather, Bentham thought the Panopticon model appropriate for a variety of other institutions, including schools, factories, and asylums. According to Spragens, Bentham worked hard all his life to get his Panopticon accepted and was sorely disappointed with his failure.

The idea of the panopticon seems amusing today, but on reflection, the omniscient and omnipotent "keeper" is ever present in contemporary society. It is the role of the physician described by Katz—the expert steeped in scientific knowledge deciding what is best for the childlike patient. It was one of the important animating ideas in the Progressive era and during the rise of the administrative agency that economic matters could be subject to scientific, neutral management. It became an important principle in private economic management, for example, Taylorism. Spragens argues that positivism has led to what he calls "technocracy"—the widespread governance by an elite group of experts concerned with the rationalization of society in terms of scientific principles. Concepts such as "liberty," "justice," and "rights" "were consigned to the realm of metaphysical nonsense" (Spragens 1981, p. 125).

In short, the argument is made that the hubris of positivism has led to the denial of those values promised by the discovery of science and the Age of Enlightenment. Liberty, autonomy, responsibility, and justice have been consigned to the irrational. Instead we have domination, hierarchy, manipulation, and instrumentalism. On the one hand, individuals are conceived of only as pleasure-seeking egoists, devoid of communitarian or social values apart from instrumental interests. On the other hand, they are considered to be objects, manipulated for their own good and the good of society. Egoistic, atomic individualism provides no coherent theory for the state, for social life, or morality.

Today philosophers are engaging in sometimes heroic efforts to establish fundamental principals of humanity on grounds other than property or pleasure (Shiffrin 1983). The results are decidedly unclear; what does seem evident is that nothing has really been settled and we are in for a long period of intense, philosophical debate. No one, claims Spragens, believes in positivism anymore—at least in its pristine form. This may be true of sophisticated scientists, but one sees much lingering evidence—the rise of conservative economics, the failure of informed consent in medicine, the failure of liberal legal ideology, as well as many other examples.

The Conditions of Discretion Compared

The conditions of discretion meet, I think, some of the major criticisms of liberalism. The doctrine of informed consent denies the fact/value distinction of positivism and the subject/object distinction of utilitarianism and atomic individualism. Informed consent, as discussed by Katz (and others in medicine) and as applied in the Madison School District, means the reaching of mutually acceptable decisions after discussion. There is no separation of fact from value, or reason from desire. The decisions of each of the participants are subjective. Thus, each person is allowed, indeed, encouraged, to assess feelings, sentiments, and intuition, as well as "facts." This is not to say that decisions are therefore arbitrary or irrational. Subjectivity is not inconsistent with rationality. The task is to explore the irrational and unconscious and to strive to reach conscious and rational decisions. This is a matter of degree, not exclusivity. But values such as the quality of life, feelings of integrity and fairness, and dignity and responsibility are at the heart of the informed consent process. Informed consent denies that knowledge can be based only on experience. With informed consent, knowledge is very different from positivism. There is no quest for simple, infallible, universalistic truths, transcending human limitations and imperfections. As Spragens says, "Instead of all knowledge aspiring to meet an unattainable standard of geometric clarity, certainty, and precision, all knowledge should be seen as potentially ambiguous and open-ended, corrigible, and groping. Instead of all real knowledge being theoretical, in short, all knowledge is incurably and indelibly 'practical.' " (Spragens 1981, p. 349).

Practical knowledge is distinguished from theoretical knowledge. Whereas theoretical knowledge is contemplative, absolute and autonomous, final and universal, and either mechanical or divine, practical knowledge holds that all knowledge is a form of problem solving, always contingent, subject to change, and "organic." "If we see know-ing not as having an essence, to be described by scientists or philoso-phers, but rather as a right, by current standards, to believe, then we are well on the way to seeing *conversation* as the ultimate context within which knowledge is to be understood" (Rorty 1979, p. 389). The idea of practical knowledge, like positivism, stems from the scientific revolution. Good science is active problem solving; it is not passive or contemplative. Both "normal" science and "extraordinary" science, in Kuhn's terms (1970), are practical in the sense of combin-ing theory with experience; the scientist is actively engaged in the environment while at the same time contemplating the mediating concepts. All scientific knowledge is contingent; "all genuinely intel-ligible 'facts' are interpreted. All theories could conceivably be sup-planted by alternative explanatory models; they therefore require judgment for their acceptance. . . . To put it another way, anything can be doubted" (Spragens 1981, p. 351). To argue that knowledge is contingent, that it ultimately depends on judgment and "rational bets," does not mean that all knowledge is arbitrary or irrational.

> Scientific claims are indeed "testable" and "confirmable." But they are "tested" and "confirmed" not by reference to some unchanging neutral algorithm but by the rational judgment of those who have the relevant experience and intellectual capaci-ties. Truth claims are "verified" or "falsified" "intersubjectively." What we call "knowledge," then, is not some eternal and change-less body of indubitably ascertained truths. In this sense, there is no "positive" knowledge. . . . What we call knowledge is our current stock of "warranted beliefs," accredited by and de-pendent on the reasoned judgments of appropriate authorities [Spragens 1981, p. 353].

The ontological correlate of viewing knowledge as "practical," accord-ing to Spragens, is that it is "organic." By this he means that it cannot be separated from the "cognitive power of living beings who are striv-ing to make their life and their world intelligible." Knowledge "is life reflecting upon itself and upon its environment" (Spragens 1981, p. 353).

> The knowing subject of "practical" reason is neither divine nor mechanical. He is neither wholly free nor wholly programmed, neither wholly "above" nature nor wholly submerged within it.

> He is part of nature, but he transcends it in that he can become conscious and reflect on both nature and himself. He is bound by his physicality, by his biology, and by his humanity, but he is a distinctive historical person, able to act on his environment as well as be subject to it. He can rise above the world far enough to "know" something about it, but he can never claim to know what he knows with finality, certainty, or perfection. He can vastly expand his historical perspective, but he can never eliminate it entirely. He is, in short, a "rational animal" [Spragens 1981, p. 354].

With informed consent, there is no subject/object distinction. The participants are simultaneously means and ends. In the Madison School District, the parents were part of the solution; there had to be communication, understanding, and agreement between parents and teachers if there was to be cooperation.

With informed consent, there is community rather than atomic individualism. Wolff (1968) defines community or social value as "a value whose definition makes essential reference to reciprocal states of awareness among two or more persons" (p. 12). He distinguishes three kinds of community—affective, productive, and rational. The affective community is not based on contractual association of egoistic satisfaction-maximizers but, instead, is bound by tradition, culture, and feelings. The example he gives is of people participating in ceremonies and rites, aware that their fellow participants are engaging in a simultaneous experience, and deriving pleasure and satisfaction from this awareness. This would be the reciprocal consciousness of a shared culture, a mutual awareness that is more than the summation of private interests.

In a productive community people are socially productive in addition to being individually productive. The rational community is the political alternative to liberal democracy. In the rational community, there is the collective deliberation and determination of social choices. Again, it is an activity, a reciprocity of consciousness, an awareness. In order to achieve a reciprocity of consciousness, there has to be a discourse by equals. "Each member must recognize his fellow citizens as rational moral agents and must freely acknowledge their right (and his) to reciprocal equality in the dialogue of politics" (Wolff 1968, p. 54). A dialogue requires the possibility of an uncoerced reply. Hence, it "takes at least two free men to conduct a political discussion" (Wolff 1968, p. 59).

With Katz's informed consent, there is a community—as Wolff describes it. The physician and patient, through the process of dialogue achieve reciprocal awareness. In the Madison School District, there is also a community. There is a community between the parents and the teachers—both want the uncoerced reply. Wolff argues that community, as he uses the concept, complements and completes private interests and does not conflict with individuality. This is also true with informed consent. Each participant—physician, patient, parent, teacher—retains autonomy and responsibility for his or her own decisions. At the same time, each is aware of the feelings of the other and each needs the other to achieve the individual and the common end.

The conditions of discretion also address the relation of the individual to the social group. The parent groups provide the second aspect of community. As conceived, these organizations combine Wolff's affective and rational communities. They provide social bonding, "easy" relationships in informal social settings, but they are also instrumental. They serve to educate the citizen and to provide the resources for individual bargaining with the schools. The groups complement and complete individuality by providing for both altruism and selective incentives. They decrease the alienation and isolation of the parents as well as their sense of powerlessness. By providing individual resources and, if necessary, advocacy resources, parents are in a better position to participate in the communitarian relationship between them and the school personnel. By addressing the distribution question, parents are in a better position to make an uncoerced reply.

In considering the function of the parent groups, it is well to repeat some basic points made in Chapter 8, since the relationship of groups to individuals is so problematic in liberal political theory. The argument is made that groups are inconsistent with autonomy, and thus inconsistent with the most fundamental value of liberalism. In the context of the parent groups, the loss of individuality could occur in a number of ways. If the groups are strongly confrontational, they would have to demand the obedience and solidarity of their membership to survive. This would mean that individual grievances would have to be subordinated to the group; and indeed, there is a good deal of empirical evidence to show that this does happen. It is important to emphasize that the context that I am discussing is not confrontational in the classic sense. One of the essential conditions for cooperative decision making is that the bureaucracy wants to cooperate; if it does not, the whole enterprise fails and we are back in the realm of liberal legalism. I do not believe that many parent groups can maintain themselves in a strongly adversarial position. The context I am talking about then, is one in which the school is seeking cooperation—of both the parents and the groups—and the purpose of the groups is to help the parents take advantage of the offer of power being made. The school wants a reciprocal arrangement, an exchange, not a fight.

Autonomy is also threatened from the other direction—the cooptation of the group. If the group is coopted, the leadership becomes dependent on relationships with the school officials, grows more hierarchical, and is less concerned about individual members. Again, there is ample evidence of cooptation. The school system has the power to coopt, just as it has the power to fight, but if it does coopt, it destroys the organization at the roots and, with it, the capacity of parents to engage in the kind of decision making necessary to make special education work. The parent groups have to be autonomous in a cooperative relationship. There must be a rational community at the institutional as well as the individual level.

If this kind of balance is to be maintained, it would seem that individuality can flourish within the group. The organization of the group is not so tight, and there is less need to be strongly cohesive. There is room for movement within the membership. There is the natural movement of the parents, who vary in terms of what they want from the group both because of their own particular resources and because of the differing interests of their children. Children differ in terms of handicaps, and as they proceed through the system, parental concerns differ as well. In order to attract and maintain members, the groups have to offer selective incentives as well as altruism. The groups cannot be exclusive; parents must be free to pursue their interests independently or to seek help elsewhere. In other words, the groups are low-key and permeable. There is movement in and out—a key requirement for the preservation of autonomy (Unger 1975). The groups provide for the collectivization of grievances (Reifner 1982; Hofrichter 1982), but participation is voluntary.

Under the conditions of discretion, the theory of the state differs sharply from the liberal/positivist perspective. Instead of the public/ private distinction and the hierarchical, bureaucratic expertise of the modern state, the conditions of discretion require decentralization and the explicit incorporation of the citizen *and* the intermediate associations in all aspects of policy. The details have been described in Chapter 6. The theory of public action views the necessary creation of discretion as an opportunity for flexibility, adaptiveness, experimentation, and participation. Public policy, at the grass roots, tracks the "practical" knowledge described by Spragens. An integral part, however, is the active, participatory role of the citizen and the group, and not the discretionary authority of the public agency alone. The state has to be willing to tolerate ambiguity and uncertainty in return for information, understanding, and cooperation. This, of course, renders policy contingent. If there is to be decentralization and discretion, if citizens and groups are to participate in all aspects of the program, there will be variation in the characteristics of the programs. In Chapter 6, the conclusion reached was that there is already variation and contingency in discretionary programs. Discretion cannot be eliminated, so it is better to confront these issues and deal with them creatively and rationally. This requires charting the permissible boundaries of discretion (for example, discrimination) and then providing for the conditions of humane, practical, liberal discretion.

The theory of the state in the conditions of discretion recognizes and supports the delegation of public power to private groups—to use the traditional liberal phraseology. Unlike the theory of the liberal state, which refuses to address this problem, the theory of public action not only recognizes the role of private groups, but considers that role essential. The theory of public action recognizes the importance of the distribution question; it also realizes that various methods will have to be devised to encourage the formation and support of these groups. The active encouragement of groups results in a redistribution of power.

Another issue that was raised concerns the growth of informalism and the threat to the citizen. This issue was also addressed in Chapter 6. The argument is that the rise of formal legal institutions was necessary to protect the citizen from absolutist government, and that the regime of rights and procedural due process still performs these functions—it limits the activities of government and when government or powerful private interests do choose to act, formal legal institutions serve to equalize the parties.

The argument against informalism (cooperative decision making) is twofold. On the one hand, there is the widening of the net. Under the guise of helping, of therapy, government extends its power. As Abel

(1982) describes, government control was confined to highly visible coercive institutions when the controls of government were limited to confinement and exclusion—courts, prisons, mental hospitals, schools. Coercive institutions, moreover, are relatively passive. Under the regime of therapy, state power is expanded. Helping agencies are purposive and proactive. The distinction between what is private and what is public, what is forbidden and what is allowed, is obliterated. The protections from state power are neutralized. Conflict is suppressed and is converted into a failure of communication. The powerless are neutralized and disarmed (Abel 1982).

While these concerns are real, I raised a number of questions. The issue is not one of an informal cooperative system versus an idealized version of the formal, adversary system. It is rare, indeed, in my opinion, that the powerless receive much protection from the formal system as it operates in the real world, or as it is likely to operate in the near future. There are a variety of reasons for this failure, but a significant one is the distribution of wealth and power. As long as this question is not addressed, there may not be much of a sacrifice in building alternative systems. But there are other answers. The argument made against the informal systems where they have been instituted is that they have focused on process rather than results. Here, the argument is different. I mentioned that the Madison School District developed its cooperative decision making as a by-product of its concern for substantive results—the improvement in the education of handicapped children—which, in turn, required the active understanding and meaningful participation of the parents. I also pointed out that informed consent in medicine seems to work with the chronically ill for the same reason—physicians need the understanding and cooperation of these patients for therapeutic purposes. In both examples, it was the nature of the substantive task—the practical knowledge—that dictated the process; it was not abstract, universalistic principles of procedure. I also pointed out that under the cooperative decision making argued for here, the distribution question is addressed. Informalism is not to be imposed from on high by the existing order. Rather, it is to be developed pragmatically out of the changed interests and concerns of the bureaucracy and the growth and development of social movement groups. Thus there will be a redistribution of power at the grass roots level.

Finally, there is no suggestion that the program of rights is to be abandoned. As will be discussed in the last section, the conditions of discretion are uncertain. They are not a program for action that, once in place, will necessarily remain so. Bureaucracies, social movement groups, teachers, and parents are in flux; what works today in a decent, humane, form could easily be repressive tomorrow. There is, unfortunately, the problem of evil. In Chapter 5, I affirmed the position of Thompson (1975) that the rule of law has been paid for with too high a price to be abandoned on the promises of tomorrow. I see no need for an either/or proposition. The point is that under a cooperative form of decision making, the importance of the formal system recedes in importance (Unger 1975). It is available if needed, but it no longer dominates. In other words, the objection to informalism is premised on the conventional view of the liberal state—the public/private distinction; the adversarial relation. Cooperative decision making is premised on a different view of the citizen and the state—for good or ill, they are locked into a continuing relationship. A different theory of the state and citizen is thus necessary.

Progress

Liberalism has failed to fulfill humanity's aspirations. Science and the Age of Enlightenment envisaged the flowering of the individual and progress in the social order. With the growth of freedom, understanding, and material wealth, humanity would begin its long delayed journey to true happiness. Instead, the opposite has happened. The market, positivism, and utilitarianism have debased humans into pleasure-seeking egoists, created an instrumental society, and denied freedom through hierarchy, domination, and poverty. All who attack the various strands of liberalism argue that once people are truly free, autonomy, community, and moral life will emerge. This view has not been the exclusive preserve of the liberal critics. Mill, for example, is exemplary in his commitment to human growth and understanding. Adam Smith, too, had an optimistic, humane view of social progress.

Nevertheless, despite the great diversity of the liberal critics, they seem united on this point—there is a conception of the basic, underlying human personality that is being distorted and suppressed by existing structures and ideologies. Once freed from this domination, society will begin to fullfill its liberal ideals and people will be truly free. Expressions of this sentiment range from the particular to the general. Katz, for example, believes that when there is informed consent between physician and patient, substance and process will merge, there will be both autonomy and better health care decisions. The Madison School District believes that there will be better substantive special education when parents participate. Rousseau (as well as Mill) believed that the end goal of participation in civic life was the education of the citizen—education in its widest sense. Habermas says:

> [O]nly in an emancipated society, whose members' autonomy and responsibility had been realized, would communication have developed into the non-authoritarian and universally practiced dialogue from which both our model of reciprocally constituted ego identity and our idea of true consensus are always implicitly derived [Habermas 1975, p. 314].

Unger takes a similar position. The universal good is the universal realization of human nature, which can only come about through the decrease of domination (liberalism) and the advance of community. Spragens also believes that once free of liberal reason, society has the capacity to pursue rationally the humane ideals of liberalism.

One could go on. Those who fear community either deny the optimistic view of humanity or are skeptical. They worry about the concept of shared values—what values, to what end? There is the tyranny of the majority, of the group. They prefer a less generous view of human nature and are content to rely on rights and legal protections to preserve autonomy. They worry about the problem of evil.

The conditions of discretion obviously rest for the most part on an optimistic view of humanity. The practical knowledge of informed consent, the possibility of mutual understanding and communication, the desirability of decentralization and discretion, fit into a conception of people who are capable of altruism and individuality, trust and autonomy, respect, responsibility, and morality. But this is a hope. It is analogous to the argument for the contingency of public policy. There is always the risk that things will turn out badly. The conditions of discretion keep an anchor to the wind. Law may be reduced; but it is not eliminated.

Utopianism

The critique of those who criticize liberalism is that they are utopian. Those who want to change the status quo, who do not accept the existing order as natural or given, who believe that man has created the chains that bind him, are dismissed as visionary. The argument of this book is also criticized as utopian—not on one but on two grounds. The vision of cooperative decision making is utopian, and the Madison special education program is an unrealistic example.

What does the Madison example show? It does not show that the conditions of discretion are working. Neither the data presented here nor other studies that I know of have done a full-scale empirical evaluation of the system; and that would be a major effort clearly beyond the scope of this work. What the Madison example does show is the *possibility* of the conditions of discretion. By possibility, I mean that there is a coherent theory about what it takes to have cooperative decision making in a bureaucracy state, and there is the plausible evidence to show that the system *seems* to be working.

There are a number of lessons to be drawn from this example. The theory that emerged from Madison agrees with the practical knowledge that Spragens is talking about as well as the eclectic liberalism of Shiffrin. There was no sharp separation of theory from practice, of ideas from fact. Each informed the other in trial-and-error fashion. There was no imposition of universal truths, nor abstract reason or ideology, on the real-life problems of the community. People had ideas and problems, and they addressed both. There was a common liberal base in terms of individual interaction; there was a recognition of mutual awareness, that people had to communicate and work together to solve their common problems. The special education officials knew the importance of parents to the program. They started off with Wolff's rational community. This was both pragmatic and idealistic. What this process implies is that though there could be consensus on the ideas of the conditions of discretion, each community would have to find its own way according to its own special circumstances. The idea of discretion means, inevitably, that each situation is unique. I do not regard this as a flaw in the argument. The recognition of uniqueness opens the opportunity to be flexible, experimental, and sensitive to the particular. "Theory can define the tensions and suggest the factors that should be taken into account in dealing with them. But only practice can yield the insights needed to correct the decisions we make" (Unger 1975, p. 288). If we are serious in rejecting the universalistic claims of positivism and the reductionism of so much of moral philosophy, then the general must be grounded in the particular.

The second lesson to be drawn from the Madison experience is its incredible complexity. Out of this example, I have specified the conditions of discretion and how justice can be achieved in the modern state. In order to do this, as the reader is by now well aware, I have had to integrate theories of implementation, organizations, social movements, informed consent, and politics. And the discussion, however long and complicated, has barely scratched the surface of these complex fields. Madison may be a special community of rather small size when considering greater conurbations, but in order to achieve its program, a great deal had to happen. And there still appear to be weaknesses in the Madison system. In order to build community, to achieve social autonomy, it is necessary to begin the task of restructuring society. Even in a community such as Madison, the task of restructuring is slow, complex, and fraught with peril. For radicals to criticize the Madison example would only lead to despair.

Having said this, I still believe that the argument presents a worthy vision. The vision is worthy, in the first place, because it is a vision. In the beginning of the book, I quote Unger: "To construct we must criticize, but criticism cannot be clear and effective unless it anticipates what is to be built." The critique of administrative justice in the modern liberal state, as well as the critique of liberalism, takes on meaning only if one knows where one wants to go.

But how realistic is the vision? Madison is not a trivial example. But, of course, it is not New York, Los Angeles, or Chicago. In Chapter 5, I discussed the implications of some of these differences. But there is no reason why large cities have to have large school districts or large units administering special education.

Although there is diversity and conflict in Madison, the community certainly appears more homogeneous and consensual than many other areas. How important is homogeneity and underlying consensus? Again, common sense would indicate that these are important characteristics. I do not think that social movement groups can exist in an autonomous, cooperative relationship with the bureaucracy in a community rent with hostility and distrust. What conclusion follows?

It seems to me that the answer is to explore the areas where communication and trust can be established and build on them. It may be that communities are divided on some issues but not on others. Katz reminds us that trustful communication is not one of humanity's more obvious qualities; he also reminds us that one does not have to accept the given state of affairs as immutable. In Chapter 8, it was pointed out that there are thousands of community groups and associations, that ordinary people did learn something from the past two decades. Foucault has taught us to look into the tiny corners in the ordinary interactions of daily life to discover the sources of power. The Madison System began with a few small cases, and depending upon your perspective, it is now either a small or a large example. It is my guess that there are myriads of other tiny examples in our cities and communities; they are there, if we know where to look for them.

The importance of the Madison System is that it is an imaginative attempt to fashion a creative structure to accommodate both community and individuality. It is a concrete step in a direction. It is a political act of freedom and liberalism. It educates those who participate; it provides guidance and hope for those who are searching for justice in contemporary life.

Living with Uncertainty

Throughout this book I have stressed uncertainty. Institutional structures are fluid; public policy is contingent; practical knowledge is tentative. The theory of public action encourages change. Discretion implies choice. There is ambiguity in the degrees of difference between autonomy and cooptation, trust and obedience, fact and value, subject and object, conflict and communication, and almost every other relationship that has been discussed. The conditions of discretion are not a blueprint. Nor is the Madison system. Indeed, that system is undergoing constant change, and there is the need for the continual reaffirmation of principles and reconstruction of programs in order to maintain the creative interactions necessary for the success of the enterprise.

Indeterminacy is hard to live with. And why should we embark on a course that only promises more uncertainty and unceasing struggle? Because that is reality. There are no fixed principles that chart a clear path. There are no laws of nature that will regulate our lives as we wish to lead them. There are no simple truths that will explain the disorders and complexities of life. If we have faith in the individual, if we believe in autonomy, we must focus on the particular. We must focus on the conditions that will allow us to act freely with each other. In the Madison system, people talk to each other; government does not talk to people (Tushnet 1981). But if people are to talk to each other, there will be uncertainty. Indeterminacy is inseparable from social autonomy.

REFERENCES

Abel, Richard L. (ed.). *The Politics of Informal Justice, Volume 1, The American Experience; Volume 2, Comparative Studies.* New York: Academic Press, 1982.

Alford, Robert R. "Paradigms of Relations Between State and Society." In Leon N. Lindberg et al. (eds.), *Stress and Contradiction in Modern Capitalism.* Lexington, Mass.: D. C. Heath & Co., 1981.

Baker, C. Edwin, "Scope of the First Amendment Freedom of Speech." *UCLA Law Review,* 25 (1978), pp. 964–1040.

Barber, Bernard. "Medical Ethics and Social Change." *The Annals* (special issue), 437 (May 1978).

Beauchamp, Tom L., and Childress, James F. *Principles of Biomedical Ethics,* 2nd ed. New York: Oxford University Press, 1983.

Berlant, Jeffrey L. "Medical Ethics and Professional Monopoly." *The Annals,* 437 (May 1978), pp. 49–62.

Berlin, Isaiah. "Two Concepts of Liberty." In *Four Essays on Liberty.* London: Oxford University Press, 1969.

Buchanan, Allen. "Medical Paternalism." *Philosophy & Public Affairs,* 7, (1978), pp. 370–390.

Cassileth, Barrie R.; Zupkis, Robert V.; Sutton-Smith, Katherine; and March, Vicki. "Informed Consent: Why Are Its Goals Imperfectly Realized?" *New England Journal of Medicine,* 302, 16 (1980), pp. 896–900.

Chevigny, Paul G. "Philosophy of Language and Free Expression." *New York University Law Review,* 55, 2 (May 1980), pp. 157–194.

Dworkin, Gerald. "Consent, Representation and Proxy Consent." In Willard Gaylin and Ruth Macklin (eds.), *Who Speaks for the Child?: The Problems of Proxy Consent.* New York: Plenum Press, 1982.

Dworkin, Gerald. "Paternalism." In S. Gorovitz et al. (eds.), *Moral Problems in Medicine.* Englewood Cliffs, N.J.: Prentice-Hall, 1976.

Edelman, Murray. "Systematic Confusions in the Evaluation of Implementing Decisions." In *Evaluating the Welfare State: Social and Political Perspectives*. New York: Academic Press, 1983.

Falk, Dennis R. "Social Development Values." *Social Development Issues*, 5, 1 (1981), pp. 67–83.

Fellner, Carl H., and Marshall, John R. "Kidney Donors—The Myth of Informed Consent." *American Journal of Psychiatry*, 126 (1970), pp. 1245–1250.

Fitzgerald, Jeffrey, and Dickens, Richard. "Disputing in Legal and Nonlegal Contexts: Some Questions for Sociologists of Law." *Law and Society Review*, 15, 3–4 (1980–1981), p. 681–701.

Foucault, Michel. *Power/Knowledge: Selected Interviews and Other Writings, 1972–1977*. Colin Gordon, ed. New York: Pantheon, 1980.

Fox, Renee C. "Some Social and Cultural Factors in American Society Conducive to Medical Research on Human Subjects." *Clinical Pharmacology and Therapeutics*, 1 (1960), pp. 432–441.

Friedman, Lawrence. *A History of American Law*. New York: Simon & Schuster, 1973.

Frug, G. "The City as a Legal Concept." *Harvard Law Review*, 93 (1980), pp. 1057–1154.

Gilligan, Carol. *In a Different Voice*. Cambridge, Mass.: Harvard University Press, 1982.

Goldberg, Gale, and Elliott, Joy. "Below the Belt: Situational Ethics for Unethical Situations." *Journal of Sociology and Social Welfare*, 7, 4 (1980), pp. 478–486.

Gordon, Robert. "New Developments in Legal Theory." In David Kairys (ed.), *The Politics of Law: A Progressive Critique*. New York: Pantheon Books, 1982.

Grad, Frank P. "Medical Ethics and the Law." *The Annals*, 437 (May 1978), pp. 19–37.

Gray, Bradford H. "Complexities of Informed Consent." *The Annals*, 437 (May 1978), pp. 37–48.

Gutmann, Amy. *Liberal Equality*. New York: Cambridge University Press, 1980.

Habermas, Jurgen. *Knowledge and Human Interests*. Boston: Beacon Press, 1968.

Habermas, Jurgen. *Legitimation Crisis*. Boston: Beacon Press, 1975.

Haug, Marie R., and Lavin, Bebe. "Practitioner or Patient—Who's in Charge?" *Journal of Health and Social Behavior*, 22, 3 (September 1981), pp. 212–229.

Himmelfarb, Gertrude. *The Idea of Poverty: England in the Early Industrial Age*. New York: Alfred A. Knopf, 1984.

Hofrichter, Richard. "Neighborhood Justice and the Social Control Problems of American Capitalism: A Perspective." In R. Abel (ed.), *The Politics of Informal Justice, Volume 1, The American Experience*. New York: Academic Press, 1982.

Hyde, Alan. "Is Liberalism Possible?" *New York University Law Review,* 57 (1982), pp. 1031–1058.

Kairys, David. *The Politics of Law: A Progressive Critique.* New York: Pantheon Books, 1982.

Katz, Jay. "Disclosure and Consent in Psychiatric Practice: Mission Impossible?" In C. Hofling (ed.), *Law and Ethics in the Practice of Psychiatry.* New York: Brunner/Mazel.

Katz, Jay. "Informed Consent—A Fairy Tale? Law's Vision." *University of Pittsburgh Law Review,* 39, 2 (Winter 1977), pp. 137–174.

Katz, Jay. *The Silent World of Doctor and Patient.* New York: Free Press, 1984.

Katz, Jay. "Why Doctors Don't Disclose Uncertainty." *Report of the Hastings Center,* 14, 1 (February 1984), pp. 35–44.

Kennedy, Duncan. "The Structure of Blackstone's Commentaries." *Buffalo Law Review,* 28 (1979), pp. 205–382.

Kidder, Robert L. "The End of the Road? Problems in the Analysis of Disputes." *Law and Society Review,* 15, 3–4 (1980–1981), pp. 717–725.

Kuhn, Thomas. *The Structure of Scientific Revolution,* 2nd ed. Chicago: University of Chicago Press, 1970.

Lempert, Richard O. "Grievances and Legitimacy: The Beginnings and End of Dispute Settlement." *Law and Society Review,* 15, 3–4, pp. 707–715.

Levine, Andrew. *Liberal Democracy: A Critique of Its Theory.* New York: Columbia University Press, 1981.

Levine, Andrew. *The Politics of Autonomy: A Kantian Reading of Rousseau's Social Contract.* Amherst: University of Massachusetts Press, 1976.

Lidz, Charles W., and Meisel, Alan. "Informed Consent and the Structure of Medical Care." In President's Commission, *Making Health Care Decisions,* Volume 2, Appendices. Washington, D.C.: U.S. Government Printing Office, 1982.

Lowi, Theodore J. *The End of Liberalism.* New York: W. W. Norton & Co., 1969.

Lustig, R. Jeffrey. *Corporate Liberalism: The Origins of Modern American Political Theory, 1890–1920.* Berkeley: University of California Press, 1982.

Lynd, Staughton. *Intellectual Origins of American Radicalism.* New York: Pantheon Books, 1968.

Macpherson, C. B. *The Political Theory of Possessive Individualism: Hobbes to Locke.* London: Oxford University Press, 1962.

Mensch, Elizabeth. "The History of Mainstream Legal Thought." In David Kairys (ed.), *The Politics of Law: A Progressive Critique.* New York: Pantheon Books, 1982.

Michelman, Frank I. "Formal and Associational Aims in Procedural Due Process." In J. W. Chapman and J. Roland Pennock (eds.), *Due Process.* New York: New York University Press, 1977.

Nedelsky, Jennifer. "Conflicting Democratic Politics: Anti-Federalists, Federalists, and the Constitution." *Harvard Law Review,* 96 (1982), pp. 340–360.

Nisbet, Robert. "Conservatism." In T. Bottomore and R. Nisbet (eds.), *A History of Sociological Analysis.* New York: Basic Books, 1978.

Nonet, Philippe, and Selznick, Philip (eds.). *Law and Society in Transition: Toward Responsive Law.* New York: Harper & Row, 1978.

Pateman, Carole. *Participation and Democratic Theory.* Cambridge: At the University Press, 1970.

Poulantzas, Nicos. *State, Power, Socialism.* London: Redwood Burn, Verso Edition, 1980.

President's Commission for the Study of Ethical Problems in Medicine and Biomedical and Behavioral Research. *Making Health Care Decisions,* Volumes I, II, III. Washington, D.C.: U.S. Government Printing Office, 1983.

Radin, Margaret Jane. "Property and Personhood." *Stanford Law Review,* 34 (May 1984), pp. 957–1015.

Rappoport, Julian. "In Praise of Paradox: A Social Policy of Empowerment over Prevention." *American Journal of Community Psychology,* 9, 1 (1981), pp. 1–25.

Reamer, Frederic G. "The Concept of Paternalism in Social Work." *Social Service Review,* 57, 2 (June 1983), pp. 254–271.

Reich, Charles. "The New Property." *Yale Law Journal,* 73 (1964), pp. 733–787.

Reifner, Udo. "Individualistic and Collective Legalization: The Theory and Practice of Legal Advice for Workers in Prefascist Germany." In R. Abel (ed.), *The Politics of Informal Justice,* Volume 2, Comparative Studies. New York: Academic Press, 1982.

Relman, Arnold. "The Power of the Doctors." (Review of *The Social Transformation of American Medicine,* by Paul Starr.) *New York Review of Books,* 31, 5 (1984), pp. 29–33.

Robertson, John A. "Taking Consent Seriously: IRB Intervention in Consent Process." *IRB,* 4, 5 (May 1982), pp. 1–5.

Rorty, Richard. *Philosophy and the Mirror of Nature.* Princeton, N.J.: Princeton University Press, 1979.

Sandel, Michael J. *Liberalism and the Limits of Justice.* New York: Cambridge University Press, 1982.

Santos, Bonaventura de Sousa. "Law and Community: The Changing Nature of State Power in Late Capitalism." In R. Abel (ed.), *The Politics of Informal Justice, Volume 1, The American Experience.* New York: Academic Press, 1982.

Shiffrin, Steven. "Liberalism, Radicalism, and Legal Scholarship." *UCLA Law Review,* 30 (1983), pp. 1103–1217.

Simon, William. "The Ideology of Advocacy: Procedural Justice and Professional Ethics." *Wisconsin Law Review,* 29 (1978), pp. 29–144.

Soskis, Carole W. "Teaching Nursing Home Staff About Patients' Rights." *The Gerontologist,* 21, 4 (1981), pp. 424–430.

Spitzer, Steven. "The Dialectics of Formal and Informal Control." In R. Abel (ed.), *The Politics of Informal Justice, Volume 1, The American Experience.* New York: Academic Press, 1982.

Spragens, Thomas A. *The Irony of Liberal Reason.* Chicago: University of Chicago Press, 1981.

Stanley, Barbara H. "Informed Consent and Competence: A Review of Empirical Research." Paper presented at MIMH Workshop, January 1981.

Stone, Alan A. "Informed Consent: Special Problems for Psychiatry." *Hospital and Community Psychiatry,* 30, 5 (May 1979), pp. 321–327.

Tancredi, Laurence. "Competency for Informed Consent Conceptual Limits of Empirical Data." *International Journal of Law and Psychiatry,* 5, 1 (1982), pp. 51–63.

Teubner, Gunther. "Substantive and Reflexive Elements in Modern Law." *Law and Society Review,* 17, 2 (1983), pp. 239–287.

Thompson, E. P. *Whigs and Hunters: The Origin of the Black Act.* London: Allan Lane, 1975.

Tribe, Laurence H. *American Constitutional Law.* Mineola, N.Y.: Foundation Press, 1978.

Tribe, Laurence H. "Structural Due Process." *Harvard Civil Rights/Civil Liberties Law Review,* 10 (1977), pp. 269–321.

Trubek, David M. "The Construction and Deconstruction of a Disputes-Focused Approach: An Afterword." *Law and Society Review,* 15, 3–4 (1980–1981), pp. 727–747.

Tushnet, Mark. "Deviant Science in Constitutional Law." *Texas Law Review,* 59 (1981), pp. 815–827.

Tushnet, Mark. "Talking to Each Other: Reflections on Yudof's 'When Government Speaks.' " *Wisconsin Law Review,* 1 (1984), pp. 129–145.

Unger, Roberto M. *Knowledge and Politics.* New York: Free Press, 1975.

Veatch, Robert M. "Three Theories of Informed Consent: Philosophical Foundations and Policy Implications." Manuscript prepared for the National Commission for the Protection of Human Subjects of Biological and Behavioral Research, February 1976.

Weimann, G. "Dealing with Bureaucracy: The Effectiveness of Different Persuasive Appeals." *Social Psychology Quarterly,* 45, 3 (1982), pp. 136–144.

Westen, Peter. "The Empty Idea of Equality." *Harvard Law Review,* 95, 3 (1982), pp. 537–596.

Wolff, Robert Paul. *The Poverty of Liberalism.* Boston: Beacon Press, 1968.

· INDEX ·